Education and Examination in Modern Japan

Education and Examination in Modern Japan

Ikuo Amano

Translated by
William K. Cummings and
Fumiko Cummings

UNIVERSITY OF TOKYO PRESS

Translation and publication of this volume were made possible by a grant from the Japan Foundation.

This volume is a translation of *Shiken no Shakai-shi*, published in 1983 by University of Tokyo Press.

ISBN   4-13-057018-8
ISBN   0-86008-448-5

Printed in Japan   Second printing, 1993

Contents

Foreword

There are few more ambiguous—or should one say multi-guous?—human institutions than academic examinations. They can be used to motivate students to study, or to shape the way they study. They can provide a check on the effectiveness of teachers. They can be used to measure competences required for further learning. They can be used to ration access to profession-al monopolies or organizational membership and may or may not offer more relevant criteria for this purpose than a road race or a chess tournament would. They can be used as a more or less random but legitimate device to reduce the applicants for valued social goods to manageable numbers. They can be used to pre-serve the public from the attentions of unqualified doctors or plumbers. They can be treated as proxy measures of native abil-ity, or of the capacity for persistent effort. They can be all kinds of mixtures of these things, and can be fiercely and openly criti-cized for failing in their ostensible purpose, while being silently but stoutly defended because they serve well other less easily acknowledged purposes.

Unless it be modern China, there is no more fascinating place to study these interplays and interconnections than in the history of modern Japan—at least when one has as guide as good an historian and sociologist as Professor Amano. Japan had both an established system of feudal ascription and a Confucian cultural legacy of government by meritocrats to draw on—and the two were already at odds with each other. It had, also (and Professor Amano is particularly illuminating on this), a tradition of social order based on conflict avoidance rather than conflict regulation, in which the competitiveness of school examinations was kept under strict control.

These traditions served to modify, but only to modify, the

attempts at wholesale educational modernization as Japan began to build a modern state capable of successfully engaging the West in the international competition for wealth and military power—and doing so by imitating the institutions which were deemed to be sources of those countries' strength. America contributed a great deal, particularly in the person of an influential advisor, David Murray, with whose speech the book begins. But in the end it was Prussia—in some ways the most Confucian country in Europe—which contributed the most. A strong sense of nationalism made the drive to mobilize the best talents in the service of the nation something more than mere rhetoric, sufficiently so for the claims of ascription and particularistic favoritism to be quite quickly pushed aside. Japan developed the most thoroughly open competitive system for rationing educational opportunity which the world had by then seen, and one of the most meritocratic systems for allocating public office.

The same nationalism, combined with Chinese traditions of the all-competent state, meant that public examinations forestalled the growth of professional self-regulation, and it was national and local government which took powers to license the lawyers, doctors, and teachers.

It is a fascinating chunk of history, and Professor Amano tells it with verve and with a wealth of historical detail. What makes his book especially rewarding is that it is a story with a theme—the theme of how modern Japan's "examination hell" came into being.

What I find especially interesting about his account, in that context, is the evidence he gives of a widespread awareness of the problematical side-effects of using examinations as a means of rationing life-chances as well as to motivate for study. He describes, for instance, the background to the decision, in the mid-1890s, to abolish grade promotion examinations and move to automatic promotion. There had been a growing feeling that the examinations did more harm than good, but the Minister wanted a systematic check and asked for a nationwide canvass of opinion. The quantity and quality of the response are a measure of the seriousness and sophistication with which those in charge of Japan's public education at the turn of the century went about their task. Let the examinations become too prominent, warned a teacher in Fukushima, and students concentrate on memorization and "their native ability is not nurtured and their imagination is barely used." As the competitive instinct grows, "their feeling of love for nature withers away while they develop a disturbing hostility to other students." The teachers begin to be preoccupied with numbers of passes and forget what education is all about.

These sorts of sensitivities clearly have long-standing roots. The idea that a genuine education should have a *moral* purpose transcending self-advancement was something Japan derived from its Confucian past, not from its American or French advisers. And who can measure the effect that this dutifulness had on Japan's industrialization? One of Amano's fascinating sources is a letter written a few years after the Meiji Restoration by a student at one of the new Western schools. He tells his step-father that there are some students who study "only for recognition"—as, his American teachers say, is commonly the case in the U.S. They only want to get good marks, please their parents, and feel proud of themselves. There are others, more solid and serious people, who are concerned about raising national productivity, or making Japan great in the arts. And he is glad to count himself among the latter.

Priggish, to be sure, but developing countries need their prigs, or at least need the sensitivities and criteria of judgement which makes that sort of priggishness the way a lot of people try to feel good about themselves. It was those sensitivities and criteria of judgement which came into play to modify (as modern developing countries like India or Kenya have found it difficult to modify) the effects of exam-oriented meritocracy. They led to the removal of grade promotion exams from elementary schools at an early stage. Since the Second World War they have been responsible, in various prefectures, for a variety of devices (including lottery within broad ability bands) designed to mitigate the effects of competitive examinations for high school entrance. (Though none of these devices have been as thoroughgoing as those adopted in that other post-Confucian country, Korea—lottery allocation of pupils between high schools and an absolute ban on all cram schools for high school students.)

But, when it came to the crucial life-chance-determining educational opportunities, such as entrance to the nation's top middle schools, high schools, and universities, the social efficiency advantages and the legitimation advantages of competitive entrance examinations proved unassailable.

The sheer effort output which these competitions evoked has been impressive. It has furnished the minds of today's average Japanese citizen with a richer stock of knowledge and skills than that possessed by the citizens of any of Japan's industrial competitors. It has also induced a great deal of mindless and ritualistic learning and regurgitation.

But always there has been some brake on those side-effects. The ideology of "learning for a higher purpose than mere self-advancement" has not been mere hypocrisy. It has ensured, for example, that public education has not concentrated exclusively on the abler children, participants in the major allocative exams, at the expense of the rest. It is notably in the achievements of the average and below-average pupils that Japan scores in international tests of academic ability.

And the ideology has affected content too. The constant curriculum revisions, the anxious deliberations of bodies like the Ad Hoc Educational Reform Council of the 1980s on the need for more individuality and creativity (a few bold spirits were rumored even to have mentioned enjoyment!), all testify to attempts—at least attempts—to make the schools places where children are educated and not just prepared for examinations. On the day that this is written, the leading article of a Japanese newspaper (*Asahi Shimbun*, 17 September 1989) complains of the excessive, convoluted difficulty of questions in entrance examinations and asks teachers to "think again, seriously, what education should be about."

Professor Amano has given us in graphic detail the story of how the foundations of today's system were laid. We must all hope that he will find the time to follow the story on through the interwar years of graduate unemployment and the American-inspired postwar reconstruction into the age of the computerized mock test and the *hensachi*—the national norm-referenced person-indexing score. And we must hope, also, that he will, for later volumes too, be interpreted by such able translators as Fumiko and William Cummings.

Ronald P. Dore

Preface

In any country, modernization promotes greater social mobility and provides opportunities for people to climb the social ladder. The more opportunities there are for upward mobility, the stronger the aspiration is to climb; and the more numerous are the channels for climbing higher in society, the faster modernization proceeds. This is exactly the process that has propelled Japan's modernization over the past century. The educational system has played a key role by giving people the incentive for upward aspirations and by providing the channels through which they could translate their dreams into reality.

Samuel Smiles's *Self-Help* (translated into Japanese in 1871) and Fukuzawa Yukichi's *Gakumon no Susume* (An Encouragement of Learning, 1872) were best-sellers during the last quarter of the nineteenth century, an indication of the strong impulse to achieve that animated young people as Japan entered the modern era. The modernized education system was there to respond to their desire for upward mobility.

A common denominator of modern societies is the presence of an educational system, or more precisely a school education system. Such systems have not always served as channels of upward mobility, but in Japan this was the case, largely because of the emergence of two factors: widespread emphasis on educational background—"educational credentialism"—and the examination system. Throughout this century, Japan's education system has both influenced and been influenced by each of these two factors.

The examination system did not exist in premodern Japan. Neither the *terakoya* (temple schools) nor the domain schools (*hankō*) supported by clan governments throughout the country conducted examinations. Nor were examinations necessary for

xi

entry into the professions or the ranks of government officialdom. The examination system was imported from Europe, along with the other elements of Western school education and the practice of professional accreditation. Once adopted, it developed very rapidly.

Initially, examinations began with elementary school. The academic progress of children and their eligibility for higher grades or for graduation were constantly tested in a continuous stream of examinations. The same was true for secondary schools and universities. Graduation rolls listed the names in order of achievement, and seating in the classroom was determined by the students' marks. This endless succession of tests was done away with at the elementary school level in the early twentieth century, but remained at other levels.

The distinguishing feature of the examination system in Japan, however, is the entrance examination. It has become standard practice for individual secondary schools and universities to prepare their own entrance examinations, a system that is the exception rather than the rule in Europe. The "examination hell," as it is known today, existed in Japan as early as the 1920s, but the cause was not competition to advance or to graduate, as in Europe, but rather to gain entrance to schools and colleges.

Examinations were also introduced for public service and for the professions, including medicine, law, and school teaching. In other words, certification in most of the professions was granted only to people who could demonstrate, through tests, a certain level of knowledge, skill, or competence. Similarly, only those who passed the government examinations were eligible to become senior officials. These screening tests were closely linked with the education system, moreover, and only students whose school background was sufficiently outstanding were exempted from taking them. Some of the tests were open only to university students.

The graduates of the Imperial universities, founded in 1886 to train the bureaucratic corps for the central government, were a case in point. Graduates of these universities (there were seven in 1945) enjoyed various advantages in finding employment. Special consideration was gradually extended, in varying degrees, to graduates of some other higher and secondary educational institutions.

The custom whereby the state granted various privileges to the graduates of certain prestigious institutions of secondary and higher education eventually gave rise to the phenomenon that is known today as *gakurekishugi*, or what I shall call "educational credentialism." Essentially it refers to the high priority placed on a person's academic background by government organizations, private employers, and society in general.

Educational credentialism became entrenched first in the civil service. In 1887, when the Japanese government established its system for hiring public officials, the factors given the greatest weight were the school from which the candidate had graduated and his scores in the civil service examinations. While the basic idea was to ensure that middle- and high-ranking bureaucrats were selected fairly, through open and competitive government-sponsored examinations, certain candidates were exempted from the exams if their educational credentials were sufficiently illustrious. Educational credentials, especially if they included graduation from an imperial university, also had an important effect on pay and promotion after hiring.

Educational background was crucial for those who sought to enter the medical profession or become secondary school teachers; if the candidates had graduated from certain government-accredited schools, they were exempted from the qualifying exams and automatically granted professional certification. However, educational credentialism did not take root in society simply because it was the norm in hiring public servants or certifying professionals. Only when it became important in the hiring of white-collar workers in the private sector did it become an overwhelming concern.

In European countries, university graduates even today tend to prefer government service or the professions over employment in a private company. The same was true of Japan in the early stages of modernization. By the beginning of the twentieth century, however, graduates not only of private universities but even of Imperial universities had begun to seek jobs in private companies. Unlike European companies, companies in Japan were quick to seek and hire university graduates, and to offer them promotions and salary increases based on educational credentials. The results of a nationwide survey conducted in 1930 show that seventy-two percent of the middle- and upper-level managers in private companies and fifty-seven percent of engineers were graduates of higher educational institutions.

The new jobs in the bureaucracy, the professions, and private businesses were created in the process of Japan's modernization and industrialization. They carried high prestige, and provided access to wealth and power. The fact that educational credentials were the basic qualification for engaging in these occupations goes far to explain why a person's educational background is still considered a major indicator of his social standing even outside officialdom and the corporate world.

The words *gakurekishugi* and *gakureki shakai* ("educational credential society") came into common use only in the 1960s. But the phenomenon had existed since the early 1920s, and had become one of the most important ways of defining a person's status and prestige in Japanese society.

In examining the relationships between the education system, the examination system, and educational credentialism, a key element to keep in mind is equality of opportunity. Examinations may be conducted fairly and educational credentials may be decisive in employment and promotion. But without equal access to education, the education system would be incapable of inspiring young people or of functioning as a ladder to the higher ranges of society. Fortunately, the far-reaching changes brought about by the Meiji Restoration of 1868 and later by Japan's defeat in 1945 contributed to making the system more open.

The first change, made in the wake of the Meiji Restoration, was the dismantling of the country's feudal status hierarchy. Schooling was made available to all, regardless of class or lineage. Of course, education at the advanced levels was still very expensive. On the other hand, even the children of the wealthiest families could not enter the higher level schools, particularly the government-run higher schools or universities that promised elite careers, unless they passed the grueling entrance examinations. It was this rigorous system of entrance examinations which made access to education equitable.

After the defeat in World War II, during the period of the Allied Occupation, Japan underwent its second great social transformation. The social structure became more fluid as a result of pervasive land reform and the dismantling of the *zaibatsu* business combines. Under the slogan of "democratization of education," the authorities introduced the new "6-3-3-4" education system (six years of elementary school, three years of junior high school, another three years of senior high school, and four years of university education). Compulsory education was extended from six to nine years. The prewar secondary schools, which had been organized in a multi-track system, were reorganized into three-year senior high schools. The higher education system, which had consisted of a few universities and many shorter-term institutions, was also reformed into a new system of four-year universities and two-year junior colleges. Universities, which had totaled only forty-eight in 1945, numbered two hundred and one in 1950. This made the education system even more open, and provided more opportunities for access.

The aspirations of both children and their parents have been nourished by the open nature of the education system and its organic relationship with the examination system and educational credentialism. It is no exaggeration to say that the social structure of the country following the Meiji Restoration was molded by the education system. The new ruling class—high-ranking officials and the managerial class of the leading enterprises—and those who worked immediately under them—the new middle- and lower echelon public servants, white-collar workers and professionals—were all products of the new education system. Academic credentials became the passport to the new, modern fields of endeavor that clustered at the pinnacle of the social structure.

Obtaining this passport required some financial wherewithal. But the prime requirement was intellectual ability and individual effort. It was possible for an intelligent child, diligent and strongly motivated but born into a poor family, to eventually acquire distinguished educational credentials. In the early stages of rapid modernization and industrialization, many people did in fact rise to the highest levels of society in just this way. The examination system stimulated their aspirations, and the intensity of their desire to succeed in turn supported the diligence and hard work required for academic achievement.

The school as a competitive arena was regarded by society, and particularly by enterprises and government offices, as a highly effective system for training and selecting able workers. As long as the children's achievements were gauged impartially and objectively by the schools, there was no need to measure their ability again upon hiring. Educational credentials provided an indicator of an individual's diligence and ability, and both industry and the government placed great weight on these credentials in basic personnel policy. This had the effect of intensifying competition within the school system.

The Japanese education system was very effective in meeting the needs of modernization and industrialization, and is often portrayed as one of the country's greatest successes. When the competition generated by the examination system for acquisition of academic credentials became overheated, however, the dark side of the system began to reveal itself.

In Japan, competition at all levels of school education was already severe in the 1890s. This was the reason that entrance examinations and examinations for eligibility to higher grades were eliminated in the nation's elementary schools at the beginning of the 1900s. That was as far as the reform went, however. Schools educating students who would occupy the top rungs of the social ladder considered examinations an unavoidable gauntlet that students must run to separate the able from the rest.

The most serious problem involved the entrance examinations. Japan had borrowed the examination system from Europe, but not without changes. In Europe, students who score acceptably on national standardized exams given at the conclusion of one level of education are automatically guaranteed admittance to the next level. The emphasis, in other words, is not on *entrance* examinations. In Japan, however, individual schools began to use examinations to select which students could enter their halls.

In the days when the education system was not yet well established, some schools found that they were not enrolling a sufficient number of students whose ability was above a certain level from the lower levels of education, and they introduced entrance examinations as a "temporary" means of selecting students who met their standards. This practice continued even after the school system took firm root, eventually becoming one of the key characteristics of the Japanese education system. The importance of entrance examinations was further inflated because the quantitative expansion of secondary and higher education was not rapid enough to accommodate the sudden large increase of students who sought to proceed to higher levels.

Although education was an important tool for achieving rapid industrialization and modernization, the government could devote only limited human and material resources to the building of the system. Emphasis was placed on achieving universal compulsory elementary education, and this goal was rapidly achieved (by 1902, over ninety percent of eligible children were enrolled). On the other hand, too few secondary schools and universities and colleges were built to respond to the rapidly growing demand for education advancement that was the natural outcome of universal elementary education.

In addition, in an effort to allocate its limited resources effectively, the government supported secondary schools and universities on a selective basis, according to the degree of their importance to the modernization and industrialization effort. This created great disparities in human and material resources among educational institutions which, at least on paper, were at the same level. This, in turn, led people to discriminate among schools in accordance with this allocation of resources, and as a consequence a clear hierarchical system based on social prestige came into being. Among universities, for example, the Imperial universities ranked highest, followed by other government-run universities, and then by the private universities.

These two factors—the paucity of institutions of secondary and higher education and their stratification—ensured that an increasingly competitive entrance examination system would remain a permanent feature of Japanese education. The system has produced phenomena that surely exist only in Japan, such as large numbers of students who have failed in one try to pass the university entrance exams to the school of their choice and who are studying for another try (known as *rōnin*, after the masterless samurai of old), the proliferation of less selective private schools, and the flourishing cram-school industry.

These distortions produced by overcompetition were already apparent in the 1920s. The government, concerned about programs that laid too much importance on preparation for entrance examinations, directed all schools to be more moderate. In 1927, entrance exams for secondary schools were done away with and an attempt was made to introduce basic reforms into the entrance exam system for universities and colleges.

However, the flames of desire for educational credentials and higher social status had been fanned; as long as they remained alight, it would be impossible to eliminate the entrance examinations. The obstacles posed by the heavy reliance on educational credentials in industry and the government became a social problem in the 1920s, and carried over without resolution to the postwar period.

Far from cooling down, the excessive competition grew even more intense after World War II. A series of social reforms implemented by the Occupation authorities brought mobility back to Japan's social structure. This mobility, together with the reformed education system emphasizing democracy and equality, provided further motivation for people to seek better educational credentials and aim for the upper rungs of the social ladder. The blossoming of aspirations is clearly shown in the sharp rise in the proportion of junior high school graduates going on to senior high school. In 1950 the proportion was forty-three percent; it increased to fifty-eight percent in 1960, then to eighty-two percent in 1970. By 1980, it was ninety-four percent. Also, in 1960 ten percent of senior high school graduates entered college. By 1970 the percentage had more than doubled, to twenty-four percent. In 1980, it stood at thirty-seven percent.

The recovery and rapid growth of Japan's economy was partly responsible for the sharp increase in the numbers of students going on to senior high school or college. Japan's industrial structure underwent enormous changes during the process of rapid economic growth and these were accompanied by great strides in technological innovation. Private enterprises, especially in the secondary sector, experienced remarkable growth, and the demand for university graduates increased rapidly. Opportunities to enter the upper strata of society were abundant. Defeated in World War II and in the throes of revolutionary change in the education system and other aspects of its society, Japan once again became a "land of opportunity," and there were many success stories, just as there had been after the Meiji Restoration. Higher wages and more equal distribution of income encouraged people to seek better education at better schools in pursuit of the academic credentials that served as the passport to success in society.

This new wave of rising aspirations made the competition in the entrance examinations even more intense than before the war. First of all, the number of competitors tremendously increased. In 1935, nineteen percent of those who had completed compulsory education (six years of schooling) went on to secondary school. Only three percent of those who had completed compulsory schooling went on to college. The competition then was among a very small elite. After the war, the scale expanded tremendously; the corresponding figures for 1960 were fifty-eight and ten percent respectively, and for 1980, ninety-four and thirty-seven percent.

Even when nearly ninety-five percent of junior high school graduates go on to senior high school, they must take entrance exams, and this means an unavoidable ordeal for virtually every fifteen-year-old. The same may be said for almost all of the seventy percent of students at general high schools (those schools which emphasize academic subjects, as opposed to commercial and technical ones). The curriculum offered at general high schools, moreover, is designed in such a way that the main emphasis is on preparation for university entrance examinations. Passing the university entrance exams is the chief educational concern of most senior high school students.

Another important reason why the competition has grown more fierce than it was before the war is that the stratified structure of secondary schools and universities has remained basically unchanged. In fact, despite the postwar reform of the educational system, stratification became even rigid as more and more senior high schools and universities were built to handle the rapidly increasing number of students seeking higher education. The progress of stratification was particularly marked in the case of universities and colleges, whose numbers quadrupled between 1945 and 1950. In 1980 there were four hundred forty-six four-year universities in Japan. Most of these newly founded institutions are private. Often they are insufficiently endowed and possess few sources of income other than the tuition paid by students. These schools form the bottom strata of higher education.

After the war, all universities, old and new, were officially ranked equally. Corporations, too, abolished the practice of starting-pay differentials determined by the rank of the school or university of the new employee. Nevertheless, the ranking of universities has continued. A small group of prestigious universities with traditions going back to before the war, including the former Imperial universities, continue to occupy the top of the hierarchy. Most of the institutions established after the war, therefore, suffer from very low social regard.

The personnel policy of businesses—the most important employers of university graduates since the war—has contributed largely to maintaining and expanding the stratification of higher education. Starting-pay differentials may have been dropped, but corporations adopted the policy of preferring graduates of certain first-class or prestige universities in hiring new workers. This forged an explicit connection between first-class universities and top-ranking corporations.

In Japan there is a very close correlation between the size of a corporation and the wages its employees receive, as well as their career stability and social prestige. It is natural, then, that people seek employment at large corporations. Because of the connection just mentioned, the competition for jobs at these large companies begins with the race to enter the prestigious universities at the top of the educational hierarchy. The university entrance exams, then, are part, a kind of first phase, of the scramble to secure a stable career.

This volume attempts to provide some perspective on the educational and societal problems facing Japan today by looking at the history of examinations and of academic credentialism. Japan is known as the land of the "examination hell," but the tradition of examinations is not an ancient one. Rather, it has definite roots in the Meiji Restoration, and the process of Japan's modernization.

The Chinese—who "invented" examinations in the sense they were the first known to have used them, beginning in the sixth century—applied their *keju* examination system only to the selection of government officials. The Western societies that learned the art of examination from China put it to other uses during the process of modernization and industrialization, using examinations not only to select officials but also to test the qualifications of professionals like physicians and lawyers.

In the West, examinations became part of the world of school education in the seventeenth century, the object of their use being to raise the level of student achievement and teacher efficiency through competition. Examination scores become the means of deciding who was admitted to schools, who would advance to higher levels, and who would receive academic degrees and qualifications. It can safely be said that Western society in the ninetheenth century was an "examination society."

Japan's deep cultural connection with China made it fertile ground for many ideas and institutions from the Asian mainland. Introduction of China's examination system for bureaucrats was also attempted in the eighth century, but without success. In the late nineteenth century, however, after the Meiji Restoration, Japan was ready for a system of examinations. The Meiji government introduced examinations as part of its policy of importing advanced technology and institutions from the West: they saw the examination as a modern institution, apparently not reflecting that its origin actually was in the Chinese *keju*.

In any event, the examination systems which had matured in the West were transplanted in their extremely purified and idealized forms to Japan, quickly took root in its sociocultural ground, and prospered. By the beginning of the twentieth century, Japan had become one of the world's most advanced "examination societies."

In this book I have attempted to describe the process by which Japan, in the last third of the nineteenth century and the early years of the twentieth, assimilated the examination systems that had developed in Europe and adapted them to the goal of modernizing education and society, and the formation of a "Japanese-style" system centering around entrance examinations in the course of industrialization. In the process, I hope to have shed some light on the roots of the problems that have been inherited by Japanese society today as it grapples with the competitiveness and credentials-consciousness that were the legacy of this history.

Acknowledgments

I owe a great deal to a group of scholars and fellow researchers in the United States and in Europe whose work stimulated me in the writing of this book: Joseph Ben-David, Ronald P. Dore, Burton R. Clark, William K. Cummings, Martin Trow, and Ronald Wheeler. My special thanks go to Professor Dore, who not only inspired through his writings and in personal discussions, but kindly agreed to write a foreword to this book. I wish to express my gratitude to the Japan Foundation for the financial support that made both translation and publication possible. Finally, I offer a special word of appreciation to William Cummings and Fumiko Cummings for their efforts in translating the original Japanese edition of *Shiken no Shakai-shi*, which contains many passages quoted from Meiji-era documents that often yield only with difficulty to contemporary understanding.

Spring 1990   IKUO AMANO

Education and Examination in Modern Japan

Chapter One

Modernization and the Rise of Examinations

The Origin of Examinations in Japan

Murray's Speech

Among the early foreign employees of the Meiji government was David Murray, an American who had been a professor of mathematics and astronomy at Rutgers University. On the recommendation of Mori Arinori, the government in 1873 invited Murray to advise it on education policy. For the next five years, Murray played an important role in building Japan's modern school system.

In December of 1877, Murray gave a brief speech at the commencement ceremony for the Faculties of Law, Science, and Letters of Tokyo University. There were two other speakers at this important ceremony, Katō Hiroyuki, the President of the University, and Nakamura Masanao, the translator of Samuel Smiles's *Self-Help* and an instructor in the Faculty of Letters.

Murray began his speech, entitled "The Ideal Educational System," by declaring, "The job of an educator is to establish the means for encouraging study." The means available to the educator, in Murray's view, included conducting examinations, awarding grades, and conferring degrees. Through these means, the educator "accustoms young people to seeking rewards for their academic effort and thereby motivates them to enjoy their studies." In a nation where the government assumed the responsibility for education, it was important to systematize encouragement by giving students academic prizes and "establishing social privileges for those who obtain degrees." The renovation of Japan's traditional approach to evaluation, award, and promotion would be an important step forward in academic history.

3

With this introduction, Murray turned to the examination systems of the East and West. First, he briefly reviewed the examination system which was initiated in sixth-century China to choose government officials, the *keju*.[1] He observed that it was important because of its long history and the influence it had on later approaches. Murray then proceeded to identify the merits and demerits of the *keju* system, and he concluded by insisting it was desirable for a country like Japan, in reforming its institutions, to draw on the merits of the Chinese system.

Next, Murray introduced the European university system. The European university developed as an independent community of scholars without reliance on the power of the state. As the university evolved a plan for educating future members of the scholarly community, it came to rely on a fixed curriculum with formal exams as a basis for academic promotion. The students who completed all of the examinations were awarded certificates qualifying them for full membership. This tradition had been maintained and had influenced other educational organizations. For example, the examination and promotion system of elementary and middle schools could be based on the model established in the universities. Just as there was a diploma system in the university, he noted, there could be a grade system in the elementary schools. Thus, in Europe, children, from the beginning of their schooling, had a positive attitude toward examinations, looking on them as a means of advancing from grade to grade until finally a diploma was awarded.

Murray allowed that the European system had its faults. He suggested Japan could bypass these, drawing only on the strong points. What was the ideal educational system for the newly developing nation of Japan? First of all, students should be educated according to ability levels, or grades. Second, examinations should be used to determine advancement between grades. Third, special steps should be introduced to motivate students to study for advancement through examinations.

After completion of the curriculum for a particular level, students should be given a general exam appropriate to that level and a certificate should be given to those students who pass. A government examination officer should witness the examination

[1] In the "old-style" (Wade-Giles) romanization, *k'o-chii*; in Japanese, *kakyo*.

and sign the certificate along with the head of the school. The certificate should guarantee admission to the next level without a further examination. Therefore, while admission to a secondary-level school or university may be relatively easy, graduation should be made difficult with a demanding graduation exam. In order to maintain a high level of education, nothing is more effective than testing the student's academic ability by a strict and fair examination system. This examination system has advantages not only for students, who are motivated to study for tests, but also for teachers, who are encouraged to maintain a high standard of education. Murray suggested that the national government assume the responsibility of administering the examination for the university degree and the authority to award degrees.

Murray's ideal education system placed the examination at the core of educational policy. He further insisted that the degree, which was given as the culmination of repeated examinations, should become an essential qualification for entrance to the professions and government service. Those without a medical degree should not be allowed to become established doctors who publicly practice medicine. The same principle should apply to lawyers and judges. And only those with professional training certified by a university degree should be qualified for positions in government service.

Summing up his speech, Murray emphasized that establishing the connection between examinations, promotion, degrees, and professional certification would lead the people to respect examinations, no matter what social class they belonged to. The ideal educational system should encompass everyone from young children to adults. If examinations were introduced to the schools and children encouraged to compete with one another, the education system could become the main road to success and wealth. Learning would become a means for the people to succeed in their undertakings. Moreover in this way, literature, art, and science would receive new stimulation and be able to develop rapidly. As a result of this ideal educational system, the incompetent would be excluded from government service. Public office would be in the hands of those who were virtuous and talented. Murray concluded his commencement speech by directly addressing the graduates: "You who are about to graduate from the university are the first generation of the 'virtuous and talented' who have passed through this hard process of selection."

The Age of the Examination

One cannot help but be impressed by Murray's unqualified optimism regarding examinations. Murray clearly identified several of the problems of both the *keju* system of China and the European examination system. However, he maintained that these problems could easily be overcome, and that examinations were a critical mechanism for promoting progress not only in education but of the nation. His unqualified faith in examinations is especially striking today, when people are so conscious of various pathological phenomena resulting from the examination system and when attempts to solve and overcome those problems have become a major social and political issue in Japan. However, Murray's optimistic view of examinations was not unique; rather, it exemplifies the orthodox view prevalent at the time of his speech.

Murray must have been familiar with the examination system that had made surprisingly rapid progress in a brief time in England, because it had been gaining acceptance in the schools and universities of the United States. America was possibly more receptive to the principle of competitive examinations than Britain. Herbert Spencer's theory of social progress had a greater impact on the United States than in his native Britain. Burton Bledstein, commenting on the American experience with examinations, writes: "Finally in the 1840s, both parents and students began to accept the competitive written exam as a matter of course. Because the grade and award system was introduced in American education, such problems as individual achievement, competition among students, and the desire to succeed attracted special attention" (Bledstein 1976). It should also be added here that Britain and the United States were rather slow in the introduction of competitive examinations. In Germany and France, emphasis on examinations started in the early nineteenth century.

In any case, in the United States and Europe the age of examinations had already begun, and although various shortcomings had been identified, on the whole examinations were considered a useful and effective means for raising educational standards and resolving various problems within society. Murray's ideas were simply in keeping with the educational trend of his time.

Moreover, for this rapidly modernizing, insular, Oriental country, he advocated transplanting the examination system in a purer and more ideal form. As we will see later, Japan had experience with the introduction of an examination system for the selection of its bureaucrats in the eighth century, when it had adopted a system based on the Chinese example. The system remained in effect for nearly three hundred years, but it never took root as a social institution as it had done in China. After that, until the Meiji Restoration, although knowledge of the system was carried forward, there was effectively no examination system in use. So Murray had good grounds for his idealism.

But he was not a mere idealist. His influence as a senior advisor to a Ministry of Education which was then seeking to build a modern school system based on the Western model allowed him to have those ideals put into practice. Both in the new school system plan (*Gakkan Kōan: Nihon Kyōiku Hō*) submitted by Murray in 1877 and in his speech at Tokyo University, examinations were included as one of the important elements.

It is difficult to evaluate how much impact Murray's advocacy of the ideal educational system actually had on the development of Japan's new educational regime. Certainly by the time of Murray's departure from Japan in 1879, examinations had at least gained a foothold in the school system. As he had hoped, children were divided into grades on the basis of academic ability at the elementary-school level. Each time they finished the curriculum of a grade, they took an examination, which determined whether they could proceed to the next level. The same principle applied to secondary schools, and even to university. Applicants also had to pass a difficult entrance examination at the university level.

Japan, it would appear, was even more receptive to examinations than Britain or the United States. In premodern Japanese society before the 1868 Meiji Restoration, competition had been strictly limited by the entrenched class system. After the Meiji Restoration, however, Japan opened its doors to the age of competition, adopting the principle that success is based on effort (*risshin shusse*). One example of the new ethos was the popularity in Japan of Samuel Smiles's *Self-Help*. Translated by Nakamura Masanao, the Tokyo University lecturer who had spoken at the same commencement ceremony as Murray, the book was first published in Japan in 1871, and sold more than one million copies in a short period. By comparison, although the original was first published in Britain in 1858, more than ten years before the translation, Smiles reported that sales came to 20,000 copies in the first year, and no more than 55,000 copies over six years. Japan may have started out a little behind Britain, but it was well on its way into the age of competition and examinations.

Institutionalization of Competition

Murray's conviction that the competition fostered by examinations leads to educational progress was elaborated at length in the commentary section of his new school system plan. There he asserted that the reason students should be divided into grades and classes was to make them competitive and to encourage them to move to higher grades by passing the standard examination. Granting a diploma was a tool to make the students academically competitive.

As Murray pointed out in his speech, the Chinese term for the traditional examination system, *keju*, actually means selection based on knowledge. The selection involved in this case was for the imperial civil service, and it was based on the mastery of several subjects or books, demonstrated by performance on the examination. The purpose of the examination was to choose the best candidates from among many applicants, so all but aspirants with the highest scores were eliminated. Thus, the examination was extremely competitive, and applicants studied intensively over a period of many years in order to better other candidates. The successive emperors of China used this competitive examination system as a means to choose talent on the basis of ability rather than status or class.

It was toward the end of the sixteenth century that Europe first learned of China's competitive examination system. The details of the *keju* system were first reported by the Jesuit priest, Matteo Ricci (Hirakawa 1969). Of course, as Murray pointed out, a more primitive type of examination system was already in use in the European university at that time. The word *universitas*,

Latin for university, means a union—in other words, a guild of scholars. Like other guilds, the university needed a qualification system to determine who could become a member. The early university examinations thus were qualifying exams.

In this qualification exam, however, there was no element of competition. For example, the examination at the University of Paris for the *baccalauréat*, the lowest degree, included three conditions: (1) whether an applicant had resided in Paris for a certain period of time and attended the required classes; (2) whether he had knowledge of the contents of the textbooks; and (3) whether the examinee had the ability to preside over a debate (Yokō 1977). Among the three conditions, the closest to what today is considered an examination was presiding over a debate. But even in this case all that was involved usually was observation of the examinee as he led junior students in debate. It was less an examination than the repetition of a ritual.

Through teaching and learning based mainly on discussion, the teachers came to know the ability of each student quite well. When the teacher found that a student's ability reached the desired standard, the teacher recommended that the student take the diploma examination. Given the nature of the system, it cannot be said that the examination was competitive. Emile Durkheim wrote: "In the University and the colleges of the Middle Ages the system of competition was completely unknown. In those days, there were no rewards to recompense merit and induce effort. Examinations were organised in such a way that for conscientious pupils they were little more than a formality" (Durkheim 1938 [trans. Collins, 1979], 261).

The competitive examination system which Matteo Ricci observed in China was fundamentally different from the prevailing practice in Europe. First, the Chinese examination system developed without any relationship with a system of formal education. China did not have a systematic education system analogous to the European schools and universities.

Second, the *keju* system was established to select officials, while the traditional European organs of government relied on other means to select their staffs. The *keju* system gained such prominence in China because the successive emperors sought able government officials who would be subject to their will. In contrast, in seventeenth-century Europe, government offices were virtually the property of the aristocracy. Important families directly participated in the sale and purchase of government offices and in the reassignment of officials, without even bothering to consult their kings. The aristocratic control of government service did not provide fertile ground for the import of a competitive civil-service examination. However superior the Chinese competitive examination system might have been, the necessary social and political conditions for its import were not found in Europe. It was not until the eighteenth century that a competitive examination system became linked to the system for employing government officials.

Nevertheless, China's competitive examination system did have some impact on Europe. One avenue was through the influence of the various schools and colleges established throughout Europe by the Jesuit order. As is well known, the Jesuits considered education to be an important part of their missionary activity. From the time of the 1599 policy statement on education of the Society of Jesus, the Jesuits established numerous mission schools, especially in France, which attracted a large number of eager students (Shimura 1975).

It would appear that Matteo Ricci's reports about the Chinese examination system contributed to the distinctive character of the Jesuit schools. In sharp contrast to the other schools of that era, the Jesuit schools, especially the *collège*, introduced competitive examinations to evaluate each student's progress. Durkheim, in *The Evolution of Educational Thought*, observes: "Then here we have [in the Jesuit *collège*], quite suddenly, a totally different system, which not only establishes itself but which instantaneously develops to the point of super-abundance." Durkheim explains why this *collège* promoted the competitive system:

> In order to train pupils in intensive formal work which was, however, pretty lacking in substance, it was not enough to surround them, to envelop them at close quarters with solicitude and vigilance; it was not enough to be constantly concerned to contain and to sustain them; it was also necessary to stimulate them. The goad which the Jesuits employed consisted exclusively in competition. Not only were they the first to organise the competitive system in the colleges, but they also developed it to a point of greater intensi-

ty than it has ever subsequently known (Durkheim, 1938/ 1979, 260).

Through the Jesuit *collèges*, the system of competition was introduced to European education. This exam-based competitive system did not immediately spread, however, to the other European countries or other schools in France. The rapid diffusion of competitive examinations did not begin until the nineteenth century when industrial society was born and the principle of competition became established in the economy, society, and sports.

Examinations in Nineteenth-Century Europe

The Civil Service Examination and the *Abitur*

Let us take a closer look at the beginning of the age of examinations in Europe (Amano 1982). Eighteenth-century Germany, and particularly Prussia under Frederick the Great, pioneered in the introduction of competitive examinations for the selection of officials. The purpose of the examinations was the same as in ancient China: to eliminate the power of the aristocracy, Frederick proposed that employment of government officers would be based on examinations. The examination system was a useful means for attracting able personnel who had a national perspective while avoiding the possible dangers of nepotism and factional favoritism (Ueyama 1964).

The selection of government officials through examinations was first introduced for judicial officials in the eighteenth century, and by 1748 it had spread to the rest of the bureaucracy, including the government administrative offices. The examination consisted of two levels: an initial examination to select candidates and a second examination to finally select the government officials. Appointment was based strictly on the examination results. In contrast to China's *keju* system, the applicants for government office in Prussia were expected to complete a program of approved courses in a field such as public administration, agriculture, or forestry in a university within the Prussian empire. University graduation, then, became a condition for employment as a government officer (Yoshimura 1950).

With the introduction of this requirement, the role of the university as a training ground for government officers was obviously strengthened. Meanwhile, another examination system developed in Prussia, the *Abitur* or middle-school graduation examination. The *Abitur*, first introduced in 1788, came to serve as a qualification examination: those who passed it were automatically admitted to the universities. Prior to the institutionalization of the *Abitur*, the examination for choosing students for German universities was so easy that it neither stimulated diligent students to study nor threatened lazy students. As the number of university students increased, the *Abitur* was introduced to upgrade the quality of the universities, rejecting youths with poor scholastic ability (Nagao 1975, 254–56).

The *Abitur* of the classical middle school, later named the *Gymnasium*, was not a competitive examination. A teacher would ask a student to sit for the exam only after he was satisfied that the student's scholarship had reached the required standard for the course. This is why the *Abitur* was also called the *Reife* (certification of maturity), and naturally the success rate was high. This systemization of the *Abitur* examination raised the standard of academic ability of university applicants. Furthermore, since the examination could be offered only by middle schools with an approved curriculum (one focusing on classical languages), those who held the *Abitur* qualification came to possess a common educational and intellectual background. On graduation from university, these were the people who, allied by that common background, took the various national qualifying examinations (which by then were held not only for the civil service but had spread to many other intellectual fields) to enter occupations in the bureaucracy, medicine, and teaching, and eventually formed a unique social group. Fritz K. Ringer speaks of this new aristocracy by virtue of academic qualifications and selection by examination as the "German Mandarins" (Ringer 1974). The Mandarins, of course, originally were the literary class of China, established through success in the examination for government service. Germany's examinations for government service, other professional examinaions, and the *Abitur* also created a special class. It might be said that the age of examinations and the correspondent elevation of the significance of academic qualifications was sparked by these developments in eighteenth-century Germany. It is no wonder that Max Weber developed such a strong interest in examinations and academic careers.

Reading Weber's *Confucianism and Taoism* makes it apparent that he was well informed concerning the *keju* system, and this helps in understanding his deep interest in the relationship between examinations and the purpose of education. Weber identified one of the characteristics of the modern bureaucracy in the rationalization of culture and education, and emphasized the importance of the links between bureaucracies, examinations, and academic preparation. According to him, the continuous development of the rational and professional examination system was sparked by the process of bureaucratization that emerged in the modern age. Weber clearly developed his theory linking education, exams, and careers from the examples of the German reality of his time and the great Chinese empire of the past.

The Examination and the *Concours*
In Europe, France followed Germany on the road to competitive examinations. Prior to the French Revolution, class and lineage determined an individual's social position. The Revolution broke down the *ancien régime* and proclaimed that all citizens were equal before the law and could not be discriminated against except on the basis of ability. Indeed the Revolution proclaimed the beginning of an age of competition based on ability. To provide all with a fair chance in this competition, free compulsory public education would be established. Up to twelve years of age, all children would receive a common education, and afterward only the most able youth would climb up the educational ladder, based on selective examinations (Piobetta 1961). But these educational reforms were not realized by the revolutionary government.

After the dissolution of the old regime's education system, it was Napoleon who reorganized and centralized the educational system. As Ringer (1979) points out, the series of educational reforms introduced by Napoleon in the early nineteenth century followed a pattern virtually identical to that of the reforms which had been carried out in Prussia somewhat earlier. In other words, both France and Prussia sought highly trained professional elites in order to establish powerful, absolutist states. For this purpose, Prussia strengthened the national civil-service examination and the graduation examination of the middle schools. Napoleon created a highly centralized and unified public education system and sought to control it through standardized examinations and a certificate system that the state monopolized.

The French and Prussian systems differed, however, in one respect. While the existence of powerful universities was a premise of the Prussian system, the French universities had been dissolved during the Revolution and were not revived until the end of the nineteenth century.

To replace the universities that had been an integral part of the *ancien régime*, Napoleon created *facultés*—schools of law, medicine, theology, humanities, and sciences—as a new type of higher educational institution. In reality, however, these institutions were too weak to be called higher educational institutions, and indeed the two central faculties of humanities and science, were merely institutions for administering the *baccalauréat* examination certifying that middle school graduates had achieved an academic level sufficient for further study. The *baccalauréat* was both the admission certificate for the *grandes écoles* and the occupational certification for government service and other professions.

Napoleon looked to a new group of institutions, the *grandes écoles*, as the vehicles for selecting and training the talented. The first *grande école*, a civil engineering school, had been founded under the old regime in 1747. The students were selected and ranked by an entrance examination. After graduation from the school, their official employment status was determined by reference to their rank in the exams taken during their school years. (Gaxotte 1956). In 1783, a mining school was added. And in the revolutionary period the famous *école polytechnique* and the *école normale supérieure* were founded. Napoleon approved of these schools and introduced measures to strengthen them. The most important characteristic of these *grandes écoles* was their severely competitive examinations, and all of their graduates were ensured jobs in the national bureaucracy. They became much more prominent institutions of higher education than the academic *facultés*.

As early as 1876, Japan's Ministry of Education published a study of the school system of France that gave considerable attention to the *grandes écoles* and especially the *école polytechnique*. According to this account, the applicants underwent an initial examination at one of the examination centers scattered across the country. Those who passed the preliminary exam were invited to Paris for the second examination, ranked in order of their score on the examination, and then were admitted according to ranking until the quota was filled. For students who gained entrance to the *grandes écoles*, examinations were given at each grade level in order to determine their relative standing. After graduation, the students with the best academic records were given first preference in filling government offices.

Even though Germany had preceded France in the introduction of competitive examinations, the Germans often expressed dismay at the complexity of the French system and France's singular reliance on such examinations. E. R. Curtius, a German scholar of European literature, wrote in his 1930 *Theory of French Culture* that the greatest difference between German and French higher education was the examination system. He noted that in France the examinations occurred more often, covered more subjects, and were more difficult than those in Germany. A more complex system of scoring was used to determine the results of French examinations as well. In general, in France only a small number of the applicants succeeded. The reason the examination was so difficult is that those who succeeded were guaranteed a government position. Moreover, according to Curtius, the French school was one of the primary factors in social selection. It was this factor, he says, that reinforced the rational tendencies of the French spirit. The state which seeks able personnel requires that they be selected through examinations. And out of deference to the republican spirit, competition among able people must take place in strict equality. Therefore, the method of frequent examination became the inevitable means of selection for France.

British Society and Competitive Examinations

Compared to Germany and France, the competitive examination system was slow to have a significant impact on British society. This is somewhat surprising, for within the British universities and middle schools, competitive examinations had been introduced in the eighteenth century. It is usually said that the British examination system started in 1747 with the tripos exam (for the honors degree) of Cambridge University (Montgomery 1965).

This examination was given to candidates for the bachelor's degree, and those students who achieved the best results received the special recognition of being granted an honors degree. As the students cherished this honor, the examination rapidly became competitive. With the increase in student interest, the examiners had to consider ways to improve the objectivity of their evaluations. Thus the written portion of the exam came to assume greater weight than the oral portion, and such subjects as mathematics which are easier to score objectively became increasingly important. This honors examination system was introduced at Oxford University in 1800 (Yasuhara 1981).

It would appear that the honors examination system was introduced to stimulate a competitive spirit in the students, and thereby improve the quality of education. The records of the Board of Oxford University state: "The examination is an important means not only to test student ability but also to encourage and lead the students in the preferred direction" (Montgomery 1965, 14). In this respect, the honors examination was similar to the examinations introduced in the Jesuit *collège*.

The competitive examination system was also introduced in the English public schools, the private schools which prepared students for Oxford and Cambridge. Shrewsbury is well known as a typical example of this phenomenon. The competitive examination system was brought into this school in the early nineteenth century, when half-year term examinations were introduced to determine the grading and promotion of students. Students who achieved excellent marks in these examinations were given intensive education in smaller classes. This educational method, which had never existed in England before, stimulated students to study, and their academic ability improved; because of these practices, the graduates of Shrewsbury came to virtually monopolize the top places in the Oxford-Cambridge scholarship examinations (Tsunogae 1975).

According to Montgomery, by the mid-nineteenth century there were numbers of people who had passed the competitive exams in the public schools and the great universities, and who believed in the importance of examinations. These people, thanks to the recognition achieved during their student days, were accorded high prestige after leaving school and came to occupy important positions in the political and educational world. Through the efforts of these people, the competitive examination system gradually came to influence the full spectrum of public life.

Compared to the well-organized educational system of Prussia, the British system was undeveloped, lacking in unity, and of a low standard. By the middle of the nineteenth century, the leading groups in Britain began to fear that this backwardness in education would affect the strength of the economy and ultimately erode national power. Unlike France and Prussia, in England education was not considered the responsibility of the state, which had neither a tradition of central education administration nor the organizational depth for it. Each social class had developed its own schools to meet its respective needs. Oxbridge and the public schools belonged to the upper strata of the society, composed of the landowning aristocracy and the upper middle class; the working class had simple elementary schools.

In this highly decentralized context, the competitive examination system was employed as an administrative device to introduce some control and unity to the educational system. In the 1840s, qualifying examinations were first introduced to select and improve the quality of teachers, and in 1861, a unique system called "payment by results" was introduced to the elementary schools. Under this system, which aimed to improve the quality of education, a government subsidy was to be distributed to each school based on the average performance of the school's students.

To determine student performance, a standardized examination was developed for each grade. The school inspectors traveled to each school to give the examination. As the subsidy was based on the number of students who passed the examination, student performance directly affected the amount of subsidy available to a school for improving teachers' salaries. Thus teachers had an incentive to improve their students' results on the examination. Despite criticisms that the system would sacrifice education to the examination, it lasted until 1897.

After the 1840s, the demand for a higher standard of middle school education also intensified. Behind this demand was the recognition, as Matthew Arnold put it, that the English middle class was the worst educated class of its type in the world (Roach 1971, 39). In both Germany and France there were well-organized middle schools, the *Gymnasium* and the *lycée*, respectively, and the examinations of these schools, the *Abitur* and the *baccalauréat*, tended to promote the quality and homogeneity of middle-class culture. The standard of the "middle schools" of Britain, however, not only varied greatly but was usually relatively low. Thus critics argued that it was time to establish a unified system of secondary education and examinations so that young people could have a common purpose.

While the arguments were sound, neither the middle class nor the middle schools of England were receptive to state intervention and control. Instead, they looked to the leading universities to establish an appropriate examination. In the late 1850s the local examination was initiated by Oxford and Cambridge in response to this demand. This was also a competitive examination. Applicants were ranked according to the results of the examination, and the names of the top students were announced and publicized.

It was during this time that the competitive examination began to be introduced to the bureaucratic world of Britain, which had up to that time been controlled by favoritism. The East India Company's introduction of open examinations for personnel selection in 1853 was said to be the first instance, and general implementation of civil-service-type examinations did not begin until the 1870s. Michael Young speaks of the ensuing period as the starting point for the age of meritocracy: "Patronage at last was abolished in the civil service and competitive entry made the rule. Merit became the arbiter, attainment the standard, for entry and advancement in a splendid profession" (Young 1958, 19).

The Ideal Examination System

What we have summarized so far are the main features of the European examination system of the mid-nineteenth century that Murray might have been familiar with. In all the advanced countries, the age of examinations—or, more precisely speaking, the age of competitive examinations—had already started. The methods of implementing these examinations, however, varied widely from country to country.

In the section on examinations in the *Encyclopedia of Education*, a 1919 American publication, the German, American, French, and British systems are compared and contrasted: "In Germany and America the tendency has been to limit the number of examinations so far as possible, and by building up a strong teaching profession and system of inspection to accept the decision of the teacher on the question whether pupils have attained required standards or not. In France every step in the education process is marked by some form of state examination. In England a system of inspection and better trained teachers has taken the place of examinations in elementary schools. But in secondary education a multiplicity of examining bodies still remains."

This description refers mainly to primary and middle school education. In the case of higher education, in France the entrance examination was emphasized at the *grandes écoles*, while in England the crucial examination took place during the course of schooling. In Germany, the various national examinations were more important than those given by the universities themselves. Similarly, in the examinations for government service and the professions there was considerable difference among these countries.

Compared with the complex reality of the implementation of the examination principle in these European countries, we can see that Murray's ideal educational system of grades, examinations, and degrees consisted of a highly selective synthesis of the merits of each country's system. In adopting a new system, any country will encounter strong resistance. Those who enjoy the privilege of status and lineage, in particular, are likely to strongly oppose competitive examinations, which evaluate the ability of individuals by a rigorous, objective standard. When the examination system for government service was proposed for England, members of the upper class ridiculed the proposal as illusionary, Prussian, Chinese, and republican, and they criticized it as a move to deprive the aristocracy of their position in government and to give people without cultivation the status of gentlemen (Yoshimura 1950). No matter how great the power of the reformer, it is difficult to eradicate old systems and customs and replace them with completely new ones. What Murray hoped to achieve in proposing his ideal educational system was sure to encounter resistance.

Yet as we proceed through the following chapters, we will gradually find that Murray's idea was realized to a remarkable degree. Before turning to the reform process, however, let us look at the history and tradition of Japanese examinations prior to the adoption of the European idea.

Chapter Two

Examinations in Traditional Society

Examinations in Premodern Society

The *Kōkyo* System: Civil Service Examinations in Old Japan

An American scholar who intensively reviewed the history of examinations found no evidence of examinations being used for selection prior to their use in China (Têng 1943). The examination system for selecting government officials was created around the end of the fifth century, and began to be referred to as the *keju* system during the seventh century. The *keju*, which might be called the world's oldest examination system, continued in China until 1904.

In Europe, the first examinations did not take place until the foundation of the medieval university. It is said that the faculty of law at the University of Bologna in Northern Italy was the first medieval university to use examinations. But in contrast to the *keju*, Bologna gave an oral examination. Nakayama Shigeru, observing this difference between testing based on written and oral responses, developed his theory of the characteristics of Eastern and Western learning (Nakayama 1974). A written examination was conducted at a European university for the first time in 1702 (Teng 1943).

How about Japan? In fact, in the early eighth century, Japan first tried an examination system modeled after the *keju* system. The Japanese system, called *kōkyo* (or *kuko*) long predates the European experience.

The Taihō Code, dating from the early eighth century, outlines the *kōkyo*. According to the Code, those who wanted to take the examination were first required to study Chinese classics at the government's college (*daigakuryō*) established in the capital, or at a local school. The *daigakuryō* had been founded around 670 by appointing as teachers scholars who had come to Japan from Paekche, an early Korean Kingdom, so that it was, in effect, a university staffed by foreign scholars. Qualifications for the students were determined according to aristocratic ranking, and except in exceptional circumstances entrance was not open to those below the fifth rank.

In the college, students underwent a systematic program of study interspersed with exams. For example, every ten days the students were given an examination testing memorization and understanding of the contents of the Chinese classical texts they were studying. These examinations were called *junshi* (periodic examinations.) In the memorization examination, three ideographs from a thousand-ideograph passage were excised, and the student was required to supply the missing characters. In the content exam, the students were required to explain the meaning of three passages, each selected from a two-thousand-character section of the text. Those who failed these exams were punished with a whipping.

In addition, each year in July, an annual examination, or *saishi*, was given. This review examination, which covered the whole year of study, only tested understanding of the content. Those who correctly answered six or more of eight questions were given a superior grade (*jōdai*), those who answered four were given an average grade (*chūdai*), and those who answered three or fewer were given a low grade (*gedai*). Three successive years with a low grade led to expulsion. The number of years of recommended study was not specified, but students who could not gain sufficient academic mastery to pass the *kōkyo* examination within nine years were ordered to leave the school.

Those who finished their study and wished to seek a position in government service were next required to take a graduation examination. This examination, administered orally, consisted of ten questions on each of several classical texts. The students who correctly answered eight of the ten questions pertaining to a particular text passed; those who mastered all of the classic texts were recognized as *kyojin*, and their names were given by the college to the government. Together with the *kōjin*, who were candidates recommended by local governors, the *kyojin* were invited to take the written examinations for employment by the central government. This second round of examinations consisted of six parts including sections called *shūsai*, *myōgyō*, and *shinshi*; of these, the *shūsai* was considered the most difficult. The applicants were ranked based on their examination scores, and only those who obtained one of the top two rankings were awarded an offiial rank and could hope for a government position (Takahashi 1978).

The *kōkyo* system differed in several respects from the *keju* system of the T'ang Dynasty on which it was modeled. The examination's relationship to employment was perhaps the most important difference. In China, those who succeeded in the examination were almost always given a high-ranking civil service position, and thus the *keju* system came to be viewed as the essential means for reaching the top levels in the bureaucracy (Murakami 1980, 268), but in Japan this was not the case. Rather, the main route to the highest positions was hereditary privilege, based on the *on'i* system. In this system, the male children of aristocrats of the fifth rank or higher were automatically given an official rank at the age of twenty-one. This rank was higher than the rank a child from an aristocratic family of the sixth or lower rank could obtain, even if through hard study he passed the *shūsai* examination. "Blood (lineage) produced government officers, not study at a college. . . . The ancient literature speaks of the colleges as places for cultivating men of wisdom as well as places where courtiers enjoy study. However, nowhere is the college described as a place for training government officers" (Takahashi 1978, 78–79).

The school system in T'ang China did not function as a training facility for civil servants, either. However, in the *keju* exams all were treated equally, regardless of lineage, and the exams were the critical gateway to the bureaucracy.

The *keju* system of China was created and developed in order to reduce the power of the aristocracy and create a bureaucratic class obedient to the emperor, whereas the *kōkyo* system in Japan was imported from China to reinforce rather than to alter a system of government based on aristocratic privilege. Thus the *kōkyo* system was rapidly reduced to little more than nominal existence once the Fujiwara clan achieved prominence. During the more than two centuries between 704 and 938, only sixty-five passed the *shūsai* examination.

In short, unlike China, the imperial system of ancient Japan was not managed by a bureaucracy. It was an aristocracy in which government posts were assigned according to family lineage. There was no place for an open, competitive examination for bureaucratic posts. This situation had a profound impact on the development of the ancient college (*daigakuryō*). "It was foolish to study hard at the college, as promotion and success were determined by family name, regardless of how hard one might study" (Takahashi 1978, 100). The *kōkyo* system, while modeled after the *keju* system, became meaningless with the rise of the aristocracy with the Fujiwara clan.

Examinations in the Shōheikō

After the abeyance of the *kōkyo* system, Japan was without a system of open, competitive examinations over the near millennium of rule by military governments (*bakufu*) until the Meiji Restoration in 1868. In the Edo period (1600–1868) when the military government reached maturity, both the shogun's central government and the local fief (*han*) governments developed bureaucratic systems staffed by members of the samurai class, and schools were established to educate samurai-class children. While some Confucian scholars, pointing to the old Chinese system, proposed to develop a general, competitive examination, this suggestion sparked no interest.

Only at the end of the Edo period, when the feudal system had reached an impasse on many fronts and both the central and local governments were in dire financial straits, did the need for selecting capable people independent of family lineage emerge as a serious proposition. According to Ronald Dore, the term *jinzai*, or "human talent," began to appear "from the middle of the seventeenth century in fief edicts announcing the establishment of schools or redefining educational policy" (Dore 1965, 44). Since many local governments began to establish their own schools in the latter half of the eighteenth century, it is apparent that the leaders of that time looked upon education as a means for developing *jinzai*. But the idea of training capable people had to be considered within the framework of the entrenched class system.

For example, in 1787, as a part of the Kansei Reform initiated by Matsudaira Sadanobu, the central government enlarged its own school for training the samurai class, the Shōheikō, and introduced a system of periodic examinations.

The enlarged school accepted both children of high-ranking samurai who held key positions in the government and children of lower-ranking samurai who seemed to show exceptional promise. The former group attended from ages seven to fourteen and each year took a noncompetitive oral examination, the *sodoku ginmi*, to test their ability to read Chinese classical texts. The latter group underwent a different examination, the *gakumon ginmi* (examination of scholarship), on which their ability in writing and comprehension was also tested; this second examination, administered every three years, had a clearly competitive character.

The *gakumon ginmi* was divided into the preliminary examination, which lasted for one day, and the final examination, which took four days. The final examination consisted of three parts: theory, history, and composition. Those who passed the exam were graded at one of three levels — upper (*ko*), intermediate (*otsu*), and lower (*hei*) — and were given awards. Not only those who had studied at the Shōheikō, but also anyone who had undertaken study of the state philosophy, *Shushigaku*, was eligible to take the examination since it was not, in fact, a Shōheikō examination, but was conducted by the *bakufu* with Shōheikō staff as the examiners. First held in 1792, the examination was conducted a total of seventeen times up to 1865. Records show that during this period a total of 66 upper-level and 415 intermediate-level grades were awarded. On the occasion of the second examination, held in 1794, there were 237 applicants, of whom five achieved the upper-level ranking, fourteen the intermediate level, and twenty-eight the lower level. With a success rate of less than 20 percent, it was indeed a difficult examination (Ōkubo 1943).

While the *gakumon ginmi* was modeled after the *keju* system of China, it differed in one important respect: success in the *gakumon ginmi* had no direct relation to appointment to a position. Of course, an outstanding performance on the exam could enhance a prospect's chances. When we consider that well-known administrators like Toyama Saemonnojō and Ōta Shokusanjin were among those receiving an A grade in the second *gakumon ginmi*, it is clear that the examination was not entirely unrelated to the selection of talented bureaucrats for the *bakufu* (Ōkubo 1943, 105). Dore (1965, 201) also notes that one of the purposes of these examinations was to identify people who might later be worthy of promotion.

Nevertheless, the fundamental objective was the promotion of scholarship, and public recognition of excellent performance was the only award students could be sure of. As performance was not tied to career success, it might be said that the *gakumon ginmi* examination was closer to the honor-degree examination of England's Oxford and Cambridge than to the *keju* examination of China.

In premodern Japan, as in England, a competitive examination which ignored the hereditary class system could not be employed to guarantee a position in government service, for there was fear that such an examination would topple the foundation of the feudal system. "Among the scholars of the Edo period, no one openly advocated the abolition of the feudal class system; what the scholars proposed was the relaxation of some of the rules so that there would be more room for talented people to make a difference" (Dore 1965, 197–99).

The Edo-period Confucian scholar and educator Hirose Tansō argued as follows: "After all, since it is impossible to do away with the established and powerful families, there is no alternative except to educate the offspring of those families so they can perform valuable services for the country." Under the circumstances of entrenched privilege, providing, not an open, competitive examination system, but an excellent education for the hereditary rulers would make the greatest social contribution. Tansō concluded: "To educate able people is a vital necessity for any fief, and there is no other means for educating able people than creating good schools" (Ōkubo 1943, 75).

The Grade System and Examinations

What, then, was the relationship between the education given at those schools and any competitiveness or examinations there? Essentially, schools are places which are established for the purpose of transmitting specified measures of knowledge at specified levels. This definition applies just as well to schools such as the Shoheikō or the fief schools, where the Chinese classics were taken as the basis for the knowledge to be imparted to achieve the goal of educating members of the ruling class in the Confucian virtues deemed appropriate to their class. Once a body of knowledge has been adopted as the foundation of an education program, and an order in which the content of that material is to be taught has been established, a curriculum emerges. And a curriculum provides a basis for dividing learners into groups according to the stage of learning reached, in other words according to their level of academic achievement. This gives rise to "grades" or "classes," a phenomenon which Philippe Ariès has identified as first occurring in Europe in the sixteenth century (Ariès 1973).

The first evidence of the introduction of grades in Japan appears in the 1660s, in the rules of the Kōbunkan, which later became the *bakufu*'s Shōheikō. These rules outline a *goka jittō no sei*: *goka* refers to five subjects, while *jittō* indicates that each subject has ten grades. Dore considers this a formal grade system for each subject, with students being classified strictly according to their academic performance (Dore 1970, 17), but how extensively this system was utilized is not known.

According to Ishikawa Matsutarō, it was as part of the school reform near the close of the Edo period that the grade system was designed and installed in many fief schools. By the early 1850s some sixty-five percent of the approximately two hundred fief schools had some type of grade system (Ishikawa 1978, 83).

The timing of the introduction of the grade system is important because of the implications for school examinations. With the establishment of a grade system, it becomes necessary to objectively evaluate the results of each student in order to place him in the proper grade. Examinations are a means for schools to carry out this objective evaluation.

Let us look at the case of Kōdōkan, the school of the Hikone fief (Ishikawa 1978, 86–87). According to the school's procedure for lessons (*kagyō shidai*), dated 1830, the grade system was such that four schools (*ryō*) were set up, and in each there were five or six "seats" or "grades." The first and second *ryō*—lower schools —provided what we might call primary education, and each had five or six grades. The third school provided middle-school education and had five grades. The fourth school, which constituted the higher school, also had five grades. The students started from the sixth grade of the first school and gradually moved up. Promotion out of the first school was based on the teachers' judgment, but from the second school up, all promotions were decided by examinations. The system practiced by the Kōdōkan is considered to be one of the most thoroughly organized of that time, but it is representative of other fief schools in its reliance on examinations to judge academic progress.

The question is the competitive nature of these examinations. The students at the fief schools came from families with different ranks in the hereditary class system. If the examinations had genuinely allowed competition based on academic ability, it would surely have led to contradictions with the class system and might possibly have eroded the feudal system. Therefore, various efforts were made to ensure that the examinations would not become too competitive.

For example, students were never ranked exclusively on the basis of examination results. When ranking was absolutely necessary, the age and year of entrance might be used as criteria. The award system based on examination performance encouraged the average students rather than arousing their jealousy by highlighting the top students. Put differently, the evaluation focused on the students' efforts instead of their abilities or other personal characteristics (Dore 1965, 202). The focus of Confucian education on the cultivation of virtue conveniently matched the exigencies of the examination and grade system.

If the purpose of education is to train capable people with a high level of professional knowledge of the military arts, economics, and agriculture, examinations have to measure the knowledge the students have acquired and evaluate their ability. Consequently, examinations cannot help but have a competitive character. In fact, toward the end of the Edo period, as the demand for capable people who possessed not only virtue but practical ability grew and as Western studies were introduced at the fief schools, examinations rapidly acquired both a competitive and a selective character.

In some fiefs, it was proposed that those who could not pass the examinations should be removed from public posts, lose their hereditary rank, or suffer a cut in their stipend. The Kumamoto fief even publicly announced that ability should be taken into consideration in personnel decisions for public posts (Dore 1965, 203). Such cases were exceedingly rare, however, and not implemented in a way that would totally contradict the class system. Thus, as Japan approached the Meiji Restoration, examinations still did not have an overtly competitive character at these governmental or public schools.

However, the *shijuku*, or private schools, were free of the restrictions of the class system, and, as we will observe below, by the end of the Edo period some of them had instituted a level of competition comparable to that found in the Jesuit colleges of seventeenth-century Europe.

Educational Methods for Chinese Studies

Before turning to the private schools, we need to look at the educational methods employed in Confucian or Chinese studies of the period, for they were closely related to the nature of examinations.

The educational method that the Japanese invented for reading and interpreting Chinese classics was truly unique (Ishikawa 1978; Ōkubo 1943). Students were first taught to read the Chinese ideographs by transliterating them into Japanese sounds, a process called *sodoku*. The first and second schools of the Kōdōkan school of Hikone concentrated on *sodoku*. There the students were divided into students who study ideographs (*shūjisei*) and students who learn how to read (*dokushosei*). After *sodoku*, the students proceeded to *kōgi* or *kōshaku*, learning to interpret the content of the textbook used for *sodoku* practice.

After acquiring a basic reading ability, in the third school of the Kōdōkan the students participated in a discussion of the contents, called *kaidoku* or *rinkō*. This was much like a seminar in a modern university. The students read and discussed the assigned parts for better understanding, while the teacher provided criticism and clarified those parts the students could not understand. More advanced students moved into independent study or research, called *dokukan*. They went to their teachers for guidance on problems they encountered during this independent study.

In *kaidoku* and *rinkō*, where students of basically the same academic level offered their respective interpretations of successive sentences, the atmosphere could easily become very competitive. In the public schools, however, special efforts were made to prevent that from happening. Even though the students were all samurai of the same clan, their lineages varied. In their classes the students were taught to observe the deference appropriate to the ranks of their classmates even as they demonstrated differences in ability.

However, the private schools were different. There, scholars who were out of office taught their followers, emphasizing their own point of view. In contrast to the public schools, these private schools stood outside of the framework of the class system that held together the clan and feudal governments.

Hirose Tansō, the founder of Kangien, one of the most renowned private schools in the later years of the Edo period, is said to have made the phrase *sandatsu*, or "three disallowances," his motto (Naramoto 1969, 136): the age, previous education, and lineage of students entering Kangien were to be disallowed, or ignored. In other words, the students lost their social identity from the moment of enrollment, and their position and status in the school was determined purely on the basis of ability and performance.

Thus, even though private schools existed within the same feudal social situation as such organizations as the Shōheikō and the fief schools, they developed into places of learning with liberal philosophies free of the yoke of the feudal society. These places of learning became fields for intellectual competition, where students competed freely against each other regardless of their age or status in the *rinkō* and *kaidoku* meetings.

Examinations and Competition at the Private Schools

The Education of Kangien

Let us take a look at an actual situation at Kangien (Inoue 1978). This school was founded in 1805, at today's Hita City in Ōita Prefecture, and in 1818 it was named Kangien. When the school was closed in the early years of the Meiji period, the number of the students totaled three thousand. As mentioned above, the school did not give any special consideration to the age, previous education, or lineage of its students. Instead, three principles of achievement were recognized at Kangien: "Seniority depended not on age but on the length of time at this school. Superiority depended not on previous schooling but on the number of courses one has finished. Honor depended not on family lineage but on scholastic performance" (Takano 1969, 137). The other side of the "three dis-allowances" of traditional privilege were the source of "three credits": for length of study, effort, and academic achievement. In this manner, Kangien became the arena for competition and the demonstration of academic ability free of the framework of the class system.

The teaching and learning approach at Kangien was not notably different from that of other schools for Chinese studies, except that competition was cleverly woven into Kangien's approach (Ishikawa 1974, 219–220). The curriculum was divided into nine grades. In each grade there was an upper and lower level. Entering students actually started at grade zero, one grade prior to first grade, and were moved from the first to the ninth grade on the basis of scholastic examinations. Following *sodoku*, the students moved into *rindoku* (reading a text in turn), where a student was asked to read three pages without any errors before the next student received his chance to read. When a reader made a mistake, the student who spotted the error got the next chance to read. After three rounds, the class ended. The next stage was *rinkō*, in which the same procedure was used, with a sentence of twenty ideographs constituting a unit. The performance of each student in *sodoku* and *rinkō* was recorded in a personal record.

After *rinkō* came *kaikō*, in which the book master Tansō used in his lectures was used as a textbook. Twenty to twenty-four students sat face to face in two rows of ten to twelve. The first seat of row A was the pivotal position in this exercise, for points could only be obtained while sitting in that position. First, the first four students of row B posed questions in succession to the individual seated at the head of row A. If he managed to answer their questions, he received three points, and then he could begin asking questions of the students in row B, starting with the fifth position. For each unanswered question he received an additional point. However, if he could not answer any of the first four questions or if those in the end seats of row B successfully answered his questions, the person from row B who had outdone him won his seat, and everyone else moved up a seat. *Kaikō* was a competitive exercise to gain and hold the first position.

On reaching the fifth grade, students began to take written

examinations. The examinations consisted of *kutō* (declamation), poetry, and composition. *Kutō* examinations were held three times a month while poetry and composition were given twice a month. Altogether seven examinations were given each month, and if a student's total score exceeded a certain standard, he was promoted to the next level of his grade. On reaching the upper level, however, the student was required to take an advancement examination in addition to these regular exams. For the advancement examination, the student was provided a textbook to memorize and then was required to reproduce or interpret selected passages, and those who passed were advanced to the next grade.

The result for each student was announced in a public list called the *gettan hyō*, and the top three students of the ninth grade whose names appeared in the first three lines of the list were respectively called the *tokō* (head boy), *fukukan* (deputy head), and *shachō* (head of the dormitory), and they were given the responsibility of managing the school. The private school thus was a sort of self-governing community. The school was also a "half-teaching and half-learning educational community," for the upper-grade students taught the students in the lower grades. These organizational principles were characteristic of most private schools of that time, and also could be observed at Keiō Gijuku, Japan's first modern private college, founded by Fukuzawa Yukichi in the decade prior to the Meiji Restoration.

What should be emphasized is that Kangien's intensely competitive system was confined to relations within the school and led neither to officially recognized qualifications nor to employment. This was not competition for worldly profit, but simply for the honor of ranking at the top. The uppermost seat was what each student aimed for. "The motivation to endure the hard daily work and the long climb, step by step, through the succession of examinations was based on the desire to see one's name at the uppermost position on the list" (Takano 1969, 141).

The College of the Jesuits

This world of meritocracy in the midst of feudalism in Japan reminds us of the college established by the Jesuits in the seventeenth century. As Émile Durkheim describes in detail, these, too, were places for competitive learning, where the reward was personal honor, divorced from worldly profit.

The collegiate institutions established by the Jesuit order were based on a grade system which made its first appearance in that period, and the principle behind that system was academic competition. First of all, "the pupils were divided into two camps, the Romans on the one hand and the Carthaginians on the other, who lived, so to speak, on the brink of war, each striving to outstrip the other. Each camp had its own dignitaries. At the head of the camp there was an *imperator*, also known as dictator or consul, then came a *praetor*, a tribune and some senators. These honours, which were naturally coveted and contested, were distributed as the outcome of a competition which was held monthly" (Durkheim 1938/1979, 260).

In addition, to stimulate competition "each camp was divided into groups consisting of ten pupils (*decuries*) each, commanded by a captain (called the *decurion*) who was selected from amongst the worthies we have just mentioned. These groups were not recruited at random. There was a hierarchy amongst them. The first groups were composed of the best pupils, the last groups of the weakest and least industrious of the scholars. Just as the camp as a whole was in competition with the opposite camp, so in each camp each group had its own immediate rival in the other camp at the equivalent level. Finally, individuals themselves were matched, and each soldier in a group had his opposite number in the opposing group. Thus academic work involved a kind of perpetual hand-to-hand combat" (Durkheim 1938/1979, 260).

In this manner, "an infinite wealth of devices maintained the self-esteem of the pupils in a constant state of extreme excitation" (Durkheim 1938/1979, 261). In this uncertain environment the students devoted all of their energies to doing their best, simply in order to stay afloat. This is the way Durkheim describes the fiercely competitive method of Jesuit education.

But why was such a competitive system adopted at the Jesuit College and widely welcomed by the society early in the the seventeenth century? Durkheim seeks the reason in the popularization of a new, more individualistic personality by society. In the seventeenth century, following the Renaissance, the concept of individual worth acquired greater value, and individuals began to assert themselves over group forces in the rhythm of everyday life. If education was to follow in the same direction, it had to impart something of value to the individual personalities of students, rather than lecturing to unspecified masses. The way to motivate students was to provide them with an education which had personal significance, to work, as Durkheim put it, "on the individual's self-esteem, his self-respect, and his *Selbstgefühl*, or self-awareness as the Germans call it," and it was in response to this new challenge that some competitive methods were adopted on a national scale. The highly competitive educational system of the Jesuit college, while it seemed like an abnormal mutation of past educational traditions, was in fact a natural reflection of the emerging modern age.

While the approach was modern in terms of its method, the curriculum still consisted of the traditional classics that had been taught since medieval times. Competition was introduced simply because it proved to be a more effective method of teaching traditional material.

The same could be said of Tansō's Kangien. By the early nineteenth century, Japan was also moving into an age when individual contributions were more highly esteemed. The emergence of the term phrase *jinsai* (person of capability) illustrates this change. Tansō founded Kangien as a means for developing *jinsai*. As we have seen, he thought it impossible to eliminate the framework of the hereditary class system. He considered it critical to improve the abilities of the ruling class through properly educating the children of the ancient and powerful families. But Tansō interpreted ability as the "virtue" idealized in Confucianism. We might question whether a competitive system is truly suitable for the development of virtue which was the aim of Confucianism, even if we recognize its effectiveness for intellectual training. Durkheim expressed similar reservations with regard to the education provided by the Jesuit colleges: "Once [the colleges] had recognized the value of rivalry and competitiveness, they made such immoderate use of them that the pupils lived in relationship to one another on a veritable war footing. How can we fail to consider immoral an academic organization that appealed only to egotistical sentiments? Was there no other means of keeping the pupils active other than by tempting them with such paltry bait?" (Durkheim 1938/1979, 264).

The Competitive System of *Tekijuku*

Another representative private academy of the late Edo period was Tekijuku, which was named after Ogata Kōan, whose literary name was Tekitekisai. From its founding in 1837 to 1864, 637 students studied at Tekijuku, including such well-known figures as Fukuzawa Yukichi, Ōmura Masujirō, and many others who played an active role in the Meiji Restoration (Koma 1969). Unlike Kangien, Tekijuku was a so-called *rangaku juku*, a school of Western sciences taught in the Dutch language. The young people came to this school neither to acquire Confucian virtue nor for personal cultivation. They came to gain knowledge that would have practical benefits and even lead to worldly profit. In this period, when the country was being pressed by foreign powers to open its doors and when the feudal system was collapsing, learning Western languages and acquiring new knowledge was practical in a way that study of Chinese classics could not be. The atmosphere in the *rangaku* academies was far more competitive than at Kangien, and the "three disallowances" were a matter of course. Here the students came to know of a totally different society and system of knowledge through an unfamiliar language, Dutch. They learned of a world outside Japan that had moved far beyond a feudal system based on class and family lineage. This school might be called a small island of modernism in the ocean of the traditional society.

The course of study at the Tekijuku in Osaka was described by Fukuzawa Yukichi in his autobiography, *Fukō Jiden*:

> This is how we studied at the *juku*. In the beginning, each new student, who usually knew nothing of Dutch, was given two books of grammar. These were texts that had been printed in Yedo, one called *Grammatica* and the other *Syntaxis*. The new student began with *Grammatica*, and was taught to read it aloud by the help of some explanatory lectures. When he had studied this through, he was likewise given *Syntaxis*. And that was the end of his instruction in Ogata academy. Whatever in addition to this he might accomplish was through his own independent study.
>
> For those who had finished these two texts, there were held what we called "reading competitions" (*kaidoku*), or class recitations. Several pages from various Dutch texts

would be assigned to a class. There being seven or eight classes, each consisting of ten or fifteen students, the members of a class would draw lots to decide on the order of reading. The monitor of each class would take the text on the day assigned and call on the student whose lot it was to read first. If he recited successfully, he would receive a circular mark; if he failed in his passage, a black dot. When a student could not make his translation, the next one by lot would take up the passage, and so on through the class until it was rendered. Whoever made a perfect recitation without a hitch would receive a triangle which had three times the value of the circle.

Our rule was that if a student received the highest mark of his class for three months in succession, he would be promoted to the higher class. This competition was held on the days of the months containing ones and sixes, or threes and eights. It may easily be seen that it was really like having examinations six times a month (Fukuzawa [trans. Kiyooka] 1960: 80–81).

Fukuzawa was admitted in 1855 to this Dutch school, and within two years he rose to the top grade. We might note that the method Fukuzawa describes for mastering Dutch studies was precisely the same as that used at Kangien for Chinese studies. Perhaps the only difference was that the students were more eager, so competition was accelerated. "Everyone thought this was the best method since the students had already become familiar with this method when they studied Chinese, and no one questioned its efficacy" (Akagi 1980, 32–33). It is natural, then, that this same method later came to be used for the study of English and other foreign languages. At Fukuzawa's Keiō Gijuku, which he founded after leaving Tekijuku, this method was used long after the Meiji Restoration not only for Dutch and English but for most other subject areas. The student's main goal in this pedagogic setting was, just as at Kangien, to triumph in the competition and thereby gain the respect of his fellow students and teachers. Successful study did not lead to a professional license or a job. Students worked hard to accumulate circles and triangles because they sought the admiration of others in the small world of their *juku*.

The original room of Tekijuku, which is still preserved in Osaka, had a floor area of only twenty-eight tatami mats—the equivalent of some forty-seven square meters. In that small space, the students studied during the day and pulled out their bedding to sleep at night. According to Nagayo Sensai, who also became the top student of this *juku* and later gained prominence in the Meiji medical world, each student was assigned his own tatami mat as a seat according to his academic rank, and on this he placed his bedding and desk and his other possessions; it is easy to imagine how crowded the *juku* was. A student allotted a place by the wall was in danger of being trodden on during the night, and even during the day it was so dark that it was impossible to study without a candle. Naturally, under these conditions, everyone sought to obtain a good place; and a chance for a change in place came at the end of every month. Strictly following the order of the results attained by the students in *rinkō* or *kaidoku* meetings, from first to last place each student was permitted to choose his place in the dormitory. Because performance affected daily life in such a practical way every student was in utter earnest during the study sessions. Nagayo noted that "to do better than the others in a *rinkō* session was a competition on which one's whole being depended." "Thus in a sense, how one fared in the *kaidoku* competition not only determined the respect you received but the very quality of your existence" (Nagayo 1904). Many of those who eventually assumed the helm of the Meiji government were brought up in this fiercely competitive environment, in which they were being challenged every five days throughout their schooldays.

The Legacy for Modern Japan

The competitive pedagogy common to Tekijuku and Kangien was introduced to other educational institutions by the graduates of these schools. For example. Ōsawa Kenji, who became the first professor of medicine at Tokyo University, reported that the way of teaching at the *bakufu*'s medical school was the same as at Tekijuku. The *bakufu* school was still in its formative stages when he was admitted, in 1866, and classes focused on the mastery of foreign languages and science rather than on medical subjects. "*Kaidoku* was the main method of teaching. A group sat around a table with the top-ranked student at the head. One by one the students read passages and gave their interpretations. If a student made a mistake he received a black mark and the next student received his chance. Those who answered well were given white marks. . . . At the end of each month, the student with the top mark was given his preference of mats in the student dormitory." Also, as at Tekijuku, "the name plates at the back of the classroom were ordered each month according to rankings of performance in the *kaidoku*" (Ōsawa 1964).

Fukuzawa adopted the same method for his school, Keiō Gijuku, which he founded in 1858. According to an early Meiji graduate of the school, "what developed our ability was the *rinkō* method, in which student A was given a half page to read and received a white mark for a good job but a black mark if he made mistakes. If A failed, then B had his chance, and so on. Because the students who answered later could learn from previous mistakes, they had a good chance of improving and advancing. Thus even the lazy students were motivated to prepare for the *kaidoku*. By doing well, they could get a better spot in the dormitory" (quoted in the *Hundred-Year History of Keiō Gijuku*, 1958). We can see from this account that the teaching approach at Keiō closely resembled the Tekijuku method.

In addition, at Keiō as at Kangien, students received monthly academic reports telling them where they stood relative to the other students. An academic report of 1871 indicates the students' scores on the *kaidoku*, the reading exam, and their attendance record. This reporting procedure was continued through the 1890s.

From its beginnings in the private schools this competition-based system gradually spread to public institutions as well. This trend was not, however, necessarily maintained in the modern school system introduced after the Meiji Restoration. For, although competitive examinations had become established as an educational practice, the context in which they were applied was traditional scholarship conveyed through traditional teaching and learning methods. Once the decision was taken to pursue modern Western knowledge through a Western school system, it was assumed that methods of learning and of evaluation and examination would also have to change. Even Keio Gijuku, which had continued to apply the old methods to the teaching of Western studies beyond the Meiji Restoration, announced amendments to its educational policies in 1873.

Keio's new regulations noted that the school had been "so eager to introduce the civilization of the West and to strengthen the nation" that its courses had been based on those aspects of Western learning which seemed to best fulfil the nation's most urgent needs rather than following the order in which such studies were taught in the West. In effect, the approach to Western learning had been the same as "Confucian scholars reading chinese Classics, not following any order but chosing topics as needs dictated." It had been decided that this approach was not appropriate for the transmission of the systematic body of Western knowlege, and the new regulations established a regular program of instruction (*The Hundred-Year History of Keio Gijuku*, 1958, pp.410-11).

The change in the instructional approach was to have a major impact on the method of evaluating students. As before, the seats of students in classes as well as their claim to preferred places in the dormitory continued to be linked to their academic performance. But the means of evaluation underwent a fundamental change. Among the private academies, Keiō was the only one to face up to the new imperatives of Western learning and make the necessary changes so that the institution could find a place in the modern school system. All the other private schools of the Edo period faltered during this transitional age. Similarly, while the names and buildings of many of the old *bakufu* and fief schools survived into the modern period, their staffs and the manner of instruction underwent a radical transformation. The introduction of the modern school system brought about a clean break with the traditional pedagogical approach. However, this did not mean that the competitive spirit that was cultivated by the traditional schools passed away as well.

The competitive spirit acquired by students educated in private schools such as Tekijuku — or to some extent at its successor, Keio Gijuku — or in other "modern" mini-worlds within traditional society was carried with them into the new society. It was these students who became the prominent opinion leaders, and whose posts in the new government called on them to establish modern institutions, of which the new school system was one example. Their understanding of the competitive and meritocratic principles underlying Western civilization helped them in the smooth integration of the new institutions, such as the competitive examination system proposed by Murray, into Meiji society. Without this legacy, it is difficult to imagine how the competitive principle could have been so rapidly introduced into a society that only a decade before had been based on feudalism.

Chapter Three

The Rise of the Modern
Educational System and Examinations

After the Restoration

Selecting Men of Talent

The period of Japanese history often referred to in English as the Meiji Restoration was in fact a period in which movements in two contradictory directions were engaged in a bitter struggle to both bring about an almost revolutionary modernization of the nation and, at the same time, to restore imperial rule. Ultimately the drive for modernization gained the upper hand, and the issues relating to the formation of a new education system were representative of the confrontation in general.

In January 1868, the new government issued a proclamation titled "The Restoration of Imperial Rule (Ōseifuko no Daigōrei)" which included an article stating that the cultivation of men of talent for government service was an urgent matter. Although a new administrative structure had not yet been established, and the new government was still essentially a league of administrative officials from the former fiefs, it was clear that in order to create a firm central government to replace the functions of the *bakufu* an autonomous administrative organization had to be created. How was the manpower for this task to be developed?

The first recruiting method employed by the new government was to nominate for high-ranking posts talented officers selected from amongst the fief administrations, or from officials of the *bakufu* living in the capital or elsewhere. By June 1869, the number of such people who had been assigned to positions with the title of *sanyo* (advisor) exceeded 100 (Yoshimura 1950, 216). We do not know what the basis for selection of these officials was. In the eighth century, as we saw, the imperial government had

41

experimented with an examination system for the selection of officials based on the *keju* system of China. But in the centuries since then, the various governments had not relied on such an objective system for the selection and promotion of officials. The new Meiji government could not refer to any established standard of qualifications or performance when selecting its officials, and as a result this early selection was influenced by personal connections and friendships. Many in the group of new rulers lacked the required skills and talents.

Ōkubo Toshimichi and Iwakura Tomomi, who had initiated this first plan, had not anticipated the negative effects personal connections would have. According to Iwakura's biography, he was most concerned to rectify the situation, and with the cooperation of Ōkubo he began to search for a more systematic approach to bureaucratic appointments. Citing a passage in the Charter Oath (*Seitaisho*) issued by the restoration faction in 1868 stating that government officials should relinquish their positions every four years, and new officials be selected by vote, Iwakura sought to hold such elections. He did not succeed, however; by that time, selection of officials had become dominated by the inner clique of former samurai from the Satsuma, Chōshū, Tosa, and Hizen domains. Of the sixty-seven top officials (*chokuninkan*) appointed through 1874, forty-four (or sixty-five percent) were from these areas (Yoshimura 1950, 220).

The first public discussion of the use of examinations to select officials appeared at the very time Iwakura and Ōkubo were trying to curb the impact of favoritism and connections in the appointment of top officials.

In 1869 the new government established a legislature, the Kōgisho, as an advisory body to the Dajokan, or cabinet. One member was invited to represent each of the fiefs, and collectively they were to present new ideas for the government to consider. The proposal for examinations first came up in this forum, and it was Kanda Takahira who made the suggestion. A teacher of mathematics at the *bakufu*'s school of Western studies, the Kaiseisho, he was among the early appointees to a top post in the new government. Kanda had originally been a scholar of Dutch, but along with Fukuzawa was among the first to take up English studies. Kanda proposed to create an examination system for the appointment of government officials, which would be modeled on the *keju*. It would not, however, be a revival of the *kōkyo* system which had been unsuccessfully introduced in the eighth century.

Kanda's Proposal to Restore Examinations

Kanda's argument, as recorded in the Diet Record of May 1869, proceeded along the following lines. There are many ways to select people, he said, but the fairest way is the old Chinese way. This is even acknowledged by Westerners. We have not used this for some time, but now that we are starting a new government, why don't we adopt the system that was once successfully used in China? Of course, it has problems: the examination subjects used are not appropriate, and the examiners are not always fair. If we can correct these weaknesses, we will be able to develop a procedure that will equal the best in the world (*Meiji Bunka Zensho* 1955, 33–47).

Kanda then provided some concrete suggestions. Examinations should be held annually for applicants invited from all over Japan. The content should focus mainly on practical subjects such as Japanese, Chinese, economics, composition, astronomy, geography, military strategy, law, medicine, and natural history. The government should appoint the examiners each year, and each examination should be evaluated by at least two examiners who do not know the names of the examinees. Examinees should be examined three times, and those who make the highest grades three times should be appointed to the fourth rank or lower of the civil service. Finally, Kanda urged that the names of the applicants, their scores, and the positions they received should all be recorded and made public.

While Kanda was a scholar of Western studies, it is not clear how detailed his knowledge was of Western examination systems. But we can at least see that he knew the Chinese system was highly regarded in Europe. Kanda argued that while the examination system had ancient origins, it was very modern in nature, and did not advocate it simply because it revived traditional Japanese practices. The reactions of the other members of the Kōgisho to his proposal centered on four points of debate: (1) the content of the examination, (2) the qualifications of applicants, (3) the type of preparatory education that should be provided to applicants, and (4) the necessity of carrying out a preliminary selection of applicants (Spaulding 1967, 23).

Perhaps the most interesting aspect of debate was the focus on preparatory education. Kanda's suggestion was based on the Chinese model, which made no provision for preparatory education, and he said nothing about this. He probably did not realize that in the West there was a close link between education and examinations of this sort. But several of the members of the advisory body, apparently drawing on common sense rather than any knowledge of Western institutions, pointed out that a careful arrangement of the educational levels prior to the examination stage would be required. Some of the opinions offered were that "local administrative bodies (the major and minor cities, and the prefectures) should be issued directives to establish schools for the purpose of developing the needed manpower," or that "before considering recruitment methods, it must be accepted that schools should be established throughout the nation so that candidates for higher education can be dealt with at the local level before going on to the *Daigakkō*, government schools" (*Meiji Bunka Zenshū* 1955, 45, 47). When Parliament voted on Kanda's proposal, 146 of the 188 attending members approved, 9 opposed, and 33 abstained.

However, most of the supporting votes came from the representatives of the small fiefs, while among the ruling clique only the representative of Hizen cast a "yes" vote. Satsuma, Chōshū, and Tosa abstained. Without the support of these key fiefs, the proposal did not stand much chance of being put into effect, and indeed, it wasn't. As we will see later, it was only in the late 1880s and the 1890s that the government began to introduce examinations, and the model they followed was that of Prussia rather than ancient China.

While Kanda's specific proposal was not adopted, the underlying concern to improve the system for selecting government personnel was not ignored. The inner clique, while desiring to favor individuals from their fiefs, recognized the critical importance of devising a way to select and train the leaders of modernization. They understood that the task of selecting a future elite required a long-term solution based on appropriate education. They turned to the development of a new school system, and their initiatives and plans were eventually summarized in the School System Order (*Gakusei*) of 1872.

Restoration and Modernization

The first actions by the new government to establish a new educational system reflected the strong influence of the restorationists (Ōkubo 1943; Kurasawa 1973). This can be seen in the selection of people who were appointed in 1868 by the government in Kyoto. For example, the National Learning scholar (*kokugakusha*) Hirata Kanetane was one of them.

The new government's expressed aim was to restore the old system described in the Taihō Code, and thus for the educational sector the National Learning scholars suggested reviving the old college (*daigakuryō*), with Japanese classical studies at the center of the new curriculum instead of Chinese studies.

Concurrent with these developments, the restorationists who favored Chinese studies opened a school on the grounds of the old Peers' School (Gakushūin), which had served for many centuries as the educational institution for the aristocrats. While the National Learning and Chinese studies factions both supported the goal of restoration, they had conflicting conceptions of the ideological foundations of the new system, and these were expressed in their plans for rival educational institutions. When the new government moved from Kyoto to Tokyo soon thereafter, these two factions carried their differences to the new capital. Both factions sought to reestablish their respective educational institutions, or at least to promote the principles underlying these institutions.

In Tokyo there were already three higher educational institutions that had been created by the *bakufu*, known respectively as Shōheikō, Yōgakusho (Institute of Western Learning) and Igakusho (Institute of Western Medical Studies). In 1869, the new government proposed to establish a university by combining the three *bakufu* institutions, and the two rival factions competed in their efforts to influence the direction of this new university. One outcome of this rivalry was a complex and somewhat confusing compromise on the organization and purpose of the new university. At the main campus (*daigakuhonkō*), which succeeded the Shōheikō, the curriculum, based on the traditional Shintō and National Learning, would teach the essence of the national polity (*kokutai*) in addition to the Chinese classics. The branch campuses would specialize in "modern" subjects: Western studies at the Kaisei Gakkō (which succeeded the Yōgakusho), and medical studies at the Igakkō (the renamed Igakusho).

The rules enacted for the main campus of this new institution indicate how determined its creators were to restore the traditional educational environment. For example, the curriculum and examination procedures were almost identical to those of the *daigakuryō* that had existed over one thousand years before. The students were to be given an examination every three years; in this they were assigned passages of two thousand words to read and given three questions; they had to correctly answer at least two (Kyōikushi Hensankai 1938, 1:118).

The branch schools—Kaisei Gakkō and Igakkō—with their Western curricula, however, were exempted from this traditional examination method. As we have seen, the medical school had already adopted a modern competitive examination system similar to those used in the private academies of the late Edo period. Promotion at the medical school was based on performance in the monthly *kaidoku* examination; prizes were given to top performers, and graduates could look forward to government employment (Kyōikushi Hensankai 1938, 1:132–33). We might say that these attached schools that focused on Western studies already were based on meritocratic principles.

As can be seen in the review of these first steps to establish a new university, the tension between modernization and restoration, and the deep rivalries between two factions among the restorationist thinkers, those who favored Chinese studies and those who favored nativist studies, were painfully evident. The conflicts between the latter two groups concerning the principles of education at the main campus of the new university were so severe that it proved impossible to develop an environment suitable for the conduct of education. It was to extract itself from this intractable dispute that the government, in 1870, issued a new set of university regulations (Kyōiku Hensankai 1938, 1:139–42).

The new university regulations, in conjunction with the new middle and lower school regulations, were the first expressions of the Meiji government's interest in emphasizing a modern Western educational system. The regulations, along with dividing schools into the three levels of university, middle school, and primary school and specifying the number of years students should spend at these levels, also proposed shifting the organization of university education from the old divisions into Japanese, Chinese, and Western studies to a new form of organization around the specialized areas of law, science, medicine, and humanities. However, when we look back at the philosophy behind the new plan, we see that it is somewhat transitory in character. It also illustrates the nature of the compromise between the forces for modernization and those whose chief conern was for the restoration of the imperial system. The new plan aimed to establish a school system which would produce the kind of skilled manpower urgently needed for modernization, but which at the same time would proceed according to old practices, such as the *kōkyo* system of selecting talented students and assigning them to government service.

The clearest example of the restorationists' influence concerns the criteria proposed for selecting university students. The new regulations proposed that lower and middle schools should be established in local governments throughout the nation to feed a single national university. Students would enter the lower school at the age of eight to undertake basic studies, then move at the age of sixteen to the middle school, where they would begin specialized studies; finally, at the age of twenty-two a select group would move on to the university. Instead of proposing a procedure for the selection of university students that stressed academic performance or outstanding performance on a formal competitive exam, the regulations simply asked the local governments to send outstanding students, or *kōshin*, to the university.

In classical Japanese, *kōshin* means the act of paying tribute to the emperor. From one point of view, therefore, the university students were offerings from the local areas to the Emperor and his new central government. There were examinations for selected students twice a year, on set days in spring and autumn. Those who achieved the "excellent" level were then assessed in terms of their performance and character and, if found suitable, were "recommended for imperial consideration to be taken into the service of the imperial offices"—in other words, were appointed as bureaucrats. In short, the selection process was virtually the same as the old *kōkyo* system.

The Kōshin System
The implementation of these new university regulations encoun-

tered immediate difficulties, and in mid-1870 the program at the main campus was terminated, and most of the students were sent back to their home areas. The advocates of nativist and Chinese studies, who were struggling for control of the main campuses, naturally felt threatened by the university regulations, with their alien principles of organization and procedure, and they joined forces to openly challenge the modernizing faction. Although the proposed new university regulations, which had been developed in an effort to create a modern education system capable of meeting the nation's new manpower needs, were not brought into effect, many of the underlying ideas, including those on selection of students, remained (Ōkubo 1943, 329–336). With the dissolution of the main campus, all that remained of higher education were the two Western-oriented institutions on branch campuses.

The more important of the branch campuses was the Southern Campus, on which the Kaisei Gakkō had been located. This Southern Campus had already begun to employ foreign teachers and openly declared its intent of providing a new form of education that would cultivate men of talent. And a Cabinet Order of July 1870 instructed the various fiefs to send from one to three students who were between the ages of 16 and 20 and had ability to the Southern Campus (Kyōikushi Hensankai 1938, 1:164). The number was to depend on the fief's importance.

The Cabinet's instructions on selecting students to attend the Southern Campus indicated that preference should be given to bright students who had some exposure to Western studies, and that their period of study should be limited to five years. The fiefs responded by sending some 319 students. While the retention of the *kōshin* concept indicates concern with preserving the past, the newly revised rules for the school made clear the desire to promote meritocratic competition among the students. However, the style of competition envisioned was closely modeled on the practices found in the private academies of the late Edo period rather than a Western model.

According to the revised regulations, the Southern Campus would take in a fixed number of students each year. In the first grade these students would be trained in spoken and written mastery of foreign languages before they moved on to advanced grades, where the focus would shift to specialized subjects. The objective was to provide a broad base and deep understanding so that the specialized knowledge could be applied in various practical contexts. The students were divided into nine grades, and had the opportunity to be tested on their achievements twice each year, in the spring and fall, in order to advance from one grade to another. Within the grades, students' seats as well as their name plates would be ranked according to their performance. And the rules indicated that diplomas would be given in both general and specialized studies.

Karasawa Tomitarō, who has completed a detailed study of the Southern Campus, reports that there was tremendous variation in the academic ability of the students (Karasawa 1974). As there was no common screening examination, the fiefs could send whomever they chose, and some decided against sending their best people, to avoid losing them permanently to the national government. While some students had had the opportunity to study foreign languages under foreign teachers, many others had virtually no such exposure. Inevitably, the school had to sift these students according to ability, in a clear example of "intellectual Darwinism" (Asō 1970).

The weakness of the *kōshin* system was soon revealed. It was difficult to carry out an effective educational program when there was such extensive variation in the abilities and motivations of the student body. It became apparent that some procedure was required to screen the intellectually able and motivated students at the point of entry. For this purpose, it was decided that a completely Western school, where entrants were selected on the basis of a competitive examination, should be considered. It became the task of Ōki Takatō, who was appointed the first Minister of Education in July 1871, to bring about this change.

Ōki Takatō and Westernization
Ōki's first step upon becoming Minister was to abolish the *kōshin* system (Karasawa 1974, 290). While the new government had hoped to gain outstanding students and then develop them into true "men of talent," unfortunately the basis for selection was flawed and many of the students lacked the will and motivation to undertake the challenging program of study. Thus an unfortunate atmosphere developed at the Southern Campus which tended to crush the will of the serious-minded students. In addi-

tion, the old fief system was replaced by the new prefecture system at this time, and as a result it was felt that a new system for selecting students needed to be devised. Ōki temporarily closed the Southern Campus, and the status of all its students was suspended.

How, then, should the university students be selected? Ōki had a very clear view on this question: the most important consideration, he said, was their academic ability. Even a student with a strong desire to study should be rejected if he lacked sufficient ability. At the Southern Campus, students should have both ability and will. However cruel it might be to have to dismiss students who were lacking in ability, without strict standards a suitable educational environment could not be created (Karasawa 1974, 292–93). Applying ability as the criterion, over half the original students sent from the fiefs were dismissed from the Southern Campus.

Ōki also reasoned that a fundamental change in the Southern Campus's educational method should be attempted. Foreign teachers had been brought in, but some of the current teachers would have to be dismissed, as they were less able than their students. Prior to deciding on the teaching staff, however, he felt it was necessary to radically alter the school so it became a truly Western school: "Everything from curriculum to living conditions and food is modeled on Western examples, so that the students will feel they are in a western country" (Karasawa 1974, 291). Ōki effectively bid farewell to the educational philosophy of the restorationists.

Ōki was a product of the Hizen (Saga) fief, where toward the end of the Edo period Western studies had reached an exceptionally high level. Guido Verbeck, who in 1870 became the assistant head of the Southern Campus, had been a teacher in Chienkan, a well-known school for Western studies located in the Saga fief. Ōki himself had not been to the school: he had been trained in Japanese and Chinese studies. But he was totally committed to the promotion of Westernization, and in this regard he resembles Etō Shimpei, also of Saga, who played a key role in the promotion of Western legal conventions. While neither of these members of the Meiji elite had been directly exposed to Western studies, they cleverly picked the brains of those who had and then pushed new systems forward. Ōki's boldest achievement was the promulgation of the *Gakusei*, or School System Order, which created the modern educational system, in August 1872. Of course, Western-style examinations were an important component of the new system.

Ōki's openness to competitive examinations may have been partly related to the fact that an examination-based educational system had already been practiced in the Saga fief school from 1853 to 1859. Samurai at that time were entitled by birth to a particular rank and stipend. At the fief school, a hierarchy of performance standards for both academic achievement and martial arts was established. The performance levels for each student were set according to their hereditary rank. Those who failed to achieve their established level faced a halving of their stipends (*Fifty-Year History of Education in Saga Prefecture*, 1927). The young Itō Hirobumi (later Prime Minister), who visited Saga at the time, expressed his amazement at the stringency of this system and at the total commitment of the fief school's young samurai to their studies. It is not clear if Ōki was tested under this system, because he was already over twenty years old at that time. But certainly he was aware of it. His radical position that ability should prevail over the will to study was certainly influenced by the highly competitive culture of Saga.

The *Gakusei* and the Examination System

Competition and Combat

Let us devote more attention to the concept of competition.

In Fukuzawa Yukichi's autobiography, there is a very interesting story that helps us understand what this concept meant at that time. Somewhat prior to the Restoration, Fukuzawa was reading a Western book on economics, and spoke about it to a top official of the *bakufu*'s Treasury, who expressed interest. When Fukuzawa had finished translating the outline he showed it to the official, who immediately raised his eyebrows on seeing Fukuzawa's selection of characters for the fundamental economic concept of competition. Fukuzawa had chosen the word *kyōsō*, and one of the component characters of this compound is *arasoi*, which means "fight." The official observed, "This character *arasoi* is disturbing. What do you mean by this?" Fukuzawa tried to explain why he had chosen that particular character, but after long discussion the official refused to accept the arguments, pointing out "it will be impossible for me to show this word *kyōsō* to the top members of the government." Eventually, Fukuzawa had to drop these characters from his translation.

This story reveals that the concept of competition was not socially acceptable prior to the Meiji Restoration. *Arasoi* had essentially the same meaning as *tōsō*, that is, combat. Miyamoto Musashi says, in his famous *Gorinsho*, "The sole objective of the warrior in battle is to defeat the enemy. It does not make a difference whether he faces a single samurai or a whole army." The samurai's duty was to fight his opponents, to destroy them, and to win. Over the three hundred peaceful years of the Edo period, however, the samurai's task had altered, at least in terms of day-to-day activities: he became a salaried bureaucrat. Indeed, fighting was outlawed (Ishida 1970, 104–7). In other words, *arasoi* was taboo.

Indeed, it is not easy to make a clear distinction between fighting (*tōsō*) and competition (*kyōsō*). According to sociologists, there are at least two differences between these concepts. First, while both are carried out to realize a goal, fighting results in the elimination of the opponent, while in competition it is not essential to destroy the opponent. Second, there are no restrictions in fighting, while competition is guided by established rules. When two samurai meet on the battlefield they fight with their swords, but when they meet in the *kendō* martial arts hall they enjoy the competition of demonstrating their relative skill with swords.

In the feudal class system, the responsibilities and privileges of samurai were fixed according to their rank, with no room for mobility. Competition was unwelcome because it could lead to results that challenged the fixed order. During this period the samurai sometimes engaged in martial contests before their lords, but many times those who lost were disgruntled and afterwards challenged their opponents to a private rematch with no restrictions. It was difficult for the samurai to accept friendly competition, because they could not draw the distinction between competition and true combat. This suggests why the *bakufu* official was reluctant to approve Fukuzawa's use of *kyōsō*.

At the end of the Edo period, the taboos against both combat and competition were disrupted. Between the *bakufu* and various fiefs, as well as within many of the fiefs, there were open power struggles that often escalated into physical combat. In these struggles, samurai of a lower rank sometimes directly confronted and prevailed over their superiors. Instead of rank and family, an individual's ability to solve the problems at hand became critical. A new age required individuals with both administrative and military skills. But how should capable people be chosen? One efficient approach might have been to define clear rules for candidates to compete openly in terms of their ability, but that approach would also strike at the very foundations of the feudal system.

What, then, was done to appoint and advance people of ability during the Edo period, without relying on formal examinations? In making personnel decisions, wise administrators sought to give as much attention to ability as to rank and family. But it was up to key authority figures such as the shogun and the *daimyō* to show this initiative, and they had no objective criteria to guide their judgments. Subjective considerations inevitably played a large part. In any case, however, in this transitional period there was firm resistance to the encouragement of open competition as a means of identifying ability.

Following the Meiji Restoration there was a radical change. During the struggle to oust the *bakufu*, lower-ranking samurai overthrew their superiors. The traditional hierarchy within the samurai class was completely destroyed, and the old personnel system with it. Still, Japanese society was not ready for open competition. First, rules for acceptable forms of competition could not be established immediately, for no one had the appropriate experience. A new system of government had to be established quickly, but how should its officials and administrators be chosen? Those in charge of these decisions only had experience in the traditional systems of their fiefs, so many of their early proposals, such as the idea of having fiefs select students to send to the government school, reflect this background.

Second, as can be seen from these examples, the leaders initially assumed that all capable people came from their own samurai class. Kanda Takahira's proposal for the promotion of able officials, while it spoke of competitive examinations as a means of selecting capable people, explicitly restricted the examinations to "ambitious samurai." There was little thought in this samurai government of equality, of opening up higher education and the civil service to commoners. This was only natural as long as the samurai class remained a separate social class with special privileges. Before the age of competition could come into full force, the warrior class would have to lose its status.

From this perspective, 1871 was a critical turning point. In July of that year, the old *bakufu* and fief system was replaced with the new central government and prefectures. Then in August the Meiji government ordered all samurai to turn in their swords and declared that commoners and samurai were free to intermarry. In December, the government indicated that all samurai, excepting those in the employ of the government, were free to pursue any occupation, including farming, commerce, crafts, and manufacturing. The government's order to abolish the *kōshin* system, then, was one piece of a larger fabric. Only after this series of reforms was it possible for a new age of freedom and competition—in other words, the age of examinations—to dawn.

Examinations under the *Gakusei*

As a result of Education Minister Ōki's efforts to draw up a blueprint for the modern educational system, the *Gakusei* was issued in August 1872. At the same time, the Cabinet issued a Preamble to the *Gakusei* outlining the fundamental philosophy of this reform (Kyōiku Hensankai 1938, 1:276–77). It declared that "it is only by studying hard according to the best of his ability that a person may make his way in the world. . . . Learning is the key to success in life, and no one can afford to neglect it." At the time, this was truly an epochal statement.

Even in the feudal society prior to the Meiji Restoration, there were a number of people who were able to achieve success through learning. Notably, medicine and scholarship were two occupations where learning was important, and it was possible for people of common origins to go far in these fields if they demonstrated exceptional ability. But the Preamble declared that learning was the key to obtaining success in all occupations, for all the people. This was truly a bold proposal.

According to the Preamble, education was an investment for success in life—that is, by educational investment and the acquisition of knowledge and skills people could achieve success and fulfillment. Therefore, everyone should study hard to acquire the necessary ability. Your position in life was determined by whether you acquired learning. Since the schools were depicted as the central institutions for distributing social opportunities, it was important for them to perform this function in a fair and equitable manner. In the past, learning had been regarded as the exclusive privilege of the samurai and his superiors: farmers, artisans, merchants, and women had been excluded from it altogether and knew nothing of its meaning. But that had to change. In the future, there should be no community with an illiterate family, nor a family with an illiterate person.

In view of the new philosophy outlined here, it would have been surprising if the *Gakusei* did not provide some guidelines for an examination system. Indeed, several references are made to examinations in this document. First, the new system proposed dividing students into grades and giving periodic tests to evaluate their performance and determine whether they were ready for promotion to a new grade. Second, there was to be a graduation examination: those who passed were entitled to a diploma qualifying them to move up to the next level, that is, from the elementary school to the middle school and from the middle school to the university. Also, those who did exceptionally well in these major examinations would be awarded special prizes.

Third, scholarships were called for. In principle, students were expected to cover their own expenses, but in the case of students who came from poor homes that could not pay the tuition, teachers were encouraged to make recommendations to the local governments based on evidence from the examinations, and when the student's performance was outstanding he might be exempted from tuition and other fees. Finally, examinations were to be used to select students who were to be sent to study abroad with national support. Candidates for basic studies overseas were chosen from among middle school graduates who received recommendations from their teachers along with certification that they had passed the middle school graduation test, which qualified them to compete in a selection examination held at the prefectural level. Candidates for advanced studies abroad were selected from university graduates on the recommendation of their academic supervisors. When there were more candidates than places available, examinations were used to determine an order for selection. All of the students sent abroad were required on their return to give evidence of having attained proficiency in their field, either in the form of a graduation diploma from an overseas institution, or by undertaking a special examination organized by the Ministry of Education.

Foreign advisers did not play a direct role in influencing the architects of the series of regulations culminating in the *Gakusei*. David Murray, who was an advisor to the Minister and a strong advocate of examinations, had not yet arrived in Japan. While these regulations were conceived by Japanese officials, it should be noted that many had a good understanding of Western practices. Of the twelve individuals who worked in the inner group drafting the *Gakusei*, nine were Western scholars familiar with the educational systems of Germany, France, the United Kingdom, and the Netherlands. Kurasawa Takashi, who has made a careful study of the process leading up to proclamation of the *Gakusei*, argues that the key figure must have been none other than the Minister of Education, Ōki Takatō. Kurasawa (1973, 400–403) argues that Ōki was an exceptionally realistic and thoughtful administrator who actively involved himself in the discussions of the document and even wrote parts of the final draft. As we have seen, he was committed to the principle of "ability first," and his attitude is evident in his writings, for instance, in his memo on the formulation of the *Gakusei*. For example, he wrote: "It is important to develop an educational structure that leads students step by step if they are to progress. It is often thought that learning should focus on abstract philosophical ideas, but these are far beyond the beginning student. The first things a student should be taught are simple, practical lessons that are close to their experience. Sound education should move step by step from the familiar to the abstract and philosophical" (Kyōiku Hensankai 1938, 342–44). We can appreciate how this line of thinking led Ōki to support a structure involving a sequence of grades with examinations to ensure mastery of each step in the process.

The Grade System
The systems of grades and exams represent two of the most concrete manifestations of meritocratic principles during this period.

The grade system consisted of splitting the subject matter into several levels and requiring students to proceed through these grades successively. To advance to a new grade, the students had to prove that they had mastered the contents of the earlier grade. This is different from the contemporary Japanese elementary or middle school, where a good attendance record seems to be the only requirement for promotion to the next grade. Because promotion depended on mastery of the grade's subject matter, some means of measuring this mastery was required, and examinations emerged as an integral part of the grade system.

As has already been noted, a grade system was found in some of the private academies of the Edo period, but at that time it was not formalized or standardized with reference to a planned curriculum. The first instance of a carefully planned system of school education based on an integrated plan of specific curriculum, grades, and exams was probably that proposed by the Southern Campus in 1870. This idea was further developed to become the basis of the entire educational system in the *Gakusei*.

In the elementary school regulations which appeared soon afterward, elementary education was divided into lower and upper divisions, and each division was divided into eight grades of six months each. A child could begin the eighth grade of the lower division when he was six years old, and if all went well could advance to a new grade every six months until the end of the first grade, at which point he had to pass the "major exam." If he passed this exam, he could graduate and move into the eighth grade of the upper division, and there again he could advance from grade to grade based on regular examinations. While the standard period for each grade was six months, some children could not pass the exam of a particular grade and had to repeat it once or even several times, while others raced through some grades in less than six months. Individual progress depended entirely on ability as demonstrated by performance on examinations.

While the same system based on the demonstration of ability was instituted in the middle schools and the university, we should keep in mind that it was still in a developmental phase. After all, there was wide variation in the abilities of both teachers and students, so there was little consistency in the quality of educational experiences among schools and even among classes in the same school. And examinations played an important role in bringing some degree of order and consistency to the various components of the system.

The introduction of the "payment by results" system in English elementary education in the 1860s stemmed from similar considerations. In England, where the local governments were strong and resistant to control from above, the task of standardizing the quality of education was daunting. The national government tried to exert indirect influence on the local educational authorities by introducing examinations to measure the average performance of students and rewarding good performance with subsidies. In this system, an agreement was reached to examine the areas of reading, writing, and arithmetic at six grade levels; this agreement even extended to the general content of the examinations. Because local school systems were aware of the content of the examination and desired the subsidy, they urged their teachers to prepare the students adequately (Narita 1966).

In Japan, while the educational system was more centralized, it was impossible to realize a uniform standard and quality of education overnight, given the great variety in local backgrounds and circumstances. Children of differing ages and abilities attended the schools. For example, in 1877 in Kyoto Prefecture only seventeen percent of the pupils entering the eighth grade of the lower elementary division were six years old; twenty percent were ten years or older (Kokuritsu Kyōiku Kenkyūjo 1974, 3, 594). While the curriculum was fixed, there were still a number of different textbooks in use, and few teachers actually had the ability and skill to teach Western subject matter successfully. In this context, the grade and examination system was an indispensable means for standardizing and upgrading the quality of education.

The Institutionalization of Examinations and Competition
Much the same can be said about the higher levels in the educational system. But since the educational content at the higher levels was more specialized and advanced, and had a clearer relation to the development of critical manpower and economic policies, the need for examinations to evaluate ability was even more apparent.

The *Gakusei* clearly stipulates that graduation from a school of the previous level is a requisite for entering a school of the next level. For example, entrants to the university had to complete the "great exam" of the upper middle school, a pattern similar to the German *Abitur* and the French *baccalauréat*. But passing a middle school graduation examination could only be imposed as a requirement for entering the university if the content of the middle school curriculum was uniform and the level of education was standardized. Otherwise, the university had two choices: to develop its own entrance examination, or to admit a diverse group of students and screen them out in the early grades through rigorous promotion examinations. In fact, difficult entrance examinations became the norm at every level of the educational system, and were required under the terms of the *Gakusei*.

Another important innovation having bearing on the examination system was the provision of scholarships, a subject we have already considered briefly. Some of the paragraphs in the policy directives to local governments concerning the *Gakusei* seem to promote the idea of scholarships. For example, "students who have the best possibilities of success should be encouraged to do so"; in other words, students with excellent abilities should be encouraged to obtain the highest education. The examinations were viewed as a means to stimulate the aspirations of students, and those with high aspirations and abilities should be supported: "If a student does well in the examination, he should be rewarded. . . . If a student with excellent performance cannot pay the tuition, then that student's tuition should be covered by public funds."

The *Gakusei* regulations on examinations incorporate nearly every expectation held of examinations by the various Western countries which had established education systems. First of all, examinations were a means of promoting educational quality. Second, they were a means to define and disseminate a common educational standard. Third, examinations were viewed as a means of motivating children to participate in education and to stimulate their aspirations. Fourth, examinations were the most effective method for the selection of excellent individuals for training as future members of the elite.

The *Gakusei* was abolished in 1879, and many of the regulations it had proposed were never put into effect. But examinations were. In a sense, the concept of examinations outlined in the *Gakusei* was even more firmly institutionalized than its architects might have anticipated. Indeed, examinations played their role at least as effectively, if not more so, than had been expected. As we will see in the next chapter, in the 1880s promotion examinations were held in every primary school throughout the nation, and in this way they played perhaps the most influential role in advancing the once forbidden ideology of competition. Examinations were repeatedly carried out in the schools, and rewards were given to students ranging from changes in their seating order to special prizes at intraschool competitions. This was the first competition that the children had experienced. Examinations, more than any other means, showed the children and their parents that the age of competition based on individual ability, regardless of social background, had arrived. In Japan it was the schools that gave birth to the meritocratic age of competition.

Chapter Four

From Elementary Schools to Middle Schools

Elementary Schools and Examinations

Examination Rules of the Elementary Schools

One book widely read by headmasters and teachers of elementary schools in the Meiji period was the *Shōgaku Kyōshi Hikkei* (Indispensable Book for Elementary School Teachers) authored by Morokuzu Nobuzumi (1873). Morokuzu was the first principal of the Tokyo Normal School, which was the first teacher-training school in Japan.

Tokyo Normal School enrolled its first class of fifty-four students, chosen by examination from more than three hundred applicants, in August 1872, and it was Marion Scott, an American, who taught courses in educational organization and modern pedagogy. In his two years at the school, Scott had a major impact through his activities not only in teaching students but also in editing the teaching rules and textbooks and importing teaching materials and equipment. Since the students taught by Scott became the core staff of the newly founded normal schools being established in each prefecture, we can see that he was well placed to shape the direction of the new educational system. Morokuzu's *Indispensable Book for Elementary School Teachers* also shows the influence of this American educator.

The book begins as follows:

> It is essential to accurately classify students according to their learning stage. Inaccurate classification will create an obstacle to learning progress.
>
> In order to advance from a lower grade to a higher grade, students should be required to pass examinations for the

subjects they have finished. Unless they pass these examinations, they should not be upgraded. Those who fail should stay in their present grade and thoroughly review the subject matter.

Monthly tests should be given for each subject, and the seating order in the class should be determined based on the results. In this way, the students will study harder and look forward to progress in each subject and better placement (Morokuzu 1873, 2–3).

The *Gakusei* formulated at this time to provide a comprehensive outline for the Meiji educational system included many of these concepts. Essentially, at the primary level students were to compete against each other in strict grade promotion examinations. Morokuzu, probably following what he had been taught by Scott, established this principle, and principals and teachers around the nation followed his instruction to introduce competition and examinatons. This is clearly demonstrated by the eagerness with which the prefectures issued their own local Primary School Examination Rules.

Tokyo, for example, in 1871 established a set of rules to guide the introduction of examinations for the elementary schools. According to these rules, examinations were to be of three kinds: (1) minor exams at the end of each month, (2) major exams given periodically, and (3) the graduation examination. The minor exams, given monthly by the teachers, were to determine each student's progress as well as their seating and the order of the name plates which were to be hung at the rear of the classrooms. The major exams were given twice a year. When a student showed exceptional performance on the major exams, he was upgraded.

The major periodic exam and the graduation exam were very important events for a school. The date was posted in advance at the front gate, and on the exam day, parents were allowed to observe. The exams were also witnessed by a local government official, the school district chief, a teacher from a nearby normal school, and the mayor of the ward. The students were first led by a teacher to a waiting room, from which they proceeded one by one into the examination room for an oral examination followed by a written examination. Each test was scored, and those who passed a certain level were given a graduation certificate. A government official presented special awards to those with outstanding scores.

The 1876 Elementary School Examination Act of Aichi Prefecture was similar in content to that of Tokyo, but provided more detailed guidance on the content and method of examinations and the rules for scoring. The exam covered twelve subjects: reading, summarizing, interpreting, spelling, dictation, composition, oral questions, memorization, arithmetic, bookkeeping, calligraphy, and drawing. A maximum of ten points was possible for each subject, with points subtracted for mistakes. Three questions were asked for each subject. For example, in subjects like reading and summarizing, good answers to all three questions received a score of eight points (rarely was a perfect ten awarded). A student who made one mistake received six points, and if he made two, he received four points. Three mistakes meant two points, while any more mistakes resulted in a zero. So long as a student did not receive a zero in any subject, he passed the exam. If a student received zeroes in up to one-third of the subjects, he could retake the test. Those who received zeros in five or more subjects failed. The examination protocol in Aichi was also more detailed than in Tokyo. The students first entered a waiting room, from which they were called one at a time to the examination room. There two seats were prepared, one for the student and another for the teacher, in front of the examination witnesses. In this room the student was given an oral examination on subjects such as reading and interpretation. Afterward, the student moved into a second waiting room where he stayed until everyone had finished the oral exam. Then all of the students took a written exam on such subjects as arithmetic, dictation, composition, and calligraphy.

Examination Procedures

The elementary school examination rules of Saitama Prefecture, prepared in 1884, provide yet another example (Horimatsu 1971). Under these rules, both the promotion and graduation exams were called regular exams. Each elementary school was responsible for reporting the names of applicants to the ward committee on school affairs. Once the ward committee handed the names over to the district office, the date and place of the examination were decided. Examination officers were chosen and appointed by the prefectural governor from among qualified teachers of different districts. The examination officer was responsible for the composition of the examination questions as well as its administration and scoring. A manual for the composition of these questions, *Shōgakkō Shiken Yōryo* (The Elementary School Exam Guide), was also prepared.

This guide provides extensive detail on what was supposed to be tested. The elementary school of that time consisted of three levels—the primary level, the middle level, and the advanced level. Both the primary and middle levels lasted three years and had six grades. The advanced level consisted of a two-year course and had four grades. The instructions for the primary-level graduation examination in Ethics said that "two of the four oral questions should be on manners and two should be on the use of proper language." Sample questions are provided, such as: (1) Describe what you are supposed to do from the time you get up until you leave for school, and (2) What are you expected to do when you meet an important person or an older person? Each answer could receive a maximum of four points, and a perfect score was twenty points including that for everyday behavior of the examinee.

The overall evaluation allocated a maximum of twenty points for each subject. If a student's average score on all subjects was fifteen or more without any subject falling below nine points, or if the average was twelve or more without any score below eleven, the student passed. An average score of eighteen points for all subjects was considered excellent.

It seems that many of the advancement and graduation examinations were carried out simultaneously for several schools. According to the memoirs of Matsuura Juntarō, who in early Meiji was a principal at one of the elementary schools in Tokyo, the contents of the graduation exams for the 1880s "were prepared at the normal school of the Tokyo area rather than at my own school" (Matsuura 1922, 62). Members of the Examination Committee were appointed by Tokyo government officials, and each committee member was assigned to a school to administer the chosen examination questions.

Combining examinations for several schools may have been instituted to lighten the load of the government officials and the board of education members who were expected to witness the exams of each school. Also, a common examination enabled a standardization of the educational level of neighboring schools. Whatever the reason for the common examination, it was indeed an important school event for both students and teachers.

According to the memoirs of one teacher who lived in Chiba Prefecture, published in the *Hundred-Year History of Education in Chiba Prefecture* (1973), the students who applied for the exam got up very early in the morning, were seen off by their parents, and gathered at the central school in the area where the exam was to take place with lanterns in their hands. Since all of them could not take the examination at the same time, they waited their turns, keeping warm with a bonfire. Inside the school, the examination started so early in the morning that "the Western-style lamp was turned on in the examination room and candles were poked in radishes to light the desk of each student. . . . The younger students usually finished during the daytime, but the older ones sometimes received their examinations on difficult subjects such as arithmetic in the evening, when they could not even read what they wrote due to the dim light." And as a result, they sometimes finished as late as at 10 o'clock, when the room was as dark as in the early morning.

It seems the difficulty of the exam varied from one prefecture to another. In Tokyo, at the first-term periodic exam of 1877, of fourteen thousand applicants, twelve thousand passed with distinction, one thousand five hundred passed, and five hundred failed (*Mombushō Daigo Nempō* 1877, 61). The four percent failure rate suggests the exam was not especially difficult; however, approximately fifteen percent of all the students enrolled in school did not take the examination. At the major graduation exam held in the same year, twenty of two hundred thirty-six applicants (eight percent) failed. As the percentage of the elementary-school-age group enrolled in school at that time in Tokyo was only fifty-six percent, those who passed the promotion and graduation examinations of the elementary school can be considered a far more select group than today's university students.

Intramural Examinations

During this period, besides these promotion and graduation examinations, there was another unique kind of examination. Although various titles were used, such as "comparative test" or "collective exam," this kind of examination was the basis for local inter-school academic contests.

In Fukushima Prefecture, these contests were called *kōshi* (competitive exam). According to the 1875 issue of Fukushima Prefecture's *Gakuji Nenpō* (Annual Bulletin of School Affairs), the examination was given once, sometimes several times, a year, at the central elementary school in the district, to two students, either boys or girls, from each primary school in the region. Both teachers and parents escorted the students to the examination room of the central school, where the teachers sat assembled on the right and left sides of the room. The examination took place "with strict fairness, as the teachers of school A questioned the students of school B, while the teachers of school B proceeded to question the students of school C, and so on. . . . After the answers of each student on each subject had been carefully recorded and checked, a discussion took place to compare the performances." The program ended with the award of a prize to the winner (*One Hundred Year History of Education in Fukushima Prefecture* 1972, 212).

The same sort of examination was held in Tokyo, though it was called the *shūgo shiken* (group exam). According to Matsuura Juntarō, this exam was so decorous that the students wore formal dress for the occasion (Matsuura 1922, 62–63).

The Special Joint Elementary Examination of Yamanashi Prefecture has been vividly described by Horimatsu Buichi (1971). For the examination held by the prefectural government in the middle of October 1886, one hundred thirty-seven students traveled to the central metropolis of Yamanashi, Kōfu City, to participate. The first-day examinations focused on ethics, arithmetic, geography, and history; the second day on composition, science, and art; and the third day on physical education and reading. The questions posed in the middle course—equivalent to the fifth and sixth grades of the contemporary elementary school—were quite challenging. One science question, for example, was put as follows: "Sometimes the lamp chimney breaks if you push it quickly so that the fire flares up. Why does that happen?" And a question in ethics was, "What is the meaning of the statement 'Even if you learn, you are ignorant unless you think; even if you think, it is dangerous if you do not learn'?'"

The examination was conducted by an examination committee and witnessed by teachers, the secretary of the district, and various government educational officials. On the fourth day, all gathered to hear the results. At the ceremony, the governor personally awarded prizes and certificates to the top students, after which a student representative expressed appreciation and a distinguished guest delivered a congratulatory speech. It was an extremely formal and impressive day for the students. At five o'clock, on the conclusion of the ceremony, all participants except the students were invited to a Western-style dinner party sponsored by the governor.

This competitive examination had the purpose of stimulating and encouraging both teachers and students to improve their studies, and it certainly had that effect. On the other hand, it became clear that there were also some ill effects. For instance, a high-ranking official of the Ministry of Education, who inspected Fukushima's 1878 intramural examination, expressed his concern that, since the subjects and methods for testing students' performance were standardized and the examination was given simultaneously to a group of students from different schools, teachers were very worried about their students' performance. This situation could lead to education becoming limited to a certain range of knowledge applicable only to the examination, a development which would stand in the way of educational progress (*Monbusho Dairoku Nenpō* 1878, 42).

Similar concerns were also felt by other members of the educational world. According to an editorial in the *Naigai Kyōiku Shimpō* (Domestic and Foreign Education News) of the time, when the comparative examination approached each year, the teachers inevitably paid attention only to the bright and good students of their class, so that they would bring honor to the teachers. At the competition, it was as if the teachers were bringing their students to a horse race or cockfight. It seemed that the teachers devoted all their energies to "choosing and training good horses and cocks, while they didn't care for the rest of the animals, whether they died or not" (Horimatsu 1971, 109).

It seems indeed that as the system of comparative examinations spread, this concern for cultivating high-scoring top students also rapidly spread. A movement to stop this kind of examination was gaining momentum in Tokyo and in other prefectures, too, as early as the 1880s, and the intramural examination soon fell into disfavor.

The cry to abolish intramural examinations so soon after their launching testifies to the deeply rooted nature of Japan's "examination hell." In Chapter 3, we noted how once the examination system was introduced in the Saga fief in the closing days of Tokugawa government, the people studied feverishly. After six years, however, this system was abolished: samurai fearing they would lose their hereditary stipend unless they passed the examination showed such an intense passion for examination preparation that the original purpose of training capable personnel quickly disappeared. The intramural examinations also brought out this same overheated competition. Just as the sons of the samurai studied hard to protect their family names, so did the elementary school students in the early days of Meiji strive to protect their school name. For the sake of their school honor (not to speak of their own honor), teachers worked hard to galvanize their students. Thus the examination system, originally created to promote education, instantly devolved into a competition to gain points on examinations.

This obsessive drive to prepare for the intramural examinations spread to other examinations, and by the beginning of the 1890s there were calls to curb the competition. An article which appeared at that time in the *Fukushima-ken Shiritsu Kyōikukai Zasshi* (Fukushima Prefecture Association Bulletin on Education) entitled "*Shiken no Kairyō*" (Improving Examinations) pointed to the following problems: (1) students treat daily classes as preparation for the examinations and try to memorize everything they are taught, so their native abilities are not nurtured and their imaginations are not stimulated; (2) since their sole desire is to surpass others and receive awards, their natural feeling of love for others withers away while they develop a disturbing hostility to other students; (3) teachers tend in daily classes to forget why they have been asked to educate young people and are constantly devoting their efforts to achieving acclaim through the success of their students in the examination hall; and (4) the expense and time consumed in examination preparation is not small.

How similar are these old arguments against the evils of examinations to those heard today! As we will see below, the

Ministry of Education in 1900 finally took action to abolish elementary school examinations for promotion and graduation.

The Role of the Examinations

The positive role played by the elementary school examinations of the early Meiji period should also be considered. Attendance at elementary schools then was still low. In 1882, according to the Ministry's survey, the percentage of the elementary school age group enrolled in schools was fifty-one percent, and only sixty-five percent of these regularly attended school. This means that the children who actually attended school were about one third of those of school age. The pupils' ages were quite wide-ranging, and, in addition, the number of teachers with proper qualifications was no more than one per school, or one for every hundred students.

Under such conditions, if standards were to be maintained and the quality of education raised, it was inevitable that the output of the educational system should be controlled by supervision of promotion and graduation. In this sense, the primary schools' examinations for promotion and graduation were a product of the age. Conversely, as educational quality reached satisfactory levels, the historical role of the examination system was fulfilled, and the examinations were no longer necessary.

In fact, in Chiba Prefecture, in the early 1880s the classroom evaluations of academic performance were so unfair that they were sometimes virtually the opposite of the results that were determined at the joint graduation examinations conducted by groups of shcools. By 1890, however, the situation had undergone such change that the government replaced its policy of sending officials to major periodic examinations with the practice of circulating inspectors to individual schools and classrooms (*The Hundred-Year History of Education in Chiba Prefecture* 1973). Once the elementary schools were well organized and the teachers well trained, it was possible to delegate decisions on promotions and graduation to the teaching staff. The abolition of the examination system in 1900 was possible only because of the improvements in primary education.

Another positive contribution of examinations was their role in spreading the ideology of competition and the principle of meritocracy. The repeated examinations must have been painful for the children who were not fond of study, but for those children with intellectual appetite and a strong desire to move up the social ladder, the examinations provided an arena where they could demonstrate their abilities. The children of farmers and merchants who previously could not even sit next to a samurai were allowed to compete equally with the children of samurai and even defeat them. The school was certainly the first place where the ideology of "the equality of the four classes"—that is, the equality of all human beings— was realized.

Naitō Konan, who established Chinese studies at Kyoto University, entered an elementary school with thirty-two other students in a remote rural school of Akita Prefecture at the age of nine. His intelligence was evident. Naitō consistently stood out in the intramural examination held at the prefecture's "central school." One official of the prefectural government was so impressed by Naitō's composition that he had it published in a newspaper, and the young Naitō gained wide recognition (Mitamura 1972).

Natsume Sōseki, one of Japan's greatest writers, was also an excellent student. He entered elementary school in Tokyo at the age of seven, and skipped rapidly through the elementary school based on his performance in the examinations, finishing the lower four grades in one year. In his novel *Michikusa* (Grass on the Wayside), there is a scene in which the protagonist, Kenzō, recalls his younger days: "Among the certificates I obtained, there were two or three certificates of merit. These always had a pattern of dragons circled around the mention of the recipient's class, and stretched out under that the prize awarded, something like 'calligraphy brush, ink, and paper'." Knowing that Sōseki was himself an excellent student, we can consider that Kenzō's recollection is Sōseki's own.

The socialist Sakai Toshihiko, who entered elementary school in 1877, seems also to have been an excellent student. In his autobiography he writes, "I started elementary school when I was seven. Later my mother told me that the neighbors often worried that I was too young to go to school. Since I was so young and also small for my age, I must have been quite conspicuous. In any case, I graduated from elementary school with distinction at thirteen. I was invited to the governor's office, where I was awarded two books, one on Japanese history and one on world geography" (Sakai 1978).

In the competitive education system of the seventeenth-century Jesuit *collèges*, Durkheim saw the awakening of self-consciousness, which he considered a major characteristic of modern society: the pride of a person, the sense of one's own dignity, or what the Germans call "self-awarenes." Thus, as the movement toward individualization proceeded, competition increased and intensified, and eventually came to play an important social role.

A similar change was taking place in the modernization of the early Meiji period. The school system, created in accordance with the *Gakusei* regulations, can be seen as a system of pipes through which "civilization and enlightenment" was to be channeled from the capital through to the rural areas, with the primary schools the ultimate outlets. The element of competitiveness in the examination system played a role in creating a strong sense of pride and self-awareness in young people such as Naitō, Sakai, and Soseki, and stimulated in them a strong desire for social advancement. Many gathered in Tokyo, the center of the "civilization and enlightenment" that had been channelled through to them via the schools, to seek fulfilment of their ambitions. By identifying talented human resources through examinations, the elementary school system which spread across Japan came to serve as an extremely efficient network for the purpose of social selection.

The Middle School and Examinations

The Beginnings of the Middle School

In Western countries, while the elementary school became a school for the general public, the middle school tended to serve the middle classes. The German *Gymnasium*, the French *collège* and *lycée*, and the English public and grammar school are all examples of this pattern. In addition to training young middle-class children for citizenship, these middle schools also provided preparatory education for the university.

The *Gakusei* of 1872 defines the middle school as a middle-level school, equivalent to the European middle school. This school was to have a six-year program for teaching general subjects to the students who had completed an elementary education. It was not designed, however, with a clear understanding of the character and function of Western middle schools. Up to that time Japanese educators had not been accustomed to planning a system of diverse schools with differing academic levels and functions. What's more, in the case of Japan, no middle stratum of the population had yet emerged as a distinct social class with the cohesiveness required to demand its own schools to encourage and sustain its own cultural and economic achievements. A middle class would emerge during the process of industrialization. In this context, it is clear that the *chūgaku* (middle school) described in the *Gakusei* was simply the generic name for a level of schooling to fill the gap between the elementary school and the university, lacking any distinctive character of its own.

The Ministry of Education was not very eager to establish the middle schools. As seen in the section on procedure for implementation in the *Gakusei*, the stress was on working hard to establish the elementary school while the middle school level was to be organized more slowly. Nevertheless, according to the statistics of the Ministry of Education, the number of both public and private middle schools rapidly increased from twenty in 1877 to three hundred eighty-nine the following year. Clearly, the appetite for a level of education beyond simple reading, writing, and abacus computation was considerable. Towards the end of the Tokugawa period, there were nearly 300 fief schools around the country, and, although no statistics are available to provide an accurate final count, several times that number of private academies, *shijuku*, certainly existed. So middle school education did have a certain tradition, and the establishment of a large number of public and private middle schools during the Meiji period built on the tradition of those fief schools and *shijuku*.

It should not be assumed, however, that all of the new middle schools included in these statistics had the same character. The middle school outlined in the *Gakusei* was to be a school with a modern curriculum and teaching practices along the lines of Western models. But the Ministry of Education was fully aware that the nation was just beginning its drive for modernization and could not easily create such middle schools overnight. The regulations for implementing the *Gakusei* state that in the transitional period, when books and equipment were still not fully prepared, even schools where old books were still used as text-books, where foreign languages and specialized subjects were taught without any set curriculum or progression of learning, and where lessons were given in teachers' homes were still considered *middle* schools. A number of middle schools counted in the statistics were in reality no more than private schools like those of the Edo period, which were attended by only several dozen students and where instruction was given in only a few subjects such as English, mathematics, and Chinese literature.

It was after 1879, when the Education Act (*Kyōikurei*) super-seded the *Gakusei*, that the Ministry of Education began focusing on the improvement of middle school education. According to the Education Act, the middle school was to be an institution where high-level general subjects were taught. Only those mid-dle schools with a comprehensive curriculum were thereafter considered "standard" middle schools, while the others were redesignated "irregular" miscellaneous schools (Kurasawa 1975, 219–22). Consequently, the number of middle schools sharply dropped, from 784 in 1879 to 187 in 1880. In addition, in 1881, the Ministry of Education clarified its educational standards in the Middle School Teaching Regulations Law, or *Chūgaku Kyōso-ku Taikō*.

What is noteworthy about this regulation is that it describes the middle school both as a place for the advanced general education required for going on to further education and as a place for the education indispensable for obtaining higher-level occupational and social status. The curriculum consists of a four-year primary course and a two-year advanced course. According to the provision, those who completed the latter course had the qualifications for a university or other highly specialized course. This regulation is the first instance of distinguishing two func-tions for the middle school: occupationally relevant general education alongside preparation for higher education. By 1884, the General Provisions for Middle Schools (*Chūgakkō Tsūsoku*) were issued to clarify the criteria for teachers' qualifications and school facilities.

Thus during the 1880s, the official standards for middle schools were progressively strengthened. There remained a gap, however, between these standards and the actual conditions in the schools. In 1884, there were one hundred thirty-two middle

schools (seventy-six run by prefectures, fifty-four run by munici-
palities, and two private institutions) with an average of eight
teachers per school and one hundred thirteen students. Relative
to the human and physical resources of that period, there were
still too many middle schools. For example, although the General Provisions for Middle Schools mentioned above stipulates that
at least three of the teaching staff of a school should be graduates
of either a middle school teaching course of a national normal
school or a university, it was extremely difficult to recruit individuals with these qualifications to teach modern subjects because of the limited number of graduates. For example, Saga
Prefectural Middle School used every conceivable means to find
teachers with these qualifications but finally was able to find
only one university graduate (Kurasawa 1975, 450).

As will be shown later, even those schools which were able to
recruit the required staff usually lacked the capability to prepare
their students for university education. Only after a major reform in 1886 that limited each prefecture to one middle school
financed by the government did middle school education begin
to develop.

The Middle School Examination System

How, then, did the middle schools fit into the education system?
The *Kyoiku Zasshi* (Education Magazine), issued by the Ministry
of Education, provides a record of the regulations of various
public middle schools around Japan up until 1877. These show
that at this early stage of the development of middle school
education, the system was still poorly organized (*Kyoiku Zasshi*
1878). In contrast to elementary schools, which benefited from
the *Indispensable Book for Elementary School Teachers*, there was no
comparable handbook for middle school teachers on curriculum,
teaching, and evaluation. The middle school lacked a clear
objective beyond providing high-level general education. There
was much variation in the ability, age, and expectations of the
students who entered the middle schools, but the middle school
lacked a curriculum and system of selection and evaluation that
was responsive to this diversity.

Nevertheless, the *Chūgaku Kyōsoku Ryaku* (Outline of Middle
School Teachers' Rules) issued in 1872 provided an outline of
the grading system to be used in the middle schools. These rules

indicated that completing the graduation exam for one grade should be the basis for moving to the next grade. And by the late 1870s, detailed rules for the conducting of examinations had been created.

According to the regulations of a public middle school in Nagano Prefecture, three types of examinations were used: (1) minor exams each month for testing progress and determining class placement; (2) regular examinations at the completion of each grade or every six months; and (3) major examinations on all the subjects covered during the four-year course to determine eligibility for graduation. The regular and major examinations were supposed to be held in the presence of government officials. All the examinations except history were to be oral exams. The regulations indicated the number of questions for each subject as well as the procedure for scoring. Less than half a perfect score was considered failure. The school history describes the perform-ance of the first six graduates on the major examination. This examination was given in 1881 and covered seven subjects: three ancient Chinese texts (*The Doctrine of the Mean, The Analects of Confucius*, and *The Zuo Zhuan*), composition, trigonometry, national laws, and psychology. The emphasis on Chinese studies and the absence of both English and the natural sciences is noteworthy. All six of the students passed the examination. To celebrate their graduation the prefectural governor gave each student an anthology of selections of the writings of eight great authors of the T'ang and Sung dynasties.

In 1884, when the General Provisions for Middle Schools were issued, this school officially became the Nagano Prefecture Mid-dle School, and for the first time the modern subjects of English and natural science were taught. The rules relating to examina-tions also became more elaborate. The seat order in classes was to be based on the results of the monthly tests. The rear seats were for the superior students and the front seats for the inferior. Student promotions from grade to grade were to be determined on the basis of performance in the monthly tests, classroom per-formance, and the biannual term examinations. According to a table included in the rules, promotion was allowed with a minimal average of 60 points and not more than one failing subject. Students with an average score of lower than 50 were to be automatically dismissed from school. Detailed rules of this kind gradually became commonplace at the public middle schools.

The Entrance Examination

According to the *Gakusei*, qualification for middle school was to be based on completion of all the subjects of elementary education. This rule reflected the European practice of making graduation from one level of schooling the qualification for entering the next level. The rules of Nagano Prefectural Middle School also stated that only those with a certificate indicating completion of all elementary subjects would be admitted. In fact, it was only in the early 1880s that students with this certificate began to appear. But even for some time after that, most of the students who entered a middle school did not have a certificate; instead, they came with various educational experiences at traditional private schools, and many of the entrants had never studied a modern curriculum. While some middle schools simply accepted the graduates of these private schools, those that sought to provide high-quality education began to rely on entrance examinations (Sakurai 1943, 140).

The regulations of the Chiba Prefectural Middle School System issued in 1878 stated that students aged fourteen years and one month who had not completed all of the elementary subjects could, for the time being, be admitted on the basis of an entrance examination covering certain subjects. The regulations for 1881 of the aforementioned Nagano Prefectural Middle School also seemed to put priority on the entrance examination, stating that applicants should be admitted to school based on the result of the entrance examination. But those with a certificate confirming completion of all elementary subjects were not required to take the examination. At the First Middle School of Tokyo Prefecture, sixty-five of the seventy-two students admitted in October of 1878 passed the examination, and seven were admitted because they had completed all of the elementary subjects (Kurasawa 1973, 970–78).

While entering students were carefully selected on the basis of their academic ability, many could not keep up with the demands of study at the middle school. Nagano Prefectural Middle School experimented with such special approaches as dividing the new students into appropriate classes on the basis of their ability and using special examinations to monitor the progress of new students; nevertheless, many dropped out. From 1876 to 1879, the school admitted one hundred fifty new students, but in the same period one hundred fifteen students left school. This phenomenon was typical of most middle schools of the period, and was to last for a long time. As the curriculum and organizational structure became more elaborate, the middle schools gradually took on the function of meritocratic selection based on academic ability.

Higher School Entrance and the Examination
The place of examinations in middle school education was also an important matter in the question of advancement to higher education.

The *Gakusei* made graduation from middle school a requirement for entering the university. However, this was an abstract regulation lacking concrete provisions for articulation between middle school and the university. The lack of articulation was reflected in the vague statement of the middle school's purpose. Only in 1881, with the Middle School Teaching Regulations Law, was it first clearly stated that the purpose of the middle school was to provide preparatory education for entering the university. Prior to that time, the Nagano Prefectural Middle School's Regulations, for example, declared only that "the school provides advanced general education suited for whatever occupation the student will engage in after graduation," without explicitly stating it was a place for preparing students for higher education.

At this time, some schools like the First Middle School of Tokyo Prefecture divided their curriculum into two courses, a regular course of advanced general subjects taught in the Japanese language and an irregular course for preparing students for the university, taught primarily in the English language (Kurasawa 1973, 906). Other schools such as the Miyagi and Okayama prefectural middle schools also established a preparatory curriculum especially for entering the university (Kurasawa 1975, 209–10). Even so, the middle school's role in preparing students for more advanced education remained ambiguous, since the graduation diploma of the middle school did not automatically guarantee university entrance.

In view of the unique character of higher education at that time, it would have been impractical to provide a definite guarantee of university admission to middle school graduates. As will be seen later, the early institutions of higher education, with Tokyo University at their summit, all conducted their classes in foreign languages, relying on foreign teachers. The middle schools simply did not have staff capable of providing the academic foundation required for these higher educational institutions. Even though the middle schools at Tokyo, Miyagi and Okayama established preparatory courses where general subjects were taught in English, the courses did not bring students up to the level required by the higher educational institutions.

Among the English teachers of that period, the graduates of Keiō Gijuku were highly regarded. Most of these graduates, however, were themselves products of English courses where they studied grammar and composition but had little exposure to the spoken language, and especially to pronunciation by native speakers. Thus they could not prepare their students to comprehend lectures given by foreign teachers. Also the academic content of these irregular courses was generally far below the level expected by the university.

The ambitious young people who sought higher education usually dropped out of the prefectural middle schools after a few years to take up study in one of the private schools in Tokyo where English was emphasized, for it was only in those schools that they could obtain the knowledge required for passing the entrance examinations to the institutions of higher education. Until the end of the 1870s, most of these private schools were classified as middle schools, but they actually functioned like today's *yobikō*, or preparatory cram schools.

The Ministry of Education sought to address this situation with a series of policies issued starting in 1880. By strengthening prefectural middle schools, young people could be kept in their home regions until they had finished middle school, and graduation from middle school could serve as the qualification for university entrance as had originally been intended. However, the gap between the academic, especially the English, ability demanded by the university and that actually provided at the rural middle schools persisted. Recognizing this situation, the Middle School Teaching Regulations of 1881, while wishfully declaring that graduation from a middle school should provide the qualification for entering an institution of higher education, felt it necessary to add that "those who seek the university course will need proficiency in foreign languages." And as one measure to compensate for the inadequacies of middle school graduates, a comprehensive English language course was established in 1883 as part of the preparatory course of Tokyo University.

According to the research of Kurasawa Takashi, the idea for this English course had actually originated with the staff of the preparatory course (Kurasawa 1975, 442–43). They reasoned that the rural middle schools were finally producing graduates, but the academic, especially the English, ability of most of the students who took the university entrance examination was so low that they failed. Therefore, the examination should be given only in the subjects that were taught in Japanese, and those who succeeded could then be given special English education for one year by the staff of the preparatory course. In this way, academic ability rather than English-language skills could become the criterion for success, and moreover, young people would no longer have to leave their local schools in order to prepare for entering the university in Tokyo. The rules of this special comprehensive English course state that it was established especially to give students who had completed the courses of rural middle schools the means of entering the faculties of law, science, and letters, and that the applicants would be tested on their academic ability in Japanese rather than on their English-language proficiency. Those who passed the examination were to specialize in English for one year and then to be admitted into the appropriate class based on their academic ability. However, the number of students actually admitted under this system between 1883 and 1885 was only ninety-eight.

The Appearance of Preparatory Schools

As we have seen, it was the numerous private preparatory schools, though not officially recognized as middle schools, that filled the wide gap between the education provided at local public middle schools and the academic ability required of university students. Especially well known among these was Kyōritsu Gakkō. This school was originally founded in 1871 as a school for the study of English, but it was closed several years later when the founder died. However, Takahashi Korekiyo, who would become Prime Minister in 1921, was at that time an English teacher in the preparatory education course of Tokyo University, and he decided to revive the school. Takahashi wrote in his autobiography: "As I fully realized how low the academic ability of the students entering the preparatory education department was, I worked to raise funds, and with the help of my colleagues was able to reopen classes in 1878. . . . . Once school opened, an unexpectedly large number came to study, and their performance was quite good. Furthermore, since the graduates of this school did best on the entrance examination for the preparatory course of the university, its reputation quickly improved" (Takahashi 1976, 172-73).

Sakai Toshihiko, in his autobiography, also praised the quality of Kyōritsu Gakkō. Sakai, after graduating in 1886 from the Toyotsu Middle School of Fukuoka Prefecture, went to Tokyo and first entered the Dōjinsha School of Nakamura Masanao. That summer he took the entrance examination for the First Higher Middle School (previously this had been the preparatory course of the university) and failed, so he entered Kyōritsu Gakkō. According to Sakai, although Dōjinsha was a well-known school, it was already declining. In contrast, Kyōritsu, headed by an English teacher from the Higher Middle School, had the reputation of training the largest number of students to succeed in the examination for the Higher Middle School. Sakai received a year of rigorous training in English at Kyōritsu and successfully entered the First Higher Middle School the following year.

Tokyo English School, a private school founded in 1880, was another famous preparatory school. Sakai wrote that "the percentage of successful students was the same at the Tokyo English School [as at Kyōritsu], and both of these schools were very popular" (Sakai 1978, 91). Certainly, these schools can be called the forerunners of today's preparatory schools. The Japanese examination industry thus was launched with the establishment of the modern school system, and has enjoyed a history of over one hundred years.

It is also interesting to note that the custom of a university student's working as a teacher at a well-known preparatory school or as a private tutor also began in this period. For example, Tsubouchi Shōyō, who eventually became a famous novelist, as a result of poor performance in his examinations at Tokyo University in 1882 was forced to find a way to support himself to continue his studies. His solution was to open a private English school, which he called Kōrokan, at his boarding house: all he had to do was to hang out a sign on the front of the boarding house. He also taught English at a preparatory school called Shinbungakusha, and even took a job tutoring the children of a wealthy rural family who were studying in Tokyo. His is an early example of the *arubaito-gakusei*, or working student (Itō 1952, 217).

Study at a preparatory school, however, did not necessarily ensure easy university entrance. To qualify for a specialized course of study, the real purpose of their university education, students had to undertake further preparatory courses, in particular in languages. The specialized university preparatory course was given at the institution which developed into the First High School. The original plan had been for middle school education to lead directly to university entrance. The reasons for the need for a specialized preparatory training institution between middle school and university are examined in the next chapter.

Chapter Five

The Examination System and Higher Education

Foreign Languages and Preparatory Education

The First Higher Middle School

In the early Meiji period "Westernization fever" often led to extreme proposals. Mori Arinori, who later became Minister of Education, seriously considered the possibility of making English the new national language of Japan and asked American scholars for their advice. As we noted in Chapter 3, the first Minister of Education, Ōki Takatō, proposed to transform the Southern Campus into a college "where everything from curriculum to living conditions and food is modeled on Western examples, so that the students will feel as if they are living in a foreign country" (Karasawa 1974, 291).

The reason the Meiji reformers moved to consider such extreme Westernization was that they strongly believed in the urgent necessity of mastering the advanced levels of Western learning in order to modernize more rapidly. And learning, so to speak, rides on the vehicle of language. Mori reasoned that, if the Japanese changed their language vehicle from Japanese to English, Western learning could be more easily obtained.

Ōki had a different plan. His first step was to create new schools along Western lines and to employ foreigners to teach advanced subjects in these schools. Japanese who had already studied foreign languages would be their students. Once these students graduated, they would teach other students using the Japanese language. Ōki's idea was to replace foreign languages with Japanese as the medium for advanced, Western-oriented studies.

The *Gakusei,* which provided the official framework for the primary and middle schools and the university, stipulated that instruction would be in Japanese, with foreign languages included as school subjects. A system to convey Western learning in Japanese could not, however, be created overnight. At the university level, where advanced education was envisioned, there were almost no Japanese with the required mastery of these subjects. Ōki believed that the solution was to establish a school that created "the West within Japan" with the help of foreign teachers, and proceeded to make plans accordingly. The process by which Tokyo University was formed from the Southern Campus can be seen as the implementation of Ōki's plans. Let us take a look at this process.

We have already seen that in 1871, as the first Minister of Education, Ōki had abolished the *kōshin* system, and then ventured into the establishment of purely Western learning-oriented schools by inviting foreign teachers to staff them. He now tried to revive the Southern Campus as an educational institution specializing in law and the sciences. But it soon became apparent that the time was not yet ripe: when the announcement was made of the availability of places for students in specialized studies, there were only twenty applicants, and only one of them passed the entrance examination. The focus on specialized education was thus temporarily postponed. In the spring of 1872, the school's curriculum focus was revised to provide general education in three languages: English, German, and French.

In August of the same year, when the *Gakusei* was promulgated, the Southern Campus became the first government middle school. A second middle school was established in Tokyo, along with one each in Osaka and Nagasaki. In terms of the *Gakusei* ordinances, all of these were "standard" schools, but they were obviously "irregular," since all of the subjects were taught in foreign languages. Indicative of their unique status was a distinct set of ministerial regulations for the four middle schools where foreigners teach. According to Ōki's plan, these schools were to serve as preparatory institutions to provide students with sufficient ability in foreign languages that they could pursue advanced specialized education in the university. The public and private middle schools where teaching was conducted mainly in Japanese could not be expected to provide equivalent preparation. But within a year, the plan to set up a special group of foreign-language middle schools was abandoned. The government middle school in Tokyo was renamed the Kaisei Gakkō, and the other foreign-language middle schools were abolished.

Kaisei Gakkō was no longer a middle school, and not a university either. As a completely independent school, no regulations were specified for it in the *Gakusei*. Minister of Education Ōki identified the school as the *senmon gakkō* (specialized school), and prepared regulations specifically for it. These regulations describe the school as a "prestigious school where education is provided by foreign teaching staff" and its goal as being chiefly "to acquire the advanced arts of the West." Graduates of the institution were expected "to go on to teach these skills to other Japanese in the Japanese language," and it was, therefore, in a sense similar to a teacher training college. By not designating this unique school as a *daigaku* (university), it becomes apparent that its place in Ōki's planning was as an institution outside the official school system which was to serve in a transitional role until a true university—one where Japanese teachers taught classes in the Japanese language—could be established.

The Birth of the English-Language Schools
The establishment of the Kaisei Gakkō did not mitigate the need for intermediate-level institutions to train students in foreign languages. The ordinary public and private middle schools recognized by the *Gakusei* were not expected to offer training in foreign languages. To supply preparatory education for applicants to the Kaisei Gakkō, special measures had to be introduced to establish foreign-language schools. Oki decided to create new schools for the purpose, and to transfer the former students of the government middle schools to these new schools.

The regulations for these government Foreign Language Schools noted that they were created because students could not study at Kaisei Gakkō unless they comprehended the language. The regulations stipulated that completion of the lower course (two years) of these schools was a minimum requirement for entry to Kaisei Gakkō. While a higher course (two additional years) was available to train students to be fluent in the language, the main emphasis in these schools was on the lower course. Based on these regulations, seven government Foreign Language Schools were founded in Tokyo, Osaka, Nagasaki, and Aichi, Niigata, Miyagi, and Hiroshima prefectures. When the Kaisei Gakkō narrowed its instructional language to English in 1874, these schools also decided to specialize in English, and they came to be known as the English Language Schools.

The annual report of the English Language Schools that was included in the Ministry of Education annual bulletin shows that the entrance examinations for these schools did not stress only the English-language facility of applicants. Those who had already studied English were tested in English as well as in Japanese translation, and based on their performance they were admitted and placed in an appropriate grade. But these were a minority of the students. At the Aichi English Language School, the majority were examined solely on passages translated from English. At the Hiroshima English Language School, the examinations tested student mastery of the Japanese-language textbooks they had used along with selected popular books.

While the admission process did not stress English-language facility, the instruction relied exclusively on English. The curriculum covered the same subjects as the regular middle schools, but all of these subjects were taught in English by foreign teachers. The English Language Schools were truly the "West in Japan." One of the graduates later recalled his experiences: "Studying at the school exclusively under English teachers was like taking a small trip to a Western country" (Ōta 1981, 81–82).

After admission, students faced a series of examinations testing their language ability. According to the school regulations of the Aichi English Language School, as recorded in the *Monbushō Daini Nenpō* statistical abstract of 1874 (p.432), the students' advancement to the next grade was based on the result of a regular grade examination. These examinations were usually conducted at the end of a half-year, but for those whose progress was irregular, they could be offered at any time. Additionally, once each month ordinary tests were administered by each teacher. Usually the teachers would set aside time to directly question each of the students in their classes. At the end of each semester, the placement of the students based on their performance in both the ordinary and regular examinations was posted on the bulletin board, and awards and prizes were given to the outstanding students. After passing the regular examination for the highest grade of the lower course, students were asked to pass the major (or graduation) examination in order to obtain the diploma, and only those who obtained the diploma were eligible to apply to the Kaisei Gakkō.

According to the regular examination results at the Aichi English Language School in 1875, of 317 who took the test, 255 were upgraded, 68 remained at the same grade, 6 fell to a lower grade, and 37 left the school. Clearly the examinations after admission were rigorous. Due to the system of frequent examinations, however, excellent students could advance quickly through the grades and graduate in a short time (Ōta 1981, 77).

The English Language Schools produced their first graduates in 1876. In that year, thirty-seven graduates from the English Language School of Tokyo, twelve from Osaka, nine each from Aichi and Hiroshima, and four each from Nagasaki and Niigata were admitted to the Kaisei Gakkō. Of the twelve students admitted in 1876 to the Sapporo Agricultural College, which was also a government higher educational institution, eleven were graduates of these schools. Thus English Language Schools were the principal suppliers of students to government institutions for specialized education.

This system of English Language Schools, however, did not last long. The new government, facing financial difficulties, decided to cut back on this effort beginning in 1877. Five of the English Language Schools were discontinued, and the students from the higher grades of these schools were moved to either the Tokyo or the Osaka school. The students of the lower grades were transferred to prefectural middle schools. The Osaka English Language School was soon reorganized into a college for specialized education, leaving the Tokyo English Language School as the sole preparatory institution.

The Preparatory Course for Tokyo University

The Tokyo English Language School had from the time of its founding a special relationship with the Kaisei Gakkō. Even after English schools were founded in other prefectures, it remained the largest supplier of students to the Kaisei Gakkō. Its educational standard was by far the highest, as it benefited from its tradition and its location in Tokyo. In Tokyo, as the center of "civilization and enlightenment," there were many private preparatory schools for English and other advanced education.

Although English proficiency was not always required to pass the entrance examination to the Kaisei Gakkō, students without a certain level of language ability faced difficulty in following classes at the school. Therefore, the typical path for local students striving to enter the Kaisei Gakkō was first to move to Tokyo, enter a private preparatory school, and gain some foreign-language proficiency before attempting the examination of the Tokyo English Language School. After the other English schools were abolished, this became the main path to the Kaisei Gakkō.

In April 1877, the same year that the system of English Language Schools was abandoned, the Kaisei Gakkō merged with the Tokyo Medical School and became Tokyo University. Kaisei was formerly the Southern Campus of the University, and Tokyo Medical School was formerly the Eastern Campus. These two schools were reunited to form the first modern university in Japan. Following the merger, the Tokyo English Language School became the official preparatory school for the university (*yobimon*) by merger with the preparatory course of the Kaisei Gakkō.

As we noted earlier, the Kaisei Gakkō began its program of specialized education in 1873. Even so, Kaisei found it necessary to provide several years of preparatory education. The school's annual bulletin of 1875 stated: "A three-year preparatory course was created, since the students do not have enough proficiency in general education to move immediately into specialized education." And it was Kaisei's dearest wish to become a genuine institution for specialized education—a university—by separating the preparatory course from its main body.

The new preparatory school (*yobimon*) for the university had a four-year curriculum, and those who completed the courses and passed the examination were allowed to pursue further studies at the Faculties of Law, Science, or Letters at Tokyo University. In other words, graduation from the preparatory school became a prerequisite for entering the university. A similar link was subsequently established between the Imperial universities and the Higher Middle Schools.

The standards for selection for the *yobimon* and those maintained in the courses were very high, and thus the failure rate for the course was extremely high. For example, in 1881, according to the *Mombushō Daiku Nenpō* statistical abstract for that year, 74 (44%) out of 170 applicants succeeded in the entrance examination held in June; in the first-term examination 83 out of 257 (32%) failed, 19 out of 176 (11%) failed in the second-term examination, and in the year-end examination 24 out of 141 (17%) failed. In fact, only 46% were able to advance to the next grade without failing or dropping out.

The high failure rate reflected the inadequate preparation of the students who entered the school. The *Mombushō Nenpō* of 1881 observed: "Many of the freshmen come from private or public schools where they became accustomed to a less rigorous education, and they lack experience in high-level, demanding studies. Therefore, though they have managed to enter, they are overwhelmed by the curriculum and have difficulty keeping up. The result is that many cannot stay at school until the end of the year as they fail in the term examination." This situation continued until the 1880s.

The preparatory school, *yobimon*, was part of neither the middle school nor the university. Since it was a school outside the formal school system, the only requirements it imposed were that the applicants be at least thirteen years old and have sufficient academic ability to pass an entrance examination. In the regulations of 1879, the examination subjects were Japanese and Chinese studies, English (reading, writing, and comprehension) and mathematics (fractions and decimals). In contrast to the English Language Schools, English proficiency was required for admission. In 1881, the term of preparatory education was shortened from four to three years and the entrance examination subjects were changed to English comprehension and grammar, arithmetic, algebra, geometry, geography, and Japanese and Chinese studies. This change was possible because education in local areas had gradually improved, according to the 1939 *Sixty-Year History of the First High School*.

Student evaluation during a school year included daily tests, a term examination, and a year-end examination. The evaluation for the first and second trimesters was based on a weighted sum for the tests and the term examination, while for the third trimester the weighted sum of the term examination and the year-end examination was considered. At the end of each trimester the names of all the students studying the same subject were customarily displayed on a bulletin board in the order of their performance. A perfect score was 100, while 60 marked the borderline between passing and failure. If a student received an average score of 60 with less than four subjects below 60 but above 50, he passed the grade. At the end of the year, only one subject could be below 60 if the student was to pass. A student had to leave school if his average was below 50 and his score was less than 50 in two or more subjects.

The Perpetuation of Preparatory Education

The preparatory school, *yobimon*, thus became the only road that led to Tokyo University. Technically, it was possible to enter the University if the result of a special examination demonstrated competence equal to that of graduates of the *yobimon*, but in fact almost no one ever tried the alternate route. Ironically, there was no provision for the preparatory school in the *Gakusei*. As we have seen, the *yobimon* for Tokyo University was originally created because rural areas lacked sufficient resources to provide the education necessary for entering the University—that is, schools where English-language and high-level general education could be provided. The *yobimon*, then, was considered a transitory provision that would disappear once the middle school system was well developed across the nation.

Around 1877, when the Kaisei Gakkō became Tokyo University, the first steps toward "Japanizing" the teaching staff and curriculum began (Amano 1977). By 1881 several specialized subjects were being taught by Japanese staff members, and it became acceptable to present a graduation thesis written in the Japanese language. This, however, did not mean that foreign-language education became unnecessary. Most of what students learned in the university came from the West. So long as Japan lacked a foundation for the indigenous production of knowledge, the dependence on Western learning would continue. By changing the *vehicle of study* from a foreign language to the national language, the prospects for indigenous research could be enhanced. And without this effort, the Japanese university would never manage to rank beside the universities of the West. The institution for preparatory education, which was outside of the formal education system and where mastery of a foreign language was the main objective, was a kind of "footstool" for steppimg up to advanced studies of international calibre.

A similar problem existed in the other government higher education institutions staffed by foreign teachers. As observed above, Tokyo Medical School provided its medical education through the medium of German teachers. Even after it became a part of Tokyo University, the Faculty of Medicine had to keep an independent five-year course for preparatory education, for there were no other public or private schools for German-language education, and the university preparatory education for the faculties of law, science, and letters was conducted in English.

The Law School created by the Ministry of Justice for training judicial officers, which had relied on French teachers, had the same problem (Tezuka 1967). Although French-language education was thriving from the end of the Edo period through the early Meiji era, its popularity declined once the Kaisei Gakkō restricted its instruction to the English language. Therefore, the Law School had to allocate four years of its eight-year program to preparatory education in French.

Compared to these two schools, both the Imperial College of Engineering attached to the Ministry of Industry and the Sapporo Agricultural College of the Land Development Bureau were fortunate to have relied on English and American teaching staff, for the number of young people exposed to English was far greater than those familiar with French or German. Many students transferred from the government English-language schools or the *yobimon*. Even so, these schools found it necessary to establish their own preparatory educational institutions in order to secure a steady supply of students of high academic ability. The Imperial College of Engineering allocated two years of its six-year curriculum for preparatory study, and the Sapporo Agricultural College established a three-year preparatory course in addition to its four-year regular course.

Except for the Sapporo Agricultural College, these institutions of higher education, along with the Komaba Agricultural School of the Ministry of Agriculture and Commerce, eventually were placed under the jurisdiction of the Ministry of Education to become a part of the Imperial University when it was inaugurated in 1886. By that time, most of the teaching staff were Japanese who had graduated from these schools and later pursued further study in Western countries. However, the necessity for the "footstool" did not totally disappear as the Japanese university sought to achieve an equal standard with the Western universities.

The Japanese education system during the Meiji period can be compared to a two-story house in which the first floor–the elementary and middle schools–was a completely different world from the second floor—the university. The university became "the West in Japan," and preparatory education, with foreign language training as its main objective, served as the stairs to go up from the first floor to the second. The preparatory course "stairs" were soon systematized as the Higher Middle School and the Higher School. As would be seen later, the Japanese "examination hell" was to form at the bottom of this staircase.

The Examinations of Higher Educational Institutions

The Law School of the Ministry of Justice

Let us take a close look at the examination practices of the various higher education institutions that had been established prior to 1886, when the Imperial University was founded.

Apart from Tokyo University, there were several important schools affiliated with various government ministries. In the manner of the French *grandes écôles*, these schools trained officials for the ministries with which they were affiliated; their students received scholarships that stipulated their obligation to serve the government for a certain period of time after graduation. Since the schools were established to train future high-ranking government officials, their admission and examination procedures were as rigorous as those at Tokyo University. Since the nationalities of the teachers at these schools differed, however, there was considerable variety among examination methods. A review of the situations of these schools enables us to understand what Japan adopted, adapted, and discarded from the examination systems it had imported from the West.

First we will consider the Law School of the Ministry of Justice, which became a part of the Law College of the Imperial University in 1886. Beginning in 1872, this school selected its students by an academic examination. In addition to evaluating mastery of Chinese studies, the examination included a French conversation test conducted by French teachers. We have already seen that many Southern Campus students majoring in French applied for this selection examination. The Southern Campus at that time was going through a difficult period since it was not able to set a definite starting date for specialized courses, and, furthermore, there was some discussion of restricting the language of instruction to English only, instead of English, French and German as proposed. According to the 1932 *Fifty-Year History of Tokyo Imperial University*, many of the students, feeling insecure about this situation, tried to transfer to other schools. The reason that the Law School of the Ministry of Justice began its courses with staff invited from France is that the Minister of Justice, Etō Shimpei, had initiated a project to draft a legal code modeled on the Napoleonic Code, which was believed to be the most complete law code in the world at that time. The French law staff at the Law School were also the legal advisers to the Ministry of Justice project.

After a one-month trial period, the first twenty students who had been admitted were divided into two groups based on their performance and started receiving specialized education. Nine of the initial class left the school, seven were sent to France for study, and sixteen new students were admitted to take their places. Finally in August 1876 the school graduated its first class of twenty students. Preceding the graduation, the Ministry of Justice asked the French teachers to provide a report on the students' performance. One of the reporters said the bottom third of the class would have great difficulty in graduating without hard work as "their knowledge was extremely poor," while the top third not only had excellent academic ability but also had "a clear goal for study" (Tezuka 1967, 60). Based on this report, the Ministry of Justice decided to send three to France to study and to employ eleven others, while the remaining six were allowed to graduate but were not offered employment.

After gaining experience with the first class, the Law School increased the size of its entering group to one hundred students. Among over eight hundred applicants for the second class, one hundred four were selected based on an examination that emphasized the thoughtful reading and comprehension of both Japanese and Chinese literature. French language ability was no longer part of the entrance examination. From the beginning the students were taught general subjects in French by French instructors who did not use any Japanese or Chinese. Individual progress was tested every week and a semester examination took place every six months. After each weekly examination, the names of the top ten or fifteen students were posted on a bulletin board. The semester examination, held in the presence of the Minister of Justice, was very demanding, and those who failed had to leave school immediately.

The students were ranked in terms of a total score which summed up their performance on the weekly minor examinations and the semester major examination. The records for the first semester indicated a large gap between the top score of 261 and the bottom score of 24. New students who had no previous knowledge of French had great difficulty following the class, which was given entirely in French. Of the original hundred students, forty-eight completed the four-year preparatory course and moved on to the regular course. After eight years thirty-one managed to graduate.

The College of Engineering

The Imperial College of Engineering of the Ministry of Industry, staffed by teachers from England, placed more reliance on continuous testing and awards.[1] The college regulations of 1877 indicate that selection of applicants was to be based on an exam covering eight subjects: Japanese translation from English, English translation from Japanese, dictation, English composition, arithmetic, beginning geometry, beginning algebra, and geography. Later, however, when the number of applicants swelled, a provisional examination covering only translation, geography, and arithmetic was used to screen qualified students for the full examination.

The first two years of the six-year program was for preparatory study, followed by two years for specialized study and a final two years for applied study. Every other week there was a weekend examination consisting of four questions for which students were allowed two hours. In addition, the professors in each subject were allowed to give subject examinations whenever they

---

[1] Data on the Imperial College of Engineering are mostly from *Kyū-Kōbu Daigakkō Shiryō* (Sourcebook on the Imperial College of Engineering), 1931.

felt the need. Yamakawa Yoshitarō, one of the early graduates of the college, wrote in a collection of student anecdotes (the 1928 *Kōbu Daigakkō Mukashi Banashi*) that he was always painfully tense and almost had a nervous breakdown because there was an examination virtually every Saturday. At the end of each semester, there was a four-hour examination consisting of from eight to ten questions. If the average score on this examination and the weekend examinations equaled forty-five points, the student was allowed to pass. Those who failed were allowed a chance to improve their performance six months after the end of the semester, but one fourth of them dropped out.

At the end of the two-year preparatory course, the students faced a major examination in which they had to demonstrate a standard level of progress in order to gain admittance to the specialized study course. At the end of this specialized study course, students once again faced a major examination of their academic ability. An interesting feature of these examinations was the recognition extended to those with outstanding performances. After each semester examination, the three best students were chosen from each class and given prizes of books or school supplies worth seven, eight, and ten yen in the order of their ranking. Similarly, at the graduation examination of the preparatory course, the two students with the fewest mistakes were awarded special prizes of twenty yen and thirty yen. Since the starting monthly salary of a graduate from this college was at most thirty yen, these were quite substantial prizes. According to the recollection of one graduate, the best student was awarded an *Encyclopedia Britannica* and the second best, a *Dictionary of Engineering*.

While there was a completion examination at the end of the six-year school term as well, students were also required during the final semester to write a graduation thesis based on their field work. Based on the cumulative record of major examinations, the thesis students were classified into three groups: first-place pass, second-place pass, and third-place completion. This system was obviously an imitation of the British honors degree system. Of the two hundred eleven graduates from 1879 to 1885, only sixty-one (twenty-nine percent) were in the first group; six were in the third group, and the remainder were in the second group. Only those in the first-place pass group were awarded a

Bachelor of Engineering degree, and those in the third group were not even given a graduation certificate.

In principle, the graduates of the Imperial College of Engineering were to become engineering officers of the Ministry of Industry, but the actual terms offered the graduates came to be associated with their academic records. The graduates of the top group became engineers of the seventh rank with a monthly salary of thirty yen, while graduates of the second group became engineers of the eighth rank with a monthly salary of twenty-five yen. The second and third group graduates, who were without a degree, were at a substantial social disadvantage. Dissatisfaction with this discrepancy gradually became so strong that in 1882, the students decided on a strike to demand that degrees be granted to all the graduates. In response, the college offered to grant a degree to second-place graduates if they could pass a special examination given two years after graduation. Later the degree was approved for all graduates of the second group, though no concession was made to those in the third group.

Another measure to stimulate a sense of pride and competitive spirit among the students was a special program that identified a small group of the top students as scholarship students and offered them the opportunity to go abroad for further study. It might be said that English examination system was faithfully reproduced at the Imperial College of Engineering.

The Sapporo Agricultural College

The Sapporo Agricultural College, founded by the Land Development Bureau, invited American teachers including William Clark, the president of the Massachusetts Institute of Agriculture, to launch its program. [2]

At this college, too, examinations quickly became a means of raising the level of study. The school began its full-scale educational program in 1876, and during the early years many of the students were transfers from preparatory institutions of the Ministry of Education. The term of the regular course was four years, preceded by a preparatory course of three years. Promotion from one grade to the next was determined by the term

[2] Data on the Sapporo Agricultural School are mostly from *Hokkaido Teikoku Daigaku Enkakushi* (The Transformation of Hokkaido Imperial University), 1926.

examinations held at the end of each semester.

By 1877, as in the Imperial College of Engineering, an award system was established for the purpose of promoting study. Awards of eight and four yen were given to the two students who scored highest in English, mathematics, botany, chemistry, and agriculture. Since some students received top scores in all five subjects, a limit of three prizes per student was set.

Examinations were held in the presence of high-ranking officials of the Land Development Bureau, and after the major exam at the end of the year an awards ceremony was held exactly as in the United States, and the ceremony was called an "exhibition," in English. The four best student compositions written during the school year were selected, memorized by their authors, and presented to the gathering (Matsukuma 1969, 57).

Uchimura Kanzō, who later achieved fame as a Christian thinker, was awarded first place in agriculture and mathematics and second place in English studies at the ceremony of 1878. Uchimura was extremely bright and had a tremendous memorization ability. It was said of him that "nobody in the history of the institute showed such outstanding performance" (Ebina 1980, 125).

Nitobe Inazō, who later became an eminent scholar and educator, had transferred from the Tokyo English Language School along with other students such as Uchimura, and joined the second class of the Sapporo Agricultural College. The letters he wrote while at the school indicate the importance of these examinations. Apparently, Nitobe was outstanding in English but weak in mathematics. In the letter sent to his foster father accompanying his report card, he wrote, "Though I placed third in geometry, I am afraid it is an accident since I am not good at mathematics." He added: "Since I entered college, I have always been top in English studies, but fourth in botany and third in physiology." He apologized that despite studying hard in chemistry, unfortunately he could not do as well as he wanted. He also wrote that he had dropped to third place in agriculture the preceding summer but subsequently regained first place because of his hard work and also "with help from Heaven." He observed, "It is hard to improve your placement when you are close to the top. I wish I could keep my third place by working hard and with the help of God" (Matsukuma 1969, 60).

Nitobe reported that there were two types of hard-working students: those with a deep-rooted aspiration to raise national productivity, to promote national art and literature, to strengthen military force, or to produce or create something by themselves; and those with the shallow aspiration of obtaining fame within the school by winning awards to please their parents and to feel proud of themselves. The latter group "study only for recognition, which teachers say is very common in the United States." Nitobe said that study "should not be for the sake of honor but for national benefit," and declared that he did not want to become one of the latter group. It is not clear, however, to what extent other students shared his skepticism about the use of examinations and competition to promote study (Matsukuma 1969, 76).

The Kaisei Gakkō

The Kaisei Gakkō, the predecessor of Tokyo University, was the sole comprehensive institution of higher education of the period.[3] Probably because of repeated reforms in its organization, however, the regulations for admissions and its examinations were not finalized until 1875. The subjects covered in the initial entrance examinations included Japanese, practical English (dictation, conversation, reading, and composition), English grammar, geography, mathematics (fractions, proportions, square roots, cube roots), and world history. In comparison to the other government schools, the coverage was more extensive and the level somewhat higher. One of the reasons Nitobe Inazō moved from the Tokyo English Language School to the Sapporo Agricultural College was his belief that he would not be able to pass the mathematics examination of the Kaisei Gakkō (Matsukuma 1969, 31). The policy of testing the overall academic ability of prospective students was clearly instituted even prior to the establishment of Tokyo University.

In the first examination for these subjects, held in September of 1985, only thirty-eight out of one hundred applicants succeeded; and twenty-nine of the successful applicants had been students at the Tokyo English Language School. The annual

---

[3] Data on the Kaisei Gakkō come mainly from annual Ministry of Education reports (*nenpō*).

bulletin of the school explains this low success rate by declaring that many had been given a one-sided rather than a well-rounded education. It was becoming apparent that the irregular education offered by many of the private schools was no longer sufficient to guarantee admission to the Kaisei Gakkō.

Examinations were also prominent in the program of study for the students who gained admission. In addition to the regular examination held at the end of each semester to measure progress, special examinations could be conducted at any time, according to each teacher's discretion. Teachers were required to record all the results and at the end of each semester to give the director the cumulative result, allowing twice as much weight for daily performance and special examinations relative to the score on the regular examination. In the first annual report of Kaisei Gakkō, the American chemistry professor stated that the progress of the students specializing in industrial chemistry was remarkable except for two students, whose ability was so low that their withdrawal from school was inevitable. The mechanical engineering professor, who was also an American, reported that generally the students' progress was great, except for three who didn't deserve praise as unlike the others they did not show any progress. The names of the students were ranked and posted in the principal's room, and the list was published in the annual report. The class head boy was appointed from the top group of his class, and it was considered a great honor to receive this recognition.

Tokyo University
Once Tokyo University was established in 1877 as the successor to Kaisei Gakkō, the various rules concerning examinations were rapidly elaborated.

According to the new rules, three indicators of student performance were authorized: evaluations during the trimester, trimester examinations, and year-end examinations. The evaluations within the trimester were to come from marks for students' daily performance on written tests, daily lessons, and compositions. And the top student of the class was awarded the title of "class leader," an honor that was considered very special.

Even the weight to be accorded to each indicator was stipulated in these regulations. Each trimester's daily performance was accorded a value of two points, as were the trimester exams. The year-end examination was worth five points. At the end of each trimester the students' names were listed in the order of their total achievement, along with their scores on each subject. The custom of listing all the students in the order of their performance in the university's annual report lasted until the second decade of the twentieth century.

The regulations for the promotion and demotion of students were also based on these objective indicators of performance. The regulations included detailed tables which stipulated that only those with a passing score of sixty or over on all subjects could be unconditionally approved for promotion, while those with an average score below forty as well as those with an average between forty and forty-nine but who had more than two subjects below fifty or more than one subject below forty should be required to leave school. Those in between these two extremes were generally required to repeat their coursework for the year. The repeaters were required to reregister in all the subjects and to retake all the examinations, though attendance was not required for those subjects they had passed in the previous year. If a student failed on his second try, he could expect permanent dismissal from the school. The rigorous application of these regulations is apparent in the report of 1881 for the Faculties of Law, Science, and Letters: 70.8 percent of the students were promoted, 11.6 percent were sent down, and the remainder had to repeat their academic year.

The Medical Faculty, which originated from the Tokyo Medical School, where teaching had been conducted in German, had a distinctive evaluation system. Since a high level of basic education was required, the Medical Faculty created its own five-year preparatory course, which it retained even after being consolidated into Tokyo University. An announcement from the Medical Faculty of 1879 says that the preparatory course was created because a high-level middle school did not exist then for those who wished to work in medicine. Completion of the preparatory course did not lead automatically, however, to admission to the regular course. Those who finished this preparatory course had to take the same entrance examination as outside applicants.

Another major difference from other faculties was the Medical Faculty's graduation examination. While the other faculties did not require a graduation examination, medical students had to pass a comprehensive examination upon completion of all the courses as a condition for receiving their graduation certificate.

The regulations for the graduation examination for the students of the Faculty of Medicine specified coverage of (1) anatomy and physiology, (2) surgery and ophthalmology, and (3) internal medicine and obstetrics. The examinations took place over a five-month period, with success in each subject a prerequisite for the next exam. The examination for each area differed in character. For example, in the examination for anatomy and physiology, groups of from one to four students met with two examiners on four separate occasions to demonstrate their skills. When a student's performance on any of these examinations was given the lowest in a series of five grades, a reexamination was given four weeks later. If the grade was second lowest, a reexamination was given two weeks later. If a student could not pass the reexamination, then he was required to wait until the next year to take all the examinations. Three failures led to permanent expulsion from school. The graduation certificates included the individual's performance on all of these subjects. This examination system may have been an exact replication of that at a German university, introduced by the German teachers who had founded the Faculty of Medicine.

By the early 1880s, Tokyo University had established a well-organized examination system. The examination regulations of the Imperial University (as Tokyo University was renamed in 1886) indicate that it retained the above procedures. By the latter half of the 1880s, examination systems had been established at both the primary and higher educational levels. The examinations for the middle school level were also falling into place. Following the establishment of these school-based examinations, the next steps in the institutionalization of examinations included the development of examinations for vocational and professional qualifications and the emergence of higher middle school entrance examinations.

Chapter Six

Qualifying Examinations for the Professions

The Qualifying Examination for Lawyers

So far, we have focused on the systematization of school-related examinations. Examinations, however, are not limited to schools. Indeed the nineteenth century is usually referred to as the age of examinations precisely because the examination spread to the world of work.

To understand the work-related use of examinations, it is important to consider the role of the professions. During the European middle ages, a variety of guilds or trade associations were established by those pursuing similar professions in order to protect their common interests. These groups drew up regulations to define the standards of work expected of members, and they organized programs to standardize and improve the knowledge and skills used by members. One outcome of these efforts was the specification by each group of the qualifications for membership.

As noted in the previous chapters, the *universitas* was one such trade association that emerged in Europe's medieval period. In the university as a "trade association," the teacher was the master and the student was his apprentice. When the student's ability reached a certain level, the teacher would administer an examination. Those students who passed the examinations were awarded a diploma, which signified membership in the teachers' guild and meant that the student possessed the qualification to teach his own students.

This diploma might also serve as a professional qualification. A medieval university typically had departments specializing in law, medicine, and theology. Those who received a diploma from these departments could engage in the practice of law, medicine, or the clergy. Many of the law graduates became officials and clerks. For each of these professions, however, there were other routes to obtaining qualifications. The church had its own system for training priests while the lawyers and doctors had their own guilds. And a diploma from a department of law was not a necessary condition for employment in government service.

In other words, each of the professions as well as the church and state organizations had, instead of relying on the university, established its own qualifying standards for admission, and had even devised means to test candidates. In fact, during the modernization process in Europe in the 18th and 19th centuries, it became established that the various professional organizations conducted qualification exams, and in some countries national governments began to conduct those tests on behalf of the professional organizations. As we have seen earlier, some nations also introduced qualification examinations for admission to employment as a government official. In Germany, a particularly advanced country in this respect, there was hardly a professional area in which the state did not conduct an examination of some kind (Ringer 1977, 540).

While these changes evolved, the number of both university students and diplomas granted increased. Consequently, the university diploma lost its meaning as a professional qualification for becoming a university professor. The diploma simply became a certificate to validate the completion of a university education, that is, an academic credential. In addition, as the status of the professional groups and the nation-states rose, both of these institutions began to carry out their own qualifying examinations, so the diploma alone no longer entitled the holder to pursue a professional practice. The diploma gradually became no more than a preliminary qualification allowing its holder to take an official qualifying examination.

These changes, which took place in Europe over the eighteenth and nineteenth centuries, could not be observed in Japan, for at that time Japan had no analogous autonomous unions of professional workers or system of qualifying examinations. While there were scholars who taught at the *bakufu* and fief schools, they had not formed a union to protect their interests. Medical doctors had not yet formed a union for the systematic training of successors or developed regulations to regulate individuals who sought to practice medicine. The legal profession, perhaps the most representative profession in Europe, did not even exist in nineteenth-century Japan. Certainly, Japan's unique *iemoto* system, which defined the proper relations between the head and the followers in, for example, schools of Noh, played a role in establishing the qualifications for these special occupations. But these schools hardly seem comparable to the European professions, since they neither openly discussed their special practices nor codified the standards required of their members. They were closer to private clubs than public professions. Indeed, when it came to establishing a modern state in Japan, not only the qualification examinations, but the very functions and organization of the professions had to be fashioned by the hands of the national government.

In feudal Japan's hierarchical society of warriors, farmers, artisans, and tradesmen, the individual's occupation was determined by heredity. In this society of restricted social mobility, the occupations of medical doctor and scholar, where knowledge and ability were the principal job requirements, were among the limited avenues for moving up the social ladder. It was in these occupations outside the established social hierarchy that a person of genuine ability could attract students and customers and rise to prominence. By the end of the Edo period, the scholars who specialized in Western studies in particular became much sought after as men with vital and useful knowledge. In a number of cases poor scholars who studied at the private academies such as Ogata Kōan's Tekijuku were recruited by feudal lords and received large salaries. The age when knowledge and skills would be recognized as a means for social mobility was about to come to Japan. It was only, however, after systematic learning gained new importance in the Meiji era that Japan established examinations for professional work and government service.

The Appearance of the Lawyer

Medical doctor, lawyer, and teacher are three of the professional occupations for which a special qualification is required. We turn now to consider how the qualifying examinations for these typical professions were established.

In the judicial system of pre-Meiji Japan, there were no specialists to speak on behalf of those involved in a legal dispute. It was in 1872 that a spokesman—an attorney—was first officially allowed to appear in court to defend litigants. But the position of spokesman, *Daigennin*, could not be considered an occupation, for no qualification was specified and anybody could serve. Each time a spokesman appeared in court, he was required to present his name card to the guard and obtain the stamp of the guard's private seal to confirm his participation. Furthermore, during the proceedings the spokesman was called by name without any mention of an honorific title, and he was even fined if he arrived late. Obviously, spokesmen were not well regarded by society; indeed, the contemptuous phrase "a spokesman for three hundred *mon*" (an old Japanese monetary unit) was sometimes used to describe the fast talkers who took up this role for such lowly remuneration (Okudaira 1971, 166). Following the *Daigennin Kisoku* (spokesman regulations) of 1876, however, the role of advocate gained greater social acceptance, becoming a profession which required licensing. According to these regulations, the Minister of Justice issued licenses only to those who passed an examination. But, at least partly because a modern legal code had not yet been formulated, the examination was an extremely simple one. At the examination held in Tokyo, some of the examinees denounced the examiners, shouting, "How could you examine us with such easy questions? You are making fools of us" (Okudaira 1971, 183). One reason the examination was so easy was that it was prepared prior to the consolidation of Japan's modern law codes. Lacking an established body of principles on which to conduct the examination, the responsible local officers placed more importance on the examinees' deportment than on their judicial knowledge.

The early educational institutions for training legal advocates were also weak (Amano 1971). The government institutions for law education included the Law School of the Ministry of Justice and the Faculty of Law of the Kaisei Gakkō. But only in the 1880s did the latter start producing graduates, and initially the number was quite small. Most of the spokesmen during this early period were trained through private apprenticeships. However, as the spokesman system became institutionalized, those with a practical knowledge of the law and trial proceedings began to create "spokesmen companies" similar to today's law firms. They also created an apprentice system in order to train successors. Hokushūsha, founded by Shimamoto Nakamichi, an officer of the Ministry of Justice, is considered to be the first such organization, and its students accounted for over half of those who succeeded in Tokyo's first examination for legal advocates (Nihon Bengōshi Rengōkai 1959).

In 1880, when the Criminal Code (Japan's first modern law code) was officially issued, the regulations covering advocates were also substantially reformed and the examination system was upgraded. According to the new regulations, a standard examination with questions prepared by the Ministry of Justice was to be administered throughout the nation. Personal conduct was omitted from this examination. When the first examination was held in 1880, only eight percent passed—a sharp contrast with the eighty-seven percent who had been approved under the old regulations. Clearly the new regulations were much more challenging (Okudaira 1971).

The new regulations raised the status and social esteem accorded advocates, who were evolving into attorneys. Until that time, attorneys could not conduct business outside their court district, but under the new regulations they were allowed to work anywhere in Japan. Furthermore, the rights to create a union and hold assemblies in order to promote professional ethical standards were also granted. The fact that three graduates from Tokyo University's Faculty of Law elected to become attorneys attests to the improving social status of this profession.

Another noteworthy provision in the regulations was the explicit prohibition of firms for attorneys. Apart from the union's assembly, forming any private firm with a special name and conducting business there was prohibited. This measure had political implications, for among the attorneys were many prominent activists in the democratic civil rights movement. The regulations made it difficult for attorneys to be trained through apprenticeship, thus creating an opportunity for the establishment of private law schools.

The Appearance of Private Law Schools
The year 1880 was pivotal for endeavors to found full-scale training institutions for attorneys. The establishment of new laws and the new qualifying examination underscored the need for sys-

tematic law education. At the same time, it was around this time that the first generation who received genuine judicial education emerged. Included in this group were those who had studied in Western countries from the end of the Edo period to the early Meiji era, the graduates of the Faculty of Law of Tokyo University and the Law School of the Ministry of Justice. Among these were several who had been selected for special studies in France. This initial crop of trained lawyers launched several distinct efforts to found law schools, which proceeded in two main directions: one modeled on French law and the other on Anglo-American law (Amano 1978).

The French-law group was largely connected with the Law School of the Ministry of Justice, where French law had been taught; they were encouraged by the fact that the first modern law codes of Japan had been modeled after French law. In 1880, a group of three people including Kishimoto Tatsuo, who had been sent to France to study by the Law School of the Ministry of Justice, founded the Meiji Law School—the predecessor of today's Meiji University. In 1881, the Tokyo Law School was founded by the graduates of the same Law School, and in 1887 it incorporated the Tokyo French School, which had been founded by a group named Futsugakkai (the Association for French Studies) composed mainly of people who had studied in France. These schools eventually merged and became Hōsei University.

In the Ango-American group, Tajiri Inajirō and others who had studied in the United States joined with several graduates of the Tokyo University Law Faculty in 1880 to found the Senshū School, the predecessor of today's Senshū University, which focused on Anglo-American law. Later, in 1882, the Tokyo Professional School was founded by the eminent politician Ōkuma Shigenobu, who invited several scholars who had studied law and political science at Tokyo University to form a teaching staff. This school, which later became Waseda University, also focused on Anglo-American law. In 1885, the English Law School, the predecessor of Chūō University, was founded.

One explanation for the founding of this extraordinary number of private law schools at this time was the wish of Meiji-era elite Japanese to repay their "debt of gratitude" to their country. Many of the founders of these schools had received a chance to study overseas from the government and now were established judicial officers, administrative officials, university professors, or attorneys. They often taught without any pay whenever they could find free time from their official duties, out of a sense of obligation. But there were other factors behind their generosity. One was the ongoing struggle between the two judicial groups, the advocates of French law and of Anglo-American law. Additionally, the power struggle between the establishmentarians and the anti-establishmentarians deserves note.

The anti-establishmentarian group was concentrated primarily in the Meiji Law School (of the French line) and the Tokyo Professional School (of the Anglo-American line). It was in order to weaken the Meiji Law School, where many of the staff supported the democratic civil rights movement, that several officials in the Ministry of Justice established the Tokyo Law School. Both schools were located in Tokyo's Kanda district, and they nearly went bankrupt when in 1883 they engaged in a tuition price war to attract students. The government also put pressure on Tokyo Professional School, which was then regarded as a "political school." The school's centenary history, published in 1932, notes that after Ōkuma left the government in 1881 following an attempted coup d'état, judicial officers and university professors were forbidden to teach there. This conflict and competition was an important driving force for the establishment and progress of the private law schools.

The Road to Success

The private law schools were founded primarily as preparatory schools for the qualifying examination to become an attorney, but this was not their sole purpose. Many of their students, who came from all over Japan, were from locally prominent families, and their main purpose in studying law was to find a place for themselves in the modern age. Some hoped to become officers of the new government, while others expected they would become politicians. The most ambitious, however, were interested in becoming private attorneys.

According to the regulations of Meiji Law School of 1883, any male over sixteen years of age could be admitted to the school. Students could hold jobs and enroll in other schools simultaneously. All three teachers of the school had other jobs and could teach only part-time. Classes were held two hours a day and as little as twelve hours a week, from eight to nine o'clock in the morning and from half-past three to half past four in the afternoon. This indicates that the students could be part-time as well. Students from wealthy families studied simultaneously at several schools, while those from impoverished families combined their studies with work.

The ratio of successful applicants in the attorney examination indicates that it was extremely difficult by contemporary standards. During the five years from 1881 to 1885, of 7,968 who took the exam, there were only 371 successful applicants, or a success ratio of only 4.7 percent (Okudaira 1971). Still, a very attractive avenue to social mobility, particularly for those able and ambitious young people from families of low status or income, lay beyond this hurdle. An academic record was not a prerequisite for taking the attorney examination, and students could prepare for the exam even while working. The competition was based entirely on ability. Once students passed the exam, they could immediately look forward to high social status and monetary reward. The attorney examination offered a short cut to success. As a route to social mobility, the path from a private law school to work as an attorney was much shorter and more economical than the "regular course" from the elementary through the middle school to the preparatory course and the university.

It should be added here that even in the early stages of the qualifying examination for attorneys, graduates of the government schools enjoyed the privilege of obtaining a certificate to practice without the examination. The first graduates of government schools to be exempted from the examination were those from the Law Faculty of Tokyo University, in 1878. The graduates from the Law School of the Ministry of Justice, which had originally been the training center for judicial officers, were not granted this privilege until 1884. Among the first group to graduate from the center, in 1876, there had been a number of unfortunate students who had not performed sufficiently well to be employed as judicial officers. They could, nonetheless, after passing the relevant examination, qualify as attorneys. The reason for the need for the Law School's graduates to take the qualifying examination was that they had been "taught only French law and nothing of the current laws of Japan" (Okudaira 1971, 571), a good indication of the unusual character of the law education of the early years of the Meiji period when no Japanese law was taught at all. Even at Tokyo University it was not until 1877 that Japanese law was included as a subject for study, and even then only the ancient laws of Japan were treated.

While the graduates of the government schools were able to become attorneys without taking an examination, the number who did so was small, since an attorney's social prestige was lower than that of a judicial or administrative officer (Amano 1978, 230). At Tokyo University, of the sixty-two graduates between 1878 and 1885, only fourteen became attorneys. The Law School of the Ministry of Justice produced sixty-two graduates in both 1876 and 1884, but most of these became judicial officers.

Thus the training of independent attorneys was mainly carried out in the private law schools. Furthermore, the government schools did not even supply enough graduates to staff the judicial service. Rules for the employment of judges drafted in 1884 created the opportunity for private-school graduates to take an examination for employment in this service. However, the Law Faculty of Tokyo University, concerned that its position in the mainstream of judicial education might be eroded by this informal arrangement, initiated a separate law course to produce a large number of judicial officers in a short time and at low cost by relying on Japanese as the language of instruction. Graduates of this intensive course, created in 1883, were also to be awarded the privilege of becoming attorneys without the qualifying examination.

This intensive course was, however, abolished after admitting altogether a little more than eighty students over a two-year period. In part this was because in 1886 Tokyo University became the Imperial University, and the content of the law courses was enriched. Furthermore, policy moved in the direction of tighter control over private law schools in a move to assimilate them into the administration-regulated system so that the private institutions might function as the providers of non-government legal practitioners, and middle- and low-level bureaucrats (Amano 1978, 221). In any case, as a result of policy modifications, a double structure emerged, with government schools producing judicial officers and private schools producing attorneys; this pattern has continued down to the present. Under this unique system, success in the examination to become an attorney functioned as a highly meritocratic and open route for poor but able and ambitious young people to climb the social ladder.

Medical Doctors and Teachers

The Qualifying Examination for Medical Doctors

Medical doctors, another recognized professional group, have a long history in Japan. But in contrast to European doctors, they neither formed a union nor created a qualifying examination. Before the Meiji period, anybody in Japan who wished to could call himself a doctor.

According to Fuse Shōichi, there were four types of doctors in the Edo period: (1) doctors with formal medical education provided by a teacher; (2) doctors who studied medicine mainly by reading Chinese medical books and who were taught to some degree by a teacher; (3) illiterate doctors or doctors who had studied medicine on their own; and (4) doctors who learned entirely through experience (Fuse 1979, 114). Those belonging to the first and second groups were few; in other words, most of the doctors never engaged in systematic study of medicine or even basic medical skills. In 1873, when the new government required all of Japan's practicing doctors to hand in professional resumés, many of the doctors could not even write a single character and had to have their resumés written by other people.

At that time, "doctoring" was considered a disreputable or mean occupation, and much of medical practice was based on folklore. Ambitious people were not inclined to become doctors. Even after the Meiji Restoration, it took some time for the profession of medicine to acquire high social prestige.

In 1873, the new government began to improve this chaotic situation by proposing a new medical system (Kawakami 1965). It was suggested that new practitioners must graduate from a formal program of medical education or pass a qualifying examination. Beginning in 1876, national qualifying examinations based entirely on Western medicine were offered at various places.

This was a truly revolutionary reform, for Japanese medicine had for centuries been based on Chinese medicine. Western medicine had only begun to be introduced in limited areas of

Japan at the end of the Edo period. A survey conducted in 1874 shows that eighty percent of physicians specialized in Chinese medicine. But after the reform, they were expected to change completely and adopt Western medicine. Since this measure was the equivalent of a death sentence for the doctors of Chinese medicine, naturally a movement opposing it emerged. But the opposition was not sufficiently well organized to be effective, and the new government successfully forced the switchover to Western medicine. However, as a concession to the protesters, in 1882 those who had already been practicing medicine were granted a license, as were any of their children over twenty-five who had been engaged as medical assistants in their family clinics.

Incidentally, while the subjects for the initial qualifying examination were stipulated in the reform regulation, the responsibility for the actual questions was left to each local government, and the content and standard naturally varied. In 1879 the central government announced a new procedure whereby it prepared the questions, did the scoring, and determined who passed. This procedure was certainly very effective in standardizing the content and level but led to a different problem: it took over six months to prepare the questions, send them back and forth for scoring, and determine who had passed among the several thousand examinees. Thus in 1883 the government again decided to change the system.

According to the revised regulations for medical practitioners, the questions would be selected by examination directors located at nine places throughout Japan, based on samples sent from both central and local government examination committees. The scoring and decisions on success or failure and even the awarding of certificates of success was to be conducted at these centers. The examination was to be divided into two parts: the first-term examination was to be on basic medicine, while the second term was to be on clinical medicine and clinical practice. This system continued for some time. The famous bacteriologist Noguchi Hideyo took and passed this examination, completing the first term in 1896 when he was twenty-one years old and the second-term examination the following year (Nakayama 1978).

According to the figures for 1887, the number of applicants for the first-term examination was 4,105, of whom 2,330 were actually tested and 741 succeeded. The number of applicants for the second-term examination was 1,429, of whom 991 were actually tested and 478 succeeded (Kawakami 1965, 127). The success ratio for the first term was 32% and for the second, 48%. The competition ratio was not as high as for the attorney examination, possibly because the need for medical doctors was increasing and therefore the number of successful applicants was high. The examinations were certainly not easy, however, for in those days it was said that three years were needed to prepare for the first and seven years for the second examination.

As a result of the reforms, three groups of doctors could be distinguished: the first consisted of long-time practitioners, the "old doctors"; the second consisted of new doctors who had completed formal medical education at a school; and the third consisted of new doctors who obtained their licenses through the qualifying examination. Until the end of the Meiji period, the majority of new doctors were in the third group.

Preparing for the Examination
The examination regulations of 1879 actually required applicants to hand in their medical academic records and a letter of certification written by their medical instructors. Similarly, the examination regulations of 1883 required a certificate of academic record indicating at least one and a half years for the first examination and the same for the second one. Where then did the applicants study?

Certainly it was not at the government's medical school, for even though in 1875 this school added a course taught in Japanese, the number of students who could study there was limited and, moreover, its graduates automatically received their qualification as medical doctors. During the early Meiji period, one way to prepare for the examination was to receive medical training as an apprentice while living in a doctor's house. But as the examination became more systematized and was upgraded, this approach proved insufficient. To respond to the demand, two types of educational institutions emerged.

One was a medical school or medical classroom attached to a local public hospital. These public hospitals had been started by prefectural governments who invited Japanese practitioners of Western medicine to create showplaces for the modernization of medicine. These first "Western doctors" often opened classes and offered training to the junior staff at the hospitals. Some of these training programs gradually became formalized into independent medical schools, gradually adding graduates of Tokyo University's Faculty of Medicine to the teaching staff.

In 1882, the government issued general rules for medical schools which set the term of study as at least four years and divided schools into two groups. Advanced schools were to be those with at least three teachers who were graduates of Tokyo University, and graduates of these schools could qualify without further examination. By the end of the 1880s twenty-one schools enjoyed the privilege of exemption from the qualifying examination. The other schools were dedicated to preparing their students for the examinations. However, neither the advanced nor the other schools enjoyed smooth progress. The establishment and maintenance of medical schools required great expenditures in those days. In the 1880s, the local governments were facing grave financial difficulties, and one after another they decided to abandon or scale down their medical schools. To make matters even worse, in 1886 the central government prohibited the expenditure of local taxes for the maintenance of medical schools. Due to this measure, only three locally supported medical schools managed to survive, while five others were converted into the medical departments of higher middle schools under the control of the central government (Amano 1978, 50-51).

In such circumstances, the contribution of private schools in preparing students for the qualifying examinations eventually proved to be greater than that of the public medical schools. Some of these schools were affiliated with private hospitals, but in Tokyo there were several independent private medical schools. The most important was Saiseigakusha, founded in 1876 by Hasegawa Yasushi, which produced a large number of successful candidates. Until it was closed in 1903, this school educated over twenty-one thousand students, of whom nearly twelve thousand passed the exam; in fact, the majority of new doctors in 1903 were Saiseigakusha graduates. Noguchi Hideyo also received his preparatory education at this school.

Hasegawa was fondly described as a "hardboiled egg" when he worked as a teacher at the Tokyo Medical School and as a principal at Nagasaki Medical School (Fuse 1979, 53). Later he became a member of the House of Representatives. Despite being called a medical school, Saiseigakusha looked exactly like a "shop on a main street" and was managed like a contemporary preparatory school. All the teachers were part-time, and most were assistants in the Medical Faculty of Tokyo University. Unlike the government medical schools, no qualifications were required for entrance, and there was neither a grading nor a promotion system. Students who paid the tuition fee of one yen could take as many classes as they wished from five in the morning to nine in the evening each day. Exceptional Saiseigakusha students were able to obtain the qualification for medical doctor in a far shorter time and at less expense than the students at the government schools (Nihon Iji Shimpōsha 1937).

Noguchi, after graduation from higher primary school, spent three years preparing for the first examination while working at a private clinic in Fukushima Prefecture as an assistant. He succeeded in the second examination after one year of study at Saiseigakusha. This sort of social mobility through success in professional examinations was possible in the Meiji period, more so than any time before or after.

Generally speaking, however, the quality of education at these private preparatory schools of medicine was not high. One student recorded in his memoirs that many of the instructors had just left university and "taught at eight o'clock in the morning what they had freshly memorized at eight o'clock the previous evening, with only twelve hours' gap between their knowledge and the students'. Consequently, they were sometimes perplexed by the students' questions. Faint-hearted teachers could not cope." Because some teachers quit after being intimidated by the students, a rule forbidding any questions was drafted. Mori Ōgai, the famous writer who had a medical degree from Tokyo University, bitterly criticized the situation in 1890: "What private schools teach is not the medicine of the twentieth century. Responding to the public demand for medical service in this way is much like trying to save a drowning person by giving him water or putting out a fire by pouring more oil on it" (Mori 1957). The reliance on private medical preparatory institutions as the main means of training new doctors naturally led to concern about not only doctors' professional knowledge and skills but their ethical training as well.

Having effectively abolished prefectural medical schools in

1886, the government opened medical departments at five higher middle schools and extended to their graduates the privilege of obtaining a licence to practice medicine without any further qualification examination. Thus even by 1890, the number of doctors who had completed formal medical education, including university graduates, was only sixteen hundred, a small number relative to the fifty-six hundred who became doctors by passing the qualification examination. The examination-based qualifying system without taking account of applicants' past education records continued until 1916.

Elementary School Teachers and the Certification Examination
Teaching, like medicine, is an old occupation. When we consider the teachers in temple schools, private academies, and fief schools, there were a large number of teachers even before the Meiji Restoration. Prior to the Meiji period, teaching was also an occupation that anybody could take up. There was no attempt to measure teaching ability objectively or to certify teachers. The qualification system for teachers was first adopted after the Meiji Restoration as a part of the process of building the modern school system.

The section on teachers in the *Gakusei* of 1872 stipulates that an elementary school teacher should have a certificate of graduation from a normal school or middle school, a middle school teacher should have a certificate indicating completion of university education, and a university teacher should have a bachelor's degree. Thus a graduation certificate from a school became a teaching license. But as the construction of schools had already begun and teachers were immediately needed for more than twenty thousand elementary schools alone, there was no time to comply with the proposed professional requirements. "The Ministry of Education could found a school in a day, but teachers were not so speedily trained. Thus the Ministry was forced to recruit those who had taught in the fief schools or were in charge of Confucian shrines, and who still subscribed to the educational philosophy of the Edo period" (*Kyoiku Seido Hattatsu Shi*, vol. I, p. 460).

The situation for middle schools was no different. According to Noda Yoshio, the middle schools, in their search for qualified teachers, had no other choice but to hire former Chinese scholars or those who had studied English irregularly. Finding proper graduates of government schools was so difficult that those who had studied at the private Keiō Gijuku were considered the most attractive candidates by local middle schools, and even those who had dropped out or had to leave government schools were sought after (Noda 1907, 247). As for higher education, there was simply no source within the country, and therefore these institutions had no alternative to hiring foreigners.

However difficult the situation was, it seemed important to base appointments on some standard of qualifications specified by the government. Again, an examination system was instituted. First, the government devised two different examinations for selecting elementary school teachers (Maki 1971). The first examination was provided by the normal schools. The proper route for becoming a teacher was to obtain a graduation certificate from a normal school or middle school, but if students succeeded in the examination provided by the normal school without actually completing the coursework they could obtain a graduation certificate entitling them to teach. Only a small number of the students could succeed in this manner. As a second method, those who succeeded in a certificate examination conducted by a local government based on certain guidelines issued by the central government were also given a teaching license. For those obtaining their qualifications by examination, this second method was the most common route. In 1880, national educational statistics show, among nearly seventy thousand elementary school teachers only thirty percent had official qualifications, and among those with qualifications only thirty-six percent had a proper graduation certificate, obtained from either completing the coursework or passing the examination offered at a normal school; the rest obtained their teaching licenses from these local examinations.

The local licensing examinations were not easy. For example, in Saitama Prefecture, the success ratio between 1880 and 1883 was only thirty-three percent (Maki 1971, 96). Moreover, three levels of licenses were given to those who passed the examination: elementary, middle, and high levels. Only those with the high-level license could teach students of all grades. Those with the elementary-level license could only teach first and second grades. In the case of Saitama Prefecture, only five percent obtained the high-level license. These licenses were valid for five years, after which another examination was required.

Although the teacher qualifying examination was most demanding, it did little to raise social acceptance of the profession or to attract large numbers of applicants. While teaching was an intellectual occupation, the salary was much too low. A report from Ehime Prefecture sent to the Ministry of Education in 1882 explained that the difficulty of recruiting quality teachers owed to the fact that not enough consideration was paid to the treatment of teachers and that the going salaries were not sufficient to support their families. The samurai class, the intelligentsia of those days, placed the highest priority on becoming government officers, and after that police officers. Only by unavoidable necessity did they choose the teaching profession.

In 1886, new regulations were issued affecting the qualification system for elementary teachers, requiring all teachers to acquire a license regardless of whether they had graduation certificates from normal schools. Graduates of normal schools were, however, exempted from the teacher's qualification examinations. All other applicants were subjected to distinctly difficult selection tests. But the low salaries and status of teachers were not redressed. The social contempt for teaching inhibited new recruitment, while many who had been teaching sought new professions. This led to a great teacher shortage which continued to the turn of the century (Ishidoya 1967, 223).

Middle School Teachers and the Certification Examination

The salaries and status of middle school teachers were far better than that of elementary school teachers. By the mid-1880s, an ordinary middle school teacher received about twenty yen, compared with an average salary of less than seven yen for an elementary school teacher. It was not unusual for a university graduate to be immediately appointed to the position of principal with a salary of more than fifty yen.

Despite the favorable status of middle school teaching, the problem of finding eligible personnel still remained. While the university diploma was designated as the formal qualification, no university was established until 1877. And even after Tokyo University started producing graduates, the social demand for them was so great that few became teachers. In 1875, the Ministry of Education Created a course for middle school teachers at the Tokyo Normal School, but the graduates were very limited in number, and most were able to find better jobs as teachers in the public normal schools. Thus there was no stable supply of middle school teachers until the late 1880s.

As we have noted, the government did not place priority on the promotion of middle school education, and thus did not take vigorous steps to cope with this situation. Only after establishing the licensing regulations for middle school teachers in 1884 were rules for qualifying examinations elaborated. According to the rules, teaching licenses were to be divided into thirty-six different subject areas, with separate exams for each area. Mathematics, for example, was divided into arithmetic, geometry, trigonometry, and algebra; science into dynamics, geodesy, astronomy, physiology, zoology, botany, mineralogy, geology, physics, and chemistry. The success ratio on the exam for the first year, 1885, was seventy-five percent, but in 1893 it had dropped to twenty-one percent due to the upgraded difficulty. Looking at the teachers in middle schools for a much later year, 1907, thirty-one percent had obtained this qualification by passing the licensing examination, twenty-eight percent were without official qualifications, and the rest were graduates of normal schools or universities (Maki 1971; Sakurai 1975; Abe 1971).

Those who passed the middle school licensing examination usually received their training at private schools. Keiō Gijuku, as noted before, was an important source of English teachers. By the early 1890s, in the Tokyo area, preparatory education for the licensing examination was mainly provided at such schools as Tokyo Eigakkai for English, Kokugakuin and Tetsugakukan for Japanese, Tokyo Physics School and Kōgyokusha for science and mathematics, and the Tokyo Physical Education Institute for physical education. A survey conducted by the Tokyo Physics School, a predecessor of today's Tokyo Science University, indicates that in 1930 about sixty percent of its graduates became middle school teachers. Much the same could be said for Tetsugakukan, the predecessor of today's Tōyō University, and Kokugakuin (now Kokugakuin University).

In addition to the students of these mostly evening schools, many studied for the license examinations on their own, using the notebooks of the lectures published by these schools and other reference books. Many elementary school teachers sat for these examinations in hopes of raising their status. A popular magazine on education of the early 1900s noted: "Now every ambitious elementary school teacher in Japan competes to become a middle school teacher, which is the highest goal" (Ishidoya 1967, 240).

The gap between elementary and middle school teachers was considerable, and both the prestige and the income of middle school teachers were much higher. Considered an intellectual occupation, middle school teaching enjoyed a status similar to that of a government official or a medical doctor. Thus the middle school teachers' examination system was another important means for climbing the social ladder.

Chapter Seven

Government Officials and Educational Credentialism

The Government Employment System and Examinations

Government Officials and Education

In addition to attorneys, medical doctors, and teachers, other professional groups such as dentists, pharmacists, and veterinarians were affected by qualifying examinations. But it is the procedures for training and selecting government officials that had the greatest role in linking the examination systems of the world of education and the world of work, thus ushering in "educational credentialism" (*gakurekishugi*).

As we have already observed, in both China and Germany, the systematization of competitive examinations began with those for selecting government officials. In Japan, Kanda Takahira in 1869 proposed adoption of a system of promoting able persons for government office through examinations, imitating the *keju* system of China. Despite considerable support within the new government, however, no action was taken on his proposal until the early 1880s.

According to the statistics for 1881, a total of seventy-five thousand government employees worked for the central and local governments, of which about four thousand were middle- and high-ranking officials who could only be appointed with the Emperor's approval and seventy percent of whom belonged to the samurai class. It would be exaggerating to say that there was absolutely no standard for selecting these top-ranking officials. At the Ministry of Industry (Kōbushō), where specialized knowledge and skills were required, some of the early recruits reported that they had been given an examination in mathematics and composition. That, however, was an exception. In fact, at most of the new government offices, those in charge initially had little concept of the type of skills needed by their office, and they relied primarily on personal ties or superficial judgments of character and experience when recruiting staff. It was only towards the end of the 1870s that the government began to seek a new type of public official who had systematically studied Western subjects, particularly law and public administration (Masumi 1966, 26-27).

At that time, however, the public educational system had not developed to the point where it could provide enough people with the desired training. Several ministries had established their own specialized training schools, including the Law School of the Ministry of Justice, the College of Engineering of the Ministry of Industry, the Sapporo Agricultural College of the Land Development Bureau, and the Komaba School of Agriculture of the Ministry of Home Affairs.

It was Keiō Gijuku, however, the well-organized private school of Western learning, that provided the largest number of Western-educated officials to the new government, especially at the Ministries of Finance and Foreign Affairs. However, the Keiō graduates acquired these jobs through personal connections rather than through an objective selection process. It is a well-known fact that the new government hired Keiō Gijuku graduates mainly because of the connection between Ōkuma Shigenobu, a powerful politician of the period, and Fukuzawa Yukichi, the founder of Keiō. It was necessary for many Keiō graduates to resign from their government posts when Ōkuma was purged in the political crisis of 1881. This political crisis also was related to the emergence of the examination system for future government officials.

The main reason for the crisis was the clash in viewpoints between Ōkuma and another powerful politician, Itō Hirobumi, concerning the nature of the state system of government to be embodied in the constitution. Itō, who came to power after expelling Ōkuma, went in the following year to Europe to study the constitutions of various Western nations. What impressed him most was the Prussian constitution, with its strong state supported by a loyal civil service (Uno 1964; Spaulding 1967). As we noted earlier, Prussia at that time had the most advanced bureaucratic system in Europe, and it relied on an examination system to select its officers. Upon returning to Japan, Itō devoted much effort to establishing an examination system for the Japanese civil service based on the example of Prussia.

As for Ōkuma, he left the government after the 1881 crisis and in 1882 founded the Tokyo Professional School, which later became Waseda University. Since most of the teachers recruited for this newly established private school were graduates of Tokyo University, the school's founding provoked a sharp reaction from the government. At that time, approximately sixty students graduated from Tokyo University annually, and only about a dozen came from the faculties of law and political science. When four of these precious graduates chose to become teachers at Ōkuma's school of political science, which officials saw as an "opposition" school, the government naturally was disappointed. In addition, several graduates of Tokyo University's faculties of law and letters (among them the well-known literary figure Tsubouchi Shōyō) also promised Ōkuma their cooperation as part-time instructors at Tokyo Professional School. These developments certainly were a blow to the government. Ernest Fenollosa, a teacher of political science in the Tokyo University Faculty of Letters, in his commencement speech directed sharp criticism at the four graduates who suddenly entered the stage of political action, giving up their specialty after six years of hard and devoted study (Kurihara 1968). This occurred only three years after Itō had presented an address on education to the Emperor, in which he had asserted that the education of advanced students should aim at cultivating their interest in scholarship rather than in politics (Kurasawa 1975).

Certainly Tokyo University was embroiled in national politics, but its connection with the government bureaucracy was quite weak until it was reorganized as the Imperial University in 1886. Up to 1883, of a total of forty-six graduates from the Faculty of Law and twenty-seven from the Faculty of Letters, only twenty-three, or one-third, became government officials, and six of these were judicial officers. Among those who did not become officials, nine became private attorneys, a not especially highly esteemed profession; three entered the private sector, and twelve became teachers at schools other than Tokyo University. Clearly the bureaucratic world, still controlled by clan and personal favoritism, was not yet attractive to the new knowledge-based elite. This situation strengthened Itō's resolve to reform the bureaucracy through the introduction of an examination system.

Itō's Proposed Rules for Civil Service Candidates

Itō's first proposal for an exam system to employ government officials was called the *Bunkan Kōhōsei Kisokuan* (Draft Rules for Candidates for Government Service). In these rules, candidates were grouped into three categories—administration, jurisprudence, and specialists—with three grades for each category. Qualification for a third-grade candidate required at least three years' education at a government school or a licensed public or private professional school, a diploma from the school, and passing the civil service examination. The qualification for a second-grade candidate included more than three years' education at a government university or a government professional school equivalent to a university and passing the civil service examination. First-grade candidates were expected to fulfill the conditions of second-grade candidates, to have three years of work experience, and to pass an additional government examination. Middle-ranking and top-level officials were to be appointed from among those who met these conditions. The proposal explained that since human knowledge had become more advanced and the laws and regulations had become more meticulous and detailed, it was natural that the people who executed them be required to demonstrate their high ability and knowledge.

The proposal went on to observe that although the Ministry of Justice trained judicial officers at its Law School and the Ministry of Industry employed the graduates of its Engineering College as engineers, there was no training school for administrative officials. Tokyo University, under the Ministry of Education, should have been in charge of this job, but there were no standardized rules for employing university graduates even though they underwent great hardship while studying and the government spent several thousand yen to train each of them. The situation, Itō said, was much like planting the seeds but forgetting the harvest. Clearly, Itō's prime target in this proposal was to assure that the elite trained at government expense should be of use to the nation, and that Tokyo University should become the central training institute for civil servants.

Itō also believed in the critical necessity of placing private schools under state control so that they would not be tempted to encourage anti-government political action, which seemed to be occurring at the Tokyo Professional School founded by Ōkuma and at some of the private law schools that focused on French law. One manifestation of this concern was his suggestion that the graduates of licensed public and private professional schools could qualify as third-level officials; through the Ministry of Education's licensing authority, he expected the government to control the private schools. Third-level officials normally would become middle-rank officers in prefectural or district bureaucracies. Itō believed that a small core of graduates from government schools should be appointed to the top positions in the central government while the remaining posts for middle and lower-level bureaucrats could be filled by the graduates of private schools. This policy would promote private schools as well. But government involvement in such matters as school regulations, curriculum, and teaching staff would have to be conceded in exchange for the privilege of allowing graduates to apply for the examination to compete for government employment. In this way, Itō justified stronger government control over private schools.

This plan, while revolutionary in comparison with the existing employment system, could not be introduced immediately, for at least two preliminary conditions had to be fulfilled.

The first was the reform of the political and administrative system. The political system created after the Meiji Restoration was the Cabinet (Dajōkan) system presupposing direct rule of the state by the Emperor. Itō, however, had concluded it was essential to establish a powerful government similar to that of Prussia, and he downgraded direct rule by the Emperor and in 1885 established a new Cabinet system in its stead, with himself as the first Prime Minister. This system, where the prime minister appoints ministers and bears full political responsibility, continues until today.

Itō, once in the seat of power as Prime Minister, immediately announced his policy of "five political principles (seikō goshō)." The second of these principles focused on "clarifying the organization of government offices," which implied the rearrangement of the bureaucratic system. The third principle was concerned with the "selection of personnel," which featured introduction of the examination system for employing government officers.

Up to that time, there had been neither criteria for the employment and promotion of government officers nor definite rules concerning their number, rank, salary, or other such details. Arguing that a powerful central government cannot exist without a capable civil service, Itō proposed a pyramid of status, rank, salary, and office as the desired structure for the civil service, based on the Prussian model. Objective standards for evaluating ability and performance would become the basis for employment and promotion in the pyramid, as in the Prussian bureaucracy.

The section on employment criteria observed that there was no definite rule for selection in the past, so usually personal acquaintance was the criterion for employment and promotion. Consequently, favoritism became a matter of course and often men of learning were not promoted. With the abolition of the old system, a limit would be placed on the number of government officials, and more care was to be exercised in hiring. In order to strengthen the civil service, the appointment of every officer except those directly appointed by the Emperor would be determined by an examination. In Itō's view, the introduction of the examination system was part and parcel of the reform of the political and administrative structure.

The second condition necessary for realizing Itō's civil service proposal was a reform of the educational system. Simply preparing for an examination was not considered sufficient training to develop an able official. Both high-quality general education and systematic professional education building on this general education were viewed as indispensable for this purpose. But for Itō, who had seen the well-organized schools and universities run by the Prussian state, the reality of Japanese education was far from satisfactory. For this difficult task of reforming the educational system, Itō turned to Mori Arinori, a young civil servant who had been sent by the Satsuma fief during the last years of the Edo period to study in both England and the United States. Mori, in charge of foreign affairs, had shown a keen interest in education since the beginning of his bureaucratic career. In 1883, when Mori was serving as the Japanese representative to England, Itō and he had had a chance to discuss educational problems. Itō was so impressed with Mori's intelligence and deep understanding that he decided to appoint Mori Minister of Education. Thus Mori became the first Minister of Education under the new Cabinet system.

The Educational Reforms of Mori Arinori

Mori focused his initial efforts on the organization of higher education by placing Tokyo University at the center. Higher education at that time had a dual structure with, on the one hand, training institutes for the various government bureaucracies managed by the respective ministries and, on the other hand, Tokyo University, administered by the Ministry of Education. This dual structure created an ambiguous role for Tokyo University. Mori developed a plan to create an "Imperial University" similar to that in Prussia; its main purpose would be to train bureaucrats who could undertake "important tasks for the state" (Nakayama 1978).

Already by the end of 1884, there was a movement to unify government schools: the Law School had been transferred from the Ministry of Justice to the Ministry of Education, and in September of 1885 it was merged with the Faculty of Law of Tokyo University. In December of the same year, the Ministry of Industry's College of Engineering was transferred to the Ministry of Education. Within Tokyo University, at the same time, various changes occurred: the Faculty of Industrial Arts became independent from the Faculty of Science; both the political science and political economy courses were moved from the Faculty of Letters to the Faculty of Law; and the faculty of Law was renamed the Faculty of Law and Politics. In 1886, the Imperial University, consisting of the five faculties of law, medicine, engineering, letters, and science, was inaugurated. As the name indicates, the Imperial University was conceived as a symbol of national prestige of the Japanese Empire, with the main purpose of training officials for the administrative service. Thus the university and the state were united.

National control over high-level educational institutions involved in the training of government officials came to be extended to private schools through the Law Faculty of the Imperial University. In August 1886, Mori ordered the president of the Imperial University to supervise "those private law schools in Tokyo metropolitan area which the president considers adequate." The *Tokubetsu Kantoku Jōki* (Special Supervision Regulations), which set out the details of the supervisory activities required, specified that control should be exercised in areas such as curriculum and examinations at the private law schools covered by the regulations (there were five such schools). Furthermore, outstanding private law school graduates were to undertake a further examination at the Law Faculty in the presence of judicial officials. Those who passed this special screening would be awarded a certificate, making them eligible to compete in the examination for the judicial service.

The intent of these regulations becomes clear when we look back at the position of private schools under the *Bunkan Kōhōsei Kisokuan* (Draft Rules for Candidates for Government Service) of 1885. In exchange for increased control, the government gave those schools the privilege of being recognized as training institutions for bureaucrats and of having their graduates eligible for a prestigious profession in the civil service. In terms of the situation in 1887, the privilege was that of having the way opened to the judiciary. Judicial officials were already being trained at the Law School of the Ministry of Justice, but there were not enough graduates to meet the demand for staff. It was to alleviate this shortage that, at the end of 1885, the Rules for Appointing Judges were issued, opening appointment to the judiciary not only to law school graduates but also to those who passed the special examination.

Initially the Law Faculty agreed to supervise five private law schools including Senshū, Meiji, and the controversial Tokyo Professional School. At the first exam, held in 1887, seventy-one "excellent students" received certificates, of whom eighteen passed the oral exam and were recommended to the Ministry of Justice for the judicial service (Terasaki and Sakai 1980).

Mori also launched a reform of pre-university education. One of the new measures involved the establishment of a system of "higher middle schools." Until then, preparatory education for the university had been given in the preparatory school (*yobimon*) of the university as a part of university education. In 1886 Mori decided to separate the *yobimon* from the university by establishing five higher middle schools at key locations throughout the nation. The university's *yobimon* became the First Higher Middle

School (Ichikō) while others were begun at Sendai (Nikō, or the Second Higher Middle School), Kyoto (Sankō, or the Third), Kanazawa (Shikō, or the Fourth), and Kumamoto (Gokō, or the Fifth).

Another important reform of Mori's was the policy of limiting each prefecture to one middle school financed by local taxes. This made even stronger the control over and raising of standards in the middle schools which the government had been pursuing since the first years of Meiji, and its effect was to dramatically reduce the number of public middle schools, from one hundred four in 1885 to forty-three the following year.

It is apparent that Mori intended through this series of educational reforms to reinforce the Imperial University as the highest institution of learning and elite training. Mori wished to create a strong middle and higher middle school system to insure a stable supply of well-educated students for the university. The university level was too late to provide an education of sufficient breadth to mold the elite bureaucrats required for the nation's modernization and industrialization. Building on a solid base of compulsory education, the students attending the middle school and above would be gradually selected for ability to create a pool of excellent candidates for the elite Imperial University. Thus the middle and higher middle school systems were expected to play the role of a pipeline extending from the periphery to the center, selecting and recruiting capable young men for the Imperial University.

The Establishment of the Examination System for Civil Servants
Once these two conditions had been fulfilled, the examination system for employing civil servants was introduced in July 1887, as Imperial Order No. 37—Examination Regulations for Probationary Officers and Apprentices. These regulations authorized a "higher" and an "ordinary" exam for government officials.

In the civil service system of that time, there were three ranks for the officers: officials appointed by the Emperor (*chokunin-kan*), officials appointed with the Emperor's approval (*sōnin-kan*), and junior officials (*hannin-kan*). The first two ranks made up the senior civil service and were to be filled by those who passed the higher exam (*kotō-shiken*), while the ordinary exam (*futsū-shiken*) was used to select middle-ranking officials. Those who succeeded in the higher exam could be appointed as *sōnin-kan* after a minimum period of three years' probation, while those appointed as *hannin-kan* had to serve at least a two-year apprenticeship before receiving their appointment. Outstanding *sōnin-kan* could be promoted to the ranks of *chokunin-kan*.

What was distinctive about this system was its relationship to the education system. First let us consider who was eligible for the senior service. Graduates of the Faculty of Law, the Faculty of Letters, and those earlier schools which had been merged into the Imperial University were allowed to join the government on a probationary basis without the exam. This privilege, which was not granted to graduates of the universities of Prussia, clearly indicated the young Japanese government's regard for the Imperial University as a truly national institution. Apart from this privileged group, others could take the higher exam only if they had the appropriate qualifications. The qualified applicants were restricted to those with graduation certificates from the government schools, such as the Higher Middle School, the Tokyo School of Commerce, and private schools where law, political science, and political economy were taught and whose regulations were approved by the Minister of Education.

Exemption from taking the ordinary exam as a basis for becoming a middle-ranking officer was extended to those with certificates from national and prefectural middle schools or the national and prefectural schools equivalent to them, as well as those from private law schools that were under the supervision of the Imperial University. All others had to take the exam.

This policy of exempting from the examinations the graduates of particular schools—that is, to those possessing the approved "graduation certificates"—naturally increased the capacity of the government for more direct control over schools and their programs so that it could be sure that graduates had acquired the knowledge needed — in short, it could exercise a form of "quality control" over the supply of candidates for the bureaucracy. The Special Supervision Provision for private law schools adopted in 1886 was an earlier illustration of the government plan, and the policy limiting public support to one middle school for each prefecture should also be seen in this light. In addition in 1888 the government issued Regulations Concerning Specially Authorized Schools which required all private schools to submit to official supervision if they wanted their graduates to be eligible to take the government examinations.

These new regulations placed special stress on facilities and teaching staffs and on the implementation of rigorous promotion and graduation examinations. Only graduates who had obtained an ordinary middle school graduation certificate, or who had passed an ordinary middle school equivalency examination, were recognized as qualified to sit for high-level civil service employment examinations. Schools were required to hand over to the Ministry of Education their examination rules, the results of the term examination given at the end of the year, the names of the students who passed the last term examination, and the names of those who were given graduation certificates. In addition, the Minister of Education had the authority to send appointed inspectors to the actual examination site.

Thus the consolidation of the civil service system and the introduction of the examination system had a profound impact on Japan's school system and soon resulted in the emergence of educational credentialism as an important characteristic of the new society. It was Itō Hirobumi and Mori Arinori who laid the foundation for this development.

The Bureaucratic System and Educational Credentialism

Let us take a close look at the initial result of introducing an examination system for the employment of government officials. Government officials of this period can be categorized as administrative, judicial, or special officers, and the first two categories were to be selected on the basis of the examination authorized under the Regulations for Employment of Probationary Officers and Apprentices which were adopted in 1887. However, beginning in 1891 when the Employment Regulations for Judges and Public Prosecutors were issued, a separate exam was used for selecting judicial officers. Special officials (including university professors) whose special academic skills were indispensable for employment could be employed directly by the concerned office without examination.

In the process of introducing the new system, however, problems soon became evident, particularly with regard to granting exemptions from the examination to the graduates of the Imperial University. Itō proposed the exemption in order to attract the most talented people to the Imperial University, which he hoped would become the central training institute for administrative officers. Itō knew that the number of graduates from the Faculty of Law at Tokyo University was not sufficient to meet the demand for the growing bureaucratic system, and thus he worried that yet another competitive examination would surely turn these carefully selected students away from the government to the private sector. Hence, he hit on the idea of recruiting as many of the graduates of the Imperial University as possible on a probationary basis by offering the incentive of exemption from the examination and then filling up the gaps with graduates of specially authorized private schools who passed the examination (Spaulding 1967, 88-89).

Once the system was put in place, however, there were several unexpected developments. First, the graduates of the Imperial University who had previously rejected government service suddenly began to favor it. Immediately after establishment of the system, eighty-one percent of the 1888 graduates of the Imperial University's Faculty of Law became government officials, followed by sixty-nine percent in 1889, seventy-nine percent in 1890, and eighty-four percent in 1891. Itō's exemption policy proved to be a greater success than he had expected.

Second, the graduates of the Imperial University expressed a much stronger interest in the administrative service than in the judicial service. Some forty-eight percent of the hundred seventy-six Imperial University graduates who became government officers between 1888 and 1891 selected the administrative service. While this may not seem an especially large number, it constituted ninety percent of all those who were newly employed as higher administrative officers. In contrast, only fifty-two percent of newly appointed judicial officers were from the University.[1]

What attracted the young law graduates to the administrative rather than the judicial service? The most obvious factor was the difference in compensation. However strong a student's university record might be, as a judicial officer, he was eligible for an

---

[1] Percentages for administrative officers are from *Meiji Shirin*, July and August issues, 1889-1892. Judicial percentage is from Spaulding (1967, 90).

annual salary of only three hundred yen. The salary for administrative officers, in contrast, not only was higher but differed according to the student's academic record: a salary of six hundred yen was extended to those with a record of eighty-five points or above, five hundred fifty yen for seventy-five to eighty-four points, five hundred yen for sixty-five to seventy-four points and four hundred fifty yen for to sixty-four points (Wada 1955). Also the probationary period for the administrative services was shorter and the opportunity for salary increases and promotions was much greater. Naturally, the law school graduates with the best academic records decided to become administrative officers.

Third, since virtually all the posts in the administrative service were taken by graduates of the Imperial University, few posts were available for the graduates of private schools. Between 1888 and 1893, only nine succeeded in the examination for administrative officers. From 1891 to 1893, all the posts were filled by graduates of the Imperial University, so the employment exam was not offered. It is easy to imagine the strong opposition expressed by the private institutions.

In the early 1880s, when Itō strongly felt the need to create a training institute for administrative officers, the number of law graduates from Tokyo University was about ten a year, and only a few of these wished to become administrative officers. By the 1890s, however, the Law Faculty of the Imperial University was producing nearly fifty graduates a year, and most of these wanted to become government administrative officers. The number of entry-level positions was not, however, increasing. In fact, due to financial difficulties, the government had to consider decreasing the number of high-ranking posts. In 1892, when Itō again assumed the position of Prime Minister, he found it necessary to reform the very system which he had conceived.

The Reform of the System

In 1893, the new Employment Law for Government Officers was issued along with the Examination Regulations for Government Officers to replace the Examination Rules for Probationary Officers and Apprentices. The major difference in the new regulations was the removal of the special privilege of employment without examination for graduates of the Imperial University. In order to obtain an appointment with the Emperor's approval, the Imperial University graduates also had to pass the examination for higher civil servants.

This, however, did not reduce the Imperial University graduates to the same starting point as the graduates of other schools, for the new higher civil service exam actually consisted of a "preliminary" and a "main" examination, and the graduates of the Imperial University only had to take the latter. The preliminary examination was supposed to determine if applicants had the academic ability of a university-level student. Its first stage required the writing of essays on preassigned topics, and for those who did well there was a second stage consisting of an oral exam and an extemporaneous composition. All the graduates of private institutions were required to take this difficult examination.

The ordinary examination for selecting middle-level officials was also reformed. Although passing the exam was an official condition for employment, the graduates of government and public middle schools were exempted from the examination. However, the graduates of those private professional schools which under the old system had also been granted exemptions from the examinations found they were denied that privilege.

Under the new system, the examinations for the administrative, judicial, and technical officials were completely separated, and an independent examination was established for the diplomatic corps. The Examination Regulations for Government Officers covered the employment of administrative officials; the Employment Regulations for Judges and Public Prosecutors applied to judicial officials; and the Employment Regulations for Diplomatic Officers and Consular Staff and Clerks covered the diplomatic officials. As for the technical officials, the Employment Law for Government Officers stated that while separate regulations for employing instructors and engineers would be prepared, officials appointed with Imperial approval were to be selected by the examination committee for higher government officials whereas junior officials were to be selected by the examination committee for ordinary government officials.

Though the Imperial University graduates lost their special privilege of exemption from examinations, the government did not intend to treat them in the same way as the graduates of other schools. Rather, the main concern of Itō and the government was simply to resolve the problems that had emerged due to the strong demand for administrative posts by Imperial University graduates. The best way to regain the balance created by the oversupply of applicants was to use a competitive examination to select the required number of superior candidates. But within the framework of the new system, the Imperial University graduates continued to enjoy certain privileges: they were exempted from the preliminary examination for administrative officers and they still retained the privilege of becoming judicial officers without an examination.

The first time the new examination was held, the graduates of the Imperial University expressed their displeasure by boycotting it. The *Hōgaku Shimpō* (*Law Journal*) of 1894, when the first examination under the new system was held, wrote: "At this first examination since the reform, two issues which attracted public attention were the removal of qualifications and the requirement that university graduates also take the examination. Placing the [Imperial] University graduates, who had monopolized the path to success, on an equal and competitive footing with the students of private schools should truly be viewed as an improvement in the examination system." At the same time, it was noted, however, that the forty-seven applicants for the new examination were all graduates of private law schools. "Of the recent [Imperial University] class of seventy-four, over sixty have received their Bachelor of Law degrees but only eleven have taken up probationary posts as judicial officers. Altogether there are nearly a hundred candidates, if we include those from previous years, who still don't have any post. . . . Why, then, has nobody stepped forward to take this first higher examination, which is the gateway to success?"

While no one from the Imperial University sat for the first year's examination, only six from the private schools passed (see Table 1). The boycott, however, lasted only one year. The following year the graduates of the Imperial University began to take the examination, pass it, and enter government service (Takenaka 1981). The fear in government circles that the holders of Bachelor of Law degrees, once stripped of their privilege, would rush to the private sector and boycott government service proved groundless. Within less than ten years of the consolidation of the bureaucratic system, the higher civil service had become an attractive career for the academic elite despite the difficult employment examination.

Table 1. Higher Civil Servants Examination — Applicants and Successful Candidates

	Imperial universities Main exam		Others Preliminary exam		Main exam	Proportion of Imperial university graduates among main exam successful candidates
	Applicants	Successful candidates	Applicants	Successful candidates	Successful candidates	
1894	—	—	45	19	6	—
1895	42	25	84	39	12	67.6
1896	66	42	144	43	8	84.0
1897	51	26	259	95	28	48.1
1898	56	23	373	163	18	56.1
1899	71	22	344	103	9	71.0
1990	94	39	377	94	19	67.2
Total	380	177	1626	556	100	63.9
%	(100.0)	(46.6)	(100.0)	(34.2)	(6.2)	

Source: This table is compiled from information found in Takenaka Teruo, "Kokka Shiken Seido to Teidai Hōka Tokken" (The National Examination System and Imperial University Admissions). In Motoyama Yukihiko (ed.), *Teikoku Jidai to Kyōiku Seisaku* (The Imperial Era and Education Policy), 1981, p. 394.

To further their dream of making Japan a rich and powerful nation, Itō and Mori worked to create a strong administrative system by relying on the education system to provide a steady supply of new talent. Occupying a strategic position in their plans were the civil service examination and the Imperial University. Although there were unexpected developments which required adjustments, on the whole a smoothly functioning system did emerge. Almost as soon as this system was put in place, many of the traits of what is today called educational credentialism (*gakurekishugi*) began to surface.

The Trend Toward Credentialism
What in the Japanese context is the meaning of educational credentials (*gakureki*)? Concrete evidence comes in the form of a graduation certificate, which describes the person's course of

study, the level, and the school. The certificate states, for example: "This person finished the required course of mechanical engineering of the Faculty of Engineering of the Imperial University." The term *gakureki* always includes these three labels, though we sometimes simplify it, as in a social survey, where the respondent is asked to indicate whether he or she finished junior high school, senior high school, or university. In the education section of a curriculum vitae we may simply list the name of the schools from which we graduated. In any case, the *gakureki* described in a graduation certificate verifies that the holder of the certificate has completed a certain course at a school of a certain level.

The certificates that establish academic credentials cannot be obtained by everyone. Only those who have mastered what is taught at a school and can demonstrate through the school's evaluation process that their learning reaches the expected standard are given the graduation certificate. Thus *gakureki* is an indication of a certain level of ability. Because examinations are used as an objective and fair means for evaluating and judging this ability, *gakureki* and examinations are inseparably related.

Gakureki does not have intrinsic value; rather, its value becomes evident only when it is used in a process of social evaluation and selection. As we have noted, *gakureki* is essentially a certificate of ability. The more strictly, fairly, and openly the evaluation process resulting in a *gakureki* is, the more likely it is that the *gakureki* will be employed as the criterion in selecting people. Modern industrial society, because it strives to evaluate and select people in terms of their ability or performance—that is, according to meritocratic principles—tends to place ever more reliance on *gakureki* as a means of selection. Hence, educational credentials also become social or occupational credentials.

First, *gakureki* is used for selection within the school system. For example, graduating from elementary school is the qualification for entering middle school, and obtaining a middle school graduation certificate is the qualification for entering a higher school. In European countries, the certificates awarded those who pass the examinations for completing the secondary level, such as the Abitur and the *baccalauréat*, even serve as the basis for university admissions. But where *gakureki* obtains its greatest significance is in relation to the world of work. Educational credentialism is most highly developed in those societies, such as Japan, where educational qualifications are extensively relied on as a basis for occupational selection (Amano 1982).

Educational credentials become closely associated with occupational credentials if the occupations are assumed to require a high level of knowledge and skills that can only be acquired through systematic schooling for an extended period of time. As we have already seen, the occupations that best fulfill these conditions are the professions and government service.

The trend of linking readiness for government service and professional work to the completion of systematic school education ending in the awarding of educational credentials started in eighteenth-century Prussia and soon spread to the other industrial societies. Japan, whose modernization started in the latter part of the nineteenth century, emerged just at the time this trend toward educational credentialism was reaching its peak.

The Beginning of Credentialism

In Japan, the equation of occupational qualifications with academic qualifications first started with the professions. As previously noted, teaching qualifications were granted to the graduates of certain schools without an examination. In the medical profession, those with a diploma from a government or public medical school were automatically granted a license to practice. Similarly, the graduates of the Law School of Tokyo University could automatically obtain a license. What played a decisive role in the development of educational credentialism in Japan was, as we have seen, the establishment of the examination system for government officials.

According to Ronald Dore, the later a nation's modernization starts, the more rapidly will that country promote the development of credentialism. Dore (1976) calls this the "late development effect." What is the cause of this effect? In late-developing countries there is a heavy reliance on school education to train the people needed in such areas of the modern sector as government, industry, the professional occupations, and teaching. There is, indeed, no other stable source for staff training and manpower supply.

In order to obtain capable personnel to build the modern sector, especially the government sector, which plays an extremely significant role at the start of the modernization process, the government should first undertake to organize the school system and create a system of social evaluation and selection based on performance and ability. Itō and Mori made an impressive effort to build such a training and selection system for Japan, in which the individual's *gakureki* occupied a strategic position.

In developing countries, especially at the early stages of modernization when private enterprises are not yet well developed, the role of government enterprises in the modern sector is overwhelmingly large. The social prestige and power of government officials is also substantial, in proportion to the presence of the government sector. Their economic compensation is also typically quite high. Thus the individual's *gakureki* becomes a passport to the most attractive occupations. Japan's credentialism was established under these circumstances.

Up to the mid-1880s, the Japanese educational system had not been consolidated into a unitary system. While a broad legal framework existed, the actual situation was that schools of various kinds and various academic standards had been established as necessity arose, and there was no organic relation among them. To enter a school or transfer between schools, young people usually had not been required to show their past educational records. The series of policies introduced by Mori began to bring order to this chaos, creating a school system with an organic unity. The result was a splendid success. The progressive route from elementary school to middle school to higher middle school to the Imperial University was systematized in a clear pattern. Each student's academic credentials became an indispensable passport for advancement along the route.

Itō's employment system for officials was premised on a systematized school system. The graduates who successfully negotiated the route that Mori had established and managed to obtain educational credentials were absorbed into the government bureaucratic organization by a selection method that meshed with their credentials. The government officials' employment examination was, so to speak, an adjustment valve.

Thus by the late 1880s the route to success in life began to take a clear shape in Japanese society. Higher officials occupied the summit, and the diploma from the Imperial University's Law

Faculty became the passport for obtaining this elite position with its benefits of high social prestige, power, and economic compensation. In order to obtain this passport, young people had to endure a tough sequence of selective examinations as they climbed up the ladder of school education step by step.

The establishment of the school system with the Imperial University at its summit and the introduction of the examination system for employing government officials thus provided a clear goal for young people with a strong desire to succeed. These new institutions also played a decisive role in putting a special premium on credentials, at least in the modern sector of society.

Chapter Eight

The Road to the Imperial University

Elementary Schools and Criticism of Examinations

Criticism of Elementary School Examinations

In 1900, the Ministry of Education issued a revised Elementary School Order along with related Regulations for Implementation.

Article 23 of the Regulations for Implementation stated: "In order to determine who shall graduate among those who complete the curriculum, daily school performance shall be the criterion, without a separate examination (Kyoikushi Hensankai 1938, 68)." Up to that time, promotion and graduation had been determined by separate examinations.

The Ministry of Education had, as we have seen, from the earliest days of the modern school system enthusiastically promoted the examination system. The *Gakusei* of 1872 included examination rules, and the education advisor David Murray, who came soon afterwards, emphasized their importance. The Ministry of Education directed each prefecture to prepare examination rules, and in 1881 it took the additional step of ordering all the public and private schools within those jurisdictions to observe these rules. By the mid-1880s children in all corners of Japan were taking examinations to determine their promotion and graduation. Why then did the Ministry of Education, which had taken such trouble to establish exams, now seek to abolish them?

Improvement in elementary education was certainly a major factor. At the early stage in the creation of the elementary school system, when the abilities of students as well as the contents and standards of teaching varied widely, the use of examinations to monitor promotions and graduation served to raise the general standard of education. As the quality of teachers and students became more uniform, however, and all children of school age began to enter school, the importance of using promotion and graduation exams as a means of quality control declined. The upgrading of quality is apparent particularly in the shift from the grade system, in which the education was based on each student's ability, to the class system, in which student assignment came to be based on age (Kokuritsu Kyōiku Kenkyūjo, 1974, 140-45).

A more significant reason for the abolition of the examinations was, however, the perception that the introduction of the competitive exam system at the elementary school level had had various undesirable effects which neither Murray nor the Ministry of Education could have anticipated. A directive issued a few days after the Elementary School Order explicitly mentions these evils: "Why was daily performance adopted as a measure of student ability rather than examinations? Because excessive study driven by the competitive spirit would have a bad effect on both the mental and physical development of young children and would produce the undesirable habit of students studying only for the examinations" (Kyoikushi Hensankai 1938, 117).

Even in the 1870s, as the examination system was spreading and planting its roots in Japanese education, some observers expressed concern. By the 1880s, critics charged that the exams, while intended as a device for motivating students and elevating educational standards, had become the main objective of the educational process. The 1889 *Fukushima Shiritsu Kyōikukai Zasshi* (Journal of Education of Fukushima Prefecture) reports one teacher's views on the evil effects of the examination on students, teachers, home, and school, and concludes by urging abolition of the elementary school regular exam system. The main points of that argument can be paraphrased as follows.

First, since the students believe that the only important thing is to get good marks on the examination, they tend to "seek instant fortune by making extreme efforts such as staying awake at night, busily studying from morning to evening, holding seminars, praying to the gods and Buddhas, or visiting their teachers."

Second, since teachers are concerned about how their students will do compared to those of other teachers, as the examination approaches they tend to ignore normal class work and "teach exclusively for the examination, for eight or nine hours straight each weekday and even on Sundays, exhorting their students to fever pitch." Some teachers "even secretly let the students know the questions that will appear on the examination day." It is said that "even such embarrassing practices as teachers writing the answers for their students are known to occur."

Third, since the parents' only concern is to encourage their children's study for the examinations, they "let their children absent themselves from classes for trifling reasons to prepare for exams," and they "become excited and visit the shrines of Monju [the Buddhist deity of wisdom] to pray for their children's success in the examinations." And the children's failure in the examinations causes "parents to feel hatred and disgust for the school and teachers."

Finally, the attitudes of school authorities are similar. "A strong result in this regular annual examination leads to a good reputation for the school and honor for the teachers." But a higher number of failing students than the previous year leads parents to protest the high tuition (even elementary school education was not free then) and the low quality of the school and its teachers. School authorities are worried only about the result of exams, not education. The examination produces a thousand evils and no good, concludes the disgruntled teacher's testament.

Abolishing the Competitive Examination

The situation described above cannot help but remind us of the "examination hell" of contemporary Japan. Other prefectural histories make it clear that Fukushima was not unique. In order to combat these evil effects, some prefectures took such remedial measures as prohibiting the use of examination competition between schools or entrusting principals and teachers with the entire responsibility for the evaluation of examinations and discontinuing attendance by the officers of the prefectural and county governments. These efforts, however, could only achieve so much. In the newly formulated Outline of Elementary School Teaching Regulations of 1891, the Ministry of Education itself had to seek to clarify the purpose of examinations and to suggest means for improving the system (Kyoikushi Hensankai 1938, 105-106).

According to these regulations, an examination should be a method of educational guidance, of evaluating how well students understand and apply what is taught at school. However, "some schools make the mistake of imposing immense amounts of work on students over a short period of time when the exams approach and thus often cause both mental and physical harm to students." Furthermore, "as far as education is concerned, it is fundamentally wrong to use the examination as a tool to rouse the competitive spirit in students." Reckless competition to improve the school's comparative position should be strictly avoided, according to the regulations.

Problems in the evaluation method were also identified. The detailed evaluation with one hundred points as the full score for each subject was described as not only time-consuming but harmful. "It would be more desirable to use an appropriate descriptive word for a student's performance rather than a comparative grade, such as upper, middle, or lower. When a score is necessary, as simple a score as possible should be used." For decisions on promotion and graduation, "daily school performance should be taken into consideration, rather than deciding on the basis of a single examination. Certificates for graduation and completion of courses should be given at the end of each course "if it is recognized, on the basis of examination results and daily performance, that the requirements prescribed by the elementary school regulations have been fulfilled."

This reconsideration by the Ministry of Education shows that within twenty years of the implementation of the system, the experience of Europe had been reproduced in even more extreme form in Japan. As Murray had pointed out, examination systems are effective in encouraging students and rousing their competitive instincts, but there always remains the danger that competition to do well on examinations becomes the sole purpose of education, and, like the Jesuit colleges, most of Japan's elementary schools had already reached that stage. According to the memoirs of one woman who entered an elementary school in Mie Prefecture in 1886, "In those days the order of name plates on the wall at the back of the classroom was changed monthly after the examination. Thus I could tell my family where I was placed. In order to figure out who would be named the next class president and vice president, we students also peeked at the name plates of the other classes." This illustrates how thoroughly institutionalized the examination competition had become.

Even with an order from the Ministry of Education, the competitive examination system, which was already firmly rooted in the elementary school, could not change immediately. While daily classroom performance was added to the evaluation, examinations still determined promotion and graduation, and the majority of schools continued to announce the examination results, providing individual rankings. In 1894 Inoue Kowashi, the Minister of Education, issued a new order to further curtail competitive examinations.

Inoue feared that excessive competition would have a negative influence on the physical and mental development of young children, and thus his instruction to limit the competitive examination was part of his order on "Physical Development and Hygiene in Elementary Schools." This order observed that the elementary school examination tended to be used as a means for praising or punishing students. Students' placement changed each semester based on examination results, with awards given only to good performers, and this had been an excessively negative influence on the average student. It not only contradicted the philosophy of basic education, Inoue wrote, but had a harmful effect on the students' physical development. Hence, he said, placement by examination should be abolished.

Inoue's speeches as the Minister of Education during this period indicate that he suspected a similar problem occurred in the advanced schools. Citing statistical data, Inoue explained that the poor physique and nearsightedness of middle and high school students, who were to be the elite of society, stemmed from the excessively long school hours and heavy load of studies they had to undergo in order to enter the more advanced schools. He did not, however, want to abolish competitive examinations for the middle and higher schools, as these competitive examinations were considered an indispensable means for encouraging and selecting elite candidates. He hoped, rather, that the negative impact of exams could be eased by other means, such as decreasing the school hours and changing the school system.

In any case, as we noted at the beginning of this chapter, examinations to determine elementary school promotions and graduations were officially abolished in 1900, and one after another the systems emphasizing competition were modified. At one elementary school in Mie Prefecture, for example, a scheme of evaluation with a total of ten points rather than one hundred was adopted in 1892, and in 1897 this was simplified to a three-level evaluation system of *kō*, *otsu*, and *hei* (A, B, and C). In the same year, the principle of ranking the name tags of class members was shifted from performance to seniority, and a new report card was introduced without examination scores and class standings. Thus, by the beginning of the twentieth century, competitive examinations had disappeared completely at the elementary school level in Japan. At around the same time, Britain abolished its elementary school examination system — the system which was known as the "payment-by-result" system.

The Road to Middle Schools

The Elementary School Act of 1886 prescribed the elementary school as being composed of two levels, the compulsory ordinary elementary school of four years and the higher elementary school of up to another four years. The Middle School Act issued at the same time established middle schools, also with two levels, the ordinary and the higher. The middle school was available to those who had reached the age of twelve and who had acquired sufficient academic preparation at elementary schools. In other words, those who entered the ordinary elementary school at the age of six and finished compulsory education at the age of ten should have at least two years' study at a higher elementary school before entering the middle school.

Completion of two years at a higher elementary school was not, however, a qualification for the middle schools. All that was required was academic ability, which could be demonstrated by passing the entrance examination. While the competitive examinations had disappeared from the elementary school, a long road of competitive examinations still awaited young people.

Those who wished to enter a middle school found it helpful to get into one of the higher elementary schools. But their number was extremely limited; in 1892 there was only one higher elementary school for every ten ordinary elementary schools, and even by 1899 the ratio had only increased to two for every ten. Quite a few counties had only one higher elementary school. Thus most of the students at these schools were from far away and had to board at the schools or stay with relatives who lived close to the schools. Watsuji Tetsurō, who was born in a farming village of Okayama Prefecture and later became a renowned philosopher, wrote about his experience staying at a relative's home so that he could attend a higher elementary school in 1899 (Watsuji 1961).

Mainly the children from economically and socially privileged families went to these higher elementary schools. According to the *Sōtei Kyōiku Teido Chōsa* (A Survey of the Education Level of Young Adult Men), among young males of conscription age (twenty years), only ten percent who began ordinary elementary school in 1887 completed a higher elementary school education, and only twenty-five percent of those who started school in 1895 completed higher elementary school. Fifty-one percent of the first group and twenty-four percent of the second group did not even complete ordinary elementary school.

The privileged handful of children who were able to enter higher elementary school were then prepared for middle school. However, even though they were twelve years old and had completed the two years of higher elementary school education, these children still found the gate to middle school tightly shut to them. An academic career survey conducted in 1892 of students who entered public middle schools in thirty-six prefectures indicates that four percent studied for two years at a higher elementary school, seventeen percent for three years, fifty-nine percent for four years, and the remaining twenty percent studied on their own (Kaigo 1968, 226). The middle school did not want to admit students with only two years of higher elementary school education. In Nagano Prefecture in 1893, for example, even among graduates who completed the four-year higher elementary education curriculum, only those with excellent scores on the examination were allowed to enter the middle school on the basis of the recommendation of their elementary school principals; all others were selected with an entrance examination. In Chiba Prefecture, from 1890 students who completed the four-year higher elementary school course were admitted without the examination, and from 1893 this was applied to the students with three years of higher elementary school education. There were usually far more applicants than vacancies, however, and at these times an examination was used to select students.

As there had been long-standing criticism of the loose connection between elementary and middle school education, in 1894 the Ministry of Education, in its Regulations on Entering Ordinary Middle Schools, issued the instruction that two years of higher elementary education—or in other words six years of elementary education—would be the official requirement for entering a middle school. According to this regulation, those who completed two years of higher elementary education should be allowed to enroll in middle school without an examination. But this could happen only when the number of applicants did not exceed the number of vacancies. Actually, in 1895 and 1898 there were 1.6 times as many applicants as vacancies, and a competitive examination was unavoidable. It is not surprising that those who succeeded had had the longer schooling. Among the middle school freshmen of 1898, according to Ministry of Education statistics, fourteen percent had completed six years of elementary education, thirty-three percent had completed seven years, and forty-seven percent had completed eight years, while seven percent took different routes to preparation. Even in 1908, only eighteen percent had had six years of elementary education, compared with thirty-eight percent who had seven years, forty-two percent with eight years, and two percent with other preparation (Kaigo 1968, 233). The higher elementary school became a preparatory school, so to speak, for the middle school, or an enclave for those waiting to gain admittance to middle school.

Graduates and Dropouts

While the middle school students were admitted on the basis of careful and rigorous selection based on their academic ability, an even tougher road of selection lay ahead, as graduation was difficult. It is estimated that during the early 1890s the graduation rate was as low as ten percent (Fukaya 1969, 82). One of the students admitted to an ordinary middle school in Chiba Prefecture in 1890 recalled: "There were about a hundred new students the year I entered. But what a surprise! So many dropped out, and there were only sixteen of us left at the time of graduation."

Furthermore, of that group of sixteen students "only nine of us" were alumni of the original class group. By the mid-1890s, the rate had climbed to the fifty percent level, but despite the passage of time it never exceeded sixty percent. Contrary to this, the dropout rate was up to twenty-six percent in 1892, and fourteen percent in 1900.

This strict winnowing of students could be partially attributed to the link between promotion and examinations. The Ordinary Middle School Regulations of Nagano Prefecture, issued in 1887, state that student evaluations were based on biannual regular exams and special exams held at least twice each semester. Promotion was decided on the basis of all these examinations. In the annual evaluation, if a student's cumulative score was higher than fifty in all subjects and the average was higher than sixty, promotion was assured. However, if one subject was lower than forty or there were more than one subject lower than fifty, the student failed. And if a student repeated the same grade twice, he was expelled. Although the regulation was reissued in 1894 and in 1900, the policy of basing promotion on examinations actually did not change at all, for unlike the elementary school, at the middle school level there was hardly any criticism of the use of competitive examinations.

Inoue Kowashi, the Minister of Education who ordered the discontinuation of examinations in elementary school, also suspected that there might be some need to reform the middle schools. In one of his letters to the principals of middle schools, he inquired about the merits and demerits of ranking and rewarding students based on examinations. Inoue noted three practices common to middle schools—publicly announcing examination results, determining ranking by academic performance, and awarding prizes—and questioned their merits:

> When examinations are restricted to their proper sphere, they provide one means for encouraging students to study; but if they go beyond that, they may engender the opposite effect of fostering jealousy among students, which would be a grave error. What are the merits and demerits of the present system of publicly announcing examination scores and changing rankings based on these results? The purpose of publicly announcing examination scores should only be

to demonstrate that there is no teacher favoritism. After all, the students are already sensitive enough to know that inferiority brings shame and superiority brings pleasure (Kaigo 1968, 285-86).

The answers to Inoue's doubts were largely negative. Katsuura Tomoo, the principal of the Ordinary Middle School of Tokyo Prefecture, collected the opinions of all the middle schools within Tokyo and its neighboring prefectures, and responded that (1) the majority of the schools announced examination scores to the students; (2) most of the schools gave awards; and (3) each school had for many years arranged the placement of students based on their performance. There was no special need to change this custom, he said (Kaigo 1968, 286). As far as middle school was concerned, it was not widely assumed that competitive examinations caused major problems.

Apart from poor academic ability, there were various other causes of dropping out. After pointing out that there were eleven thousand dropouts out of twenty-eight thousand students admitted, the *Mombushō Nenpō* (Annual Bulletin of the Ministry of Education) for 1900 concluded that there were too many who had entered by "being tempted simply to follow their peers without strong will and without assurance of financial support."

It also should be noted, however, that the dropout figures may have been inflated, for many students left a particular school halfway through their studies for another school. Of the dropouts for 1901, fifty-three percent left because of family circumstances and twelve percent were expelled; however, at least nineteen percent left to enroll in another school (Sakurai 1975, 320). In order to understand why there were so many dropouts and transfers, we need to consider the relationship between the middle schools and the higher schools, which were considered the gateway to success.

From Middle School to Higher School

After proclamation of the *Gakusei*, for a long time there remained a wide gap between the educational ideal and its reality. Mori Arinori, the Minister of Education from 1885 to 1889, began the task of bringing these two closer together. In four key school orders of 1886—the Elementary School Order, the Middle School Order, the Imperial University Order, and the Normal School Order—he created the backbone for an integrated educational system. Both the elementary and middle schools were divided into ordinary and higher levels, and progression through these four steps became the regular route to the Imperial University.

Mori's reforms clarified the relationships among the various schools and created a unified system. But it took some time for this new system to function smoothly. While the route to the Imperial University was defined, initially only a minority of entering students followed it.

As we have already shown, Mori's aim in these reforms was to solidify the status of the Imperial University as an institution to train members of the elite, including government officers, to perform tasks of national importance. The Imperial University should have as high a standard as the European universities, and for this purpose nothing was more essential than students of high academic ability. Schools below the university level were expected to serve as the pipeline through which excellent students would be sent for selection by the Imperial University, the highest academic institution. However, the schools preceding higher middle school were slow in attaining a sufficiently high academic level to respond to this expectation.

To raise the level of middle school education, Mori laid down the principle of one ordinary middle school for each prefecture. Moreover, as we saw in the previous chapter, the admission standard to ordinary middle schools was so high that entrants required considerable preparation: fewer than ten percent entered with six years of elementary education; the majority had eight years. And despite the rigorous selection of ordinary middle schools, only a fraction of their graduates could continue on to the higher middle schools.

The higher middle schools located at five places across the nation provided preparatory education for entering the Imperial University. Graduates of these schools could automatically — that is, without an examination — gain admission to the Imperial University, so the quality of the students attending the Imperial universities was in fact determined by the kind of students admitted to the higher middle schools. It was therefore inevitable that the selection of students for the higher middle schools was far more rigorous than for ordinary middle schools.

Foreign language education received the most emphasis among the subjects taught at the higher middle schools. Continuous adoption of the latest developments in Western learning was considered necessary in order to make the Imperial University equal to those of the West.

All the predecessors of the Imperial University, including Tokyo University, had tried to import Western learning through relying on instruction in foreign languages by foreign teachers. Compared to these predecessors, the Imperial University was certainly more Japanized. Most of the teaching staff were Japanese, and many classes were given in the Japanese language. But in these early years there still was not an adequate scholarly foundation and accumulation of modern Western learning in Japan, so foreign language was still an indispensable means for both teaching and learning at the highest academic institutions. This made the higher middle school necessary as a preparatory institution for the university in addition to the regular middle school. The selection standard for the higher middle school had to be established independently of the actual academic level of the ordinary middle schools so as to satisfy the academic demand from the Imperial University above.

Selection Based on Academic Ability

The gap between expected and actual academic ability being wide, some measure was necessary to close it, and selection by examinations was one such measure.

Admission to the predecessors of the Imperial University was granted on the basis of success in the entrance examination, and preparation for the examination was taken either at separate institutions or through independent courses of study providing foreign-language and other specialized training prerequisite for success in the chosen field of study. Under this system, applicants were required to have sufficient proficiency to pass the entrance examination, and no more than that. The level of educational institutions attended did not come into consideration. Young people discovered that the most efficient way to obtain this proficiency was to attend one of the preparatory schools in Tokyo, rather than to study at a local middle school which might have less competent teachers and a lower academic standard. By the early 1880s, a large number of students from rural areas were going to Tokyo to pursue their studies, and the privately run preparatory schools there flourished.

Mori, in organizing the middle school system, aimed to reduce the dependence on these preparatory schools. He proposed that the graduates of improved ordinary middle schools should be allowed to move directly into higher middle schools. Thus the regulation on admission requirements for entering the higher middle school stated that "those who qualify for the first grade must be seventeen years of age or older, with good conduct and health, and must have completed an ordinary middle school or must have equivalent academic ability."

However, Mori's objective was not easily realized, for the academic gap between the higher and ordinary middle schools was too great to be solved by a simple reorganization of the system. Mori's Middle School Order indicated that a higher middle school should have a two-year course and that the five-year ordinary middle school graduates should be able to enter directly. But realistically, since these graduates were not sufficiently prepared to start education at the higher middle school, Mori approved the provisional adoption of a three-year preparatory course in addition to the two-year main course at the higher middle school. In other words, the higher middle school would itself include a curriculum equivalent to what had formally been the upper level course of the ordinary middle school. This, however, was still not enough to produce an adequate level of proficiency in the students, so in 1887 a supplementary course equivalent to the two lower grades of the ordinary middle school was added to all of the higher middle schools except the First Higher Middle School. It was only after they established a five-year preparatory course under their own supervision that the higher middle schools could secure a supply of students with the desired level of proficiency.

What, then, was the relationship between these ordinary middle school-level preparatory courses, known as "the preparatory course plus supplementary course" now attached to the higher middle schools, and the ordinary middle schools? The major point is that admission to the higher middle schools depended solely on the individual student's proficiency.

With the addition of the preparatory courses, the higher middle school was able to accommodate a wide range of student abilities. Examinations were given to students in each grade of the main, preparatory, and supplementary courses to see if they had attained the appropriate level of ability. Conversely, regardless of whether an applicant had graduated from an ordinary middle school or not, he was admitted to the grade suited to his ability. In an extreme case, a graduate of an ordinary middle school might start from the first grade of the supplementary course. On the other hand, a student with exceptional ability might enter the main course of the higher middle school even though he had not graduated from an ordinary middle school. The criterion was not the academic career but academic ability.

For example, the average age of the first grade students at the preparatory course of the Third Higher Middle School was eighteen years and nine months, and at the Fifth Higher Middle School it was eighteen years and five months (Toita 1975). If the system had been working as planned, students of this age should have completed the main course of the higher middle school. This illustrates how wide a gap there was between the education actually provided at ordinary middle schools and what was expected by the higher middle schools as gateways to the Imperial University.

The Ministry of Education, in its annual report for 1889, indicated that it fully appreciated this reality: "Although the graduates from the ordinary middle school should go directly to the main course of the higher middle school, the present graduates cannot due to their insufficient ability, and, moreover, many of them cannot even enter the preparatory course. It is because of the preparatory course of the higher middle school and the private preparatory schools in Tokyo that a minimally acceptable level of continuity of schooling is being realized."

The System of Admission Without Examination
One of the reasons there were so many dropouts from the ordinary middle schools in the late 1880s was this weak link between the ordinary and higher middle schools. As long as sufficient ability, rather than academic career, was the requirement for entering the higher middle school, why should a student remain at school? For those who were confident of their ability, it was

much more efficient to leave school as soon as possible and aim at the preparatory or supplementary courses of a higher middle school, or otherwise to go to Tokyo to develop their ability through studying at a preparatory school where the best teachers were assembled. By the early 1890s, when the numerous public middle schools had been cut back to one school per prefecture, both the numbers of private preparatory schools and the size of each increased. Such well-known schools as Kyōritsu School came to enroll more than fifteen hundred students.

This was not a welcome situation for the Ministry of Education. Hamao Arata, the Ministry's Director of Professional Studies, when attending an opening ceremony for a new building at the Fifth Higher Middle School in Kumamoto Prefecture, commented on the problem: "At present there are more than seventy schools in Tokyo teaching a variety of general courses to some twenty-eight thousand students. Since half of these students are from other parts of Japan, an incredible amount of money has to be sent to Tokyo. In addition, a large, bustling city is not a suitable place for minors to study. The policy for improving ordinary middle schools and establishing higher middle schools at various places was directed to reforming the current situation by ensuring that high level general education is possible in other parts of Japan with little expense. The result has fallen short of expectations, however. Although many tend to believe that it is essential to attend the First Higher Middle School if they wish to enter the Imperial University, this is contrary to the facts."

Hamao asked the educators in attendance to make efforts to remedy this situation by telling young people they can be well prepared for the Imperial University through studying general education at a nearby higher middle school and urged that the prefectural government improve the ordinary middle school so that it had better communication with the higher middle school.

This situation also created problems for the higher middle schools. While these schools selected students by examination, they nonetheless faced difficulties in attracting students since the ordinary middle schools, which were their primary source of students, were weak. In fact, in 1889 the number of those admitted to the various courses of the higher middle schools filled only fifty-nine percent of the places available, and admissions were only up to sixty-nine percent of capacity by 1893. On top of this, in 1889 only twenty-one percent of all students were in the main course, and by 1893 this had risen to no more than thirty-one percent (Uchida 1968). To improve this situation, the higher middle schools initiated a liaison system with the ordinary middle schools of their areas.

For example, the July 1889 document describing the system adopted by the First Higher Middle School states that those whose good conduct, academic excellence, and good health were approved by the principals of their schools should be admitted without an examination. Only when the applicants from these liaison schools did not exceed the number of available places in this school might it fill the vacant places by selecting students with examinations. This entrance examination was a type of qualifying exam, and only those who achieved more than the minimum prescribed score (at least sixty out of a perfect score of one hundred in each subject) passed. Admission was then granted according to the priority of the highest overall scores until the number of vacant places was filled. The examination was a demanding one which consisted of three parts testing a total of ten subjects, with applicants screened at each of the three stages. Gradually it was introduced at the other higher middle schools.

While the liaison system was introduced to strengthen the ordinary middle schools in rural areas, in fact in 1890 at the First Higher Middle School only thirty-eight (thirteen percent) of the three hundred four students admitted to the third grade of the preparatory course—the lowest grade—were selected by recommendation without an examination, and among them thirteen were from ordinary middle schools in Tokyo, five each from schools in the nearby prefectures of Aichi, Shizuoka, Ibaragi, and Nagano, and four from Gakushūin School. Though the minimum age for the third grade of the preparatory course was fourteen, the youngest admitted was actually sixteen, and most were over eighteen. Furthermore, none were admitted by the liaison system to the higher grades. This suggests there was at least a three-year gap between what the ordinary middle school taught students and what was expected of entrants to the main course of the higher middle school. It is not surprising that eighty-seven percent were selected by entrance examination.

Inoue Reforms the System

However, admission without examinations based on the liaison system gradually began to have an impact. Most directly affected were the private preparatory schools of Tokyo. An increasing number of people gave up studying in Tokyo once the route from a local ordinary middle school to the Imperial University through a higher middle school became established. The Ministry of Education accelerated this trend with an order proposing measures to reduce the student flow to Tokyo. Consequently even such a famous school as Kyōritsu, whose students in 1890 made up twenty-one percent of those admitted to the First Higher Middle School, suddenly lost enrollees: from about fifteen hundred in 1888 its enrollment dropped in three years to a little over seven hundred. To survive this crisis, the preparatory schools began to transform themselves, one after another, into ordinary middle schools.

Another hurdle had to be overcome, however, by these newly established private ordinary middle schools, for the government proposed to grant official recognition and liaison privileges only to public schools. The private schools started a campaign against this policy, and the Diet was forced to discuss the issue. As a result, in 1892 each higher middle school was instructed to develop its own accrediting system for private middle schools. The Kyōritsu School History indicates that all except the Fourth Higher Middle School authorized Kyōritsu Middle School as one of their liaison schools. The Nihon Middle School, which formerly had been known as the Tokyo English School, was also authorized by the First, Second, and Fourth Higher Middle Schools.

The steady improvement in the quality of the ordinary middle school was another outcome. As a consequence of this trend, the supplementary course of the higher middle schools was abolished. In 1891 the Second Higher Middle School eliminated its course, and in the following year the Third and Fourth Higher Schools followed suit. Finally, in 1893 the Fifth Higher Middle School stopped recruiting for the course. Furthermore, the First Higher Middle School shortened its three-year preparatory course to two years. One manifestation of the improved quality of the ordinary middle school was the fact that by 1892 some thirty-four percent of those admitted to the higher middle schools were graduates of the ordinary middle schools.

While the relationship between the ordinary middle schools and the higher middle schools was being formalized, in 1894 Minister of Education Inoue Kowashi began a major reform of the higher middle school. In a new Higher School Law he decided to change the existing higher middle school into a "higher school" where professional subjects were taught and a preparatory course could be offered to those who intended to attend the Imperial University (Kaigo 1968).

As we have already seen, the higher middle school that Mori had created was conceived as a preparatory school for those who intended to go to the university. It was also designed to provide courses for professional education, and a medical department was actually established at each higher middle school, and a law department at the Third Higher Middle School. Inoue attempted to relocate the higher middle school from its position of involvement in both professional and university preparatory roles to one emphasizing specialized education. In particular, he reorganized the Third Higher School, which already had the two professional education departments of medicine and law, into a full-scale institution for professional education by adding a department of engineering and dropping the preparatory course.

Behind this policy was Inoue's personal philosophy of higher education and his reservations about the purpose of the existing higher middle school.

The reason that the higher middle school, an institution not found in the West, had come into existence in Japan was that an extremely high level of academic and foreign language proficiency had been set for studies in the Imperial university. And, in the pursuit of levels of academic achievement equal to those of the West, there was a very real need for institutions with such high academic standards. However, there was also an urgent need for high-level specialized education and the development of a broad manpower base from among the limited resources of those graduating from ordinary middle schools. It was necessary to open a route for these people into higher schools where they could take specialized courses taught in the Japanese language. In budgetary debates in the Diet the abolition of higher middle schools was a topic of frequent debate.

Inoue's view of higher education thus included an image of a new kind of university, but Inoue's proposals for replacing the higher middle schools with higher schools which offered university-type education quite different from that of the Imperial university were never accepted.

In the event, the only additional establishment of a department of professional education was at the Fifth Higher School. The preparatory course for the university which Inoue had sought to abolish began to accept an ever-increasing number of students, while the departments for professional education experienced a decline. Thus in the late 1890s the Ministry of Education began to transform the higher schools into institutions whose main objective was preparatory education for the university.

The Entrance Examination for the Higher School

In any case, one outcome of Inoue's reform was to telescope the higher middle school's five-year curriculum into a three-year preparatory course for university education, at what he called the "higher school." The link between the middle school and the higher school finally became stabilized. Comparison of the figures for the number of higher school entrants who were graduates of ordinary middle schools shows steady and significant improvement from 1894, when only forty-five percent of middle school graduates were admitted to higher schools, to sixty-eight percent in 1895, seventy-one percent in 1896, eighty percent in 1897, and eighty-six percent in 1898. By 1899 the proportion gaining admission was as high as eighty-eight percent.

In the process of strengthening this linkage, the method for selecting students also changed. The 1895 admission rules for the First Higher School specified that there were two kinds of entrance examination: the "special" examination, testing a selection of subjects taught at middle schools; and the "general" examination, or examination on all subjects. The special examination was to be administered to "those who were graduates of middle schools which were accredited by contract with the First Higher School and had received the recommendation of their principal." For top students there was a provision exempting applicants recommended by their principals as "excellent in scholastic achievement" from the entrance examination altogether. The general examination was taken by students who did not qualify for exemption or for the special examination. The following year, 1896, the rule requiring an accrediting contract between the middle schools and the higher school was abolished, and any student from any middle school could, with the principal's recommendation, attempt the special examination. Those not qualified for the special examination could apply for the general examination.

Selection by a special examination was reemphasized by the Ministry of Education in 1898. Examination on all subjects would be held only when the number of applicants for the special examination exceeded the number of vacancies. In the same year the Ministry of Education instructed that unless the number of applicants from public and private middle schools exceeded the number of vacancies, the applicants would be admitted without an examination. Moreover, those who had not graduated from the middle schools should be admitted only when the number of the applicants from the middle schools was insufficient to fill the vacancies.

In this way it is clear that the Ministry of Education was doing its best to establish a firm route from the middle to the higher school. The alternate route from the various types of private preparatory schools was virtually closed by the late 1890s. Despite the regulations, however, the route to a higher school without examination was not automatically open to middle school graduates. For at all five higher schools, applications were far greater than the number of vacancies. The ratio of the number admitted to the number of applicants was forty-nine percent in 1899 and forty-two percent in 1900. While it was now impossible to enter a higher school without graduating from middle school, graduation alone was still not sufficient.

Professional and Industrial Schools and the Examinations

The Problem of Vocational Schools

Among the many schools created to respond to social demands after the establishment of the *Gakusei* were a number which could not be covered by the Elementary, Middle, Imperial University, and Normal School Laws. One example was the women's high school (*kōtōjogakkō*). While this middle-level institution for women was legally an ordinary middle school, in many respects, such as the curriculum and number of years of study, it was quite different. The industrial schools (*jitsugyō gakkō*) for agriculture, engineering, and commerce were another example. These schools were alternately called professional schools (*senmon gakkō*) and technical schools (*gigei gakkō*), and their programs were intended for youths who had the background to attend anything from a higher elementary school to a higher school. Yet another type was the professional school where such professions as medicine, pharmacy, law, economics, literature, and science were taught. Though these were basically higher educational institutions, they also included classes at the middle school level to provide preparatory education. Finally there was a category of miscellaneous schools (*kakushu gakkō*), mainly schools that provided preparatory education for other schools.

In the mid-1890s there was still no law covering these schools, and it was only around the turn of the century, with the Women's High School Law, the Vocational School Law (both 1899) and the Professional School Law (1903), that these schools finally gained official status. Among these laws the Professional School Law had the greatest impact.

The professional schools (*senmon gakkō*) occupied an unusual position. As we have seen, there was no provision for them in the original *Gakusei* regulations—their role was in fact seen as being that of interim institutions filling in until a full-fledged university was established. The case of Tokyo University's immediate predecessor, Kaisei Gakkō, reflects this, and even after Tokyo University was established in 1877 the "professional school" title was retained in the education laws. In 1879 the *Kyōiku-rei* (Education Act) replaced the *Gakusei*. The new regulations defined the professional schools (*senmon gakkō*) as "institutions where one specialized subject is taught," in contrast to the university (*daigaku*) which was "an institution where various specialized subjects were taught." Thus, the institution which offered comprehensive higher education was called the university, and institutions which offered courses in single, specialized fields were called professional schools. While neither the educational standard nor the organization of these professional schools would qualify them as universities, by the 1880s they were providing highly specialized education which cannot be overlooked.

The most important of all these professional schools was the group of "great schools" established by the various government ministries such as the Law School of the Ministry of Law, the College of Engineering of the Ministry of Industry, the Sapporo College of Agriculture, and the Tokyo Forestry and Agriculture School. Besides these, the Ministry of Education created during this period a professional school in Osaka and other high-level institutions for professional education such as the Tokyo Foreign Language School, the Tokyo Commercial School, and the Tokyo Technical School. Also among the schools founded and run by local governments were professional schools for literature and science studies in Ishikawa Prefecture and medical schools in several prefectures. Private institutions also began offering specialized education, mostly in the legal field. Initially, however, many of these schools tended to be fly-by-night operations concentrating on preparing applicants for licensing examinations.

After 1886, when the first Imperial University was established, the character of these professional schools was dramatically changed. First, all the government "great schools" were absorbed into the Imperial University, with the sole exception of the Sapporo College of Agriculture. Second, all but three of the prefectural medical schools had to cease operation, and instead departments of medicine were added to the five higher middle schools. Third, the government professional schools became more substantial, with many focused on commerce and engineering. Fourth, government control of private professional schools became stricter in exchange for the privilege of having their graduates sit for the official vocational license examinations, and consequently the standard of these schools began to improve. Finally, private professional schools such as Keiō Gijuku and the Tokyo Professional School (today's Waseda University) began to feature multiple departments or courses.

In short, after 1887 "professional school" (*senmon gakkō*) became a name for higher educational institutions including those schools whose quality was lower than the Imperial University and furthermore which could not be categorized under the laws of either the Imperial University, the Higher School, or the Normal Schools. The Professional School Law issued in 1903 was what legally defined the character of these schools for lower-level professional education.

In this law a professional school was defined as a school offering at least three years of study, where high-level academic and professional education was provided to those who had graduated from a middle school or completed no less than than four years at a women's high school, or to those who had proven equivalent ability on an examination. Furthermore, an industrial school equivalent to these schools was to be called "an industrial professional school" (*jitsugyō senmon gakkō*). It also clarified the distinctions not only between *daigaku* (universities) and *senmon gakkō* (professional schools), but also between the professional schools and other institutions, the *jitsugyo gakkō* (industrial schools) and the *kakushu gakkō* (miscellaneous school).

Ministry of Education annual reports record that in 1902 the number of public and private professional schools was fifty, but just one year later, following the enactment of the Professional School Law, the number had fallen dramatically, to thirty-one. The private preparatory schools or fly-by-night professional schools were downgraded to "miscellaneous" schools or were closed as a result of the standards set out in this regulation. For example, Saiseigakusha, which had attracted many students seeking to prepare for the medical license examination, was closed, and most of the other private schools for medicine, dentistry, and pharmacy were designated "miscellaneous" schools. In addition, the professional departments for law, engineering, and medicine which had been attached to the higher schools were either abolished or made separate government professional schools.

The Main Road and the Side Roads of Higher Education

One of the distinctive features of the professional schools, when compared to the higher schools and the Imperial University, was their reliance on the Japanese language to transmit the curriculum.

The professional education of the Imperial University was premised on ability in at least two foreign languages, and a large portion of the higher schools' curriculum was devoted to foreign language study. A professional school, where all the classes were taught in Japanese by Japanese teaching staff, did not require special proficiency in foreign languages, and the graduates of middle schools could be admitted without further preparation.

When he took office as Minister of Education in 1893, Inoue Kowashi tried to change the higher middle school into a higher school for professional education, and he believed these new institutions for professional education should become the new "universities," while the Imperial University might become a separate institution for advanced research and the training of researchers. Not a few people shared his idea and vision of changing the professional schools into universities (Amano 1979). In fact, as far as quantity was concerned, these professional schools where the majority of students were studying could have been considered the main road of Japanese higher education.

But however strong the professional and industrial schools were in terms of numbers, they were still clearly a lower priority educational choice, a detour route for those blocked from the main road established under Mori—of advancing from ordinary middle school, to higher school, and so on to the Imperial University. This is the reason that the professional departments of law, engineering, and medicine established by Inoue at the higher schools had many vacancies, particularly during the 1890s. The number of applicants to the departments of law and engineering of the Third Higher School never exceeded the number of vacancies, and the admission standard set by the departments of medicine at the higher schools was lower than that set for the preparatory course of the university. For example, in 1895, while the university preparatory course of the Second Higher School used an entrance examination to select students from among the graduates of the middle schools, the only requirement for admission to the department of medicine for graduates from the middle school was a physical check-up; there was no examination.

This illustrates how strong the attraction of the Imperial University was for young people, how intensive was the investment of national resources in the main road with the Imperial University at its end, and how extensive were the measures to protect and enhance this road in order to attract the best candidates from all over the nation to the elite civil service.

Graduates of the professional departments of the higher schools could hope for no better career than that of a middle-level bureaucrat, engineer, or private medical practitioner, while it was expected that graduates of the government professional schools would find employment as clerical or technical staff with private firms, or else as middle school teachers. Even so, the graduates of government institutions fared somewhat better than those of private institutions, because they were at least granted the privilege of exemption from the qualification examinations for professions such as teaching and medicine. It was not until after the late 1890s that provisions were made for private professional school graduates to qualify for those exemptions. In other words, there was a clear ranking of educational choices for young people seeking social advancement, with the higher school to Imperial University route at the top, followed by the government professional schools and the private professional schools in that order.

While university entrants thus received their preparatory education at a variety of schools, both higher schools and professional schools relied on the middle schools for their students. Since the most desirable educational track for middle school graduates was the route from a higher school to the Imperial University, the social prestige of these professional schools tended to be determined by the quantity and quality of the middle school graduates each of them could attract. And so the professional schools had to build themselves up and make their way forward along the sidelines of the path established and nurtured by national policy for progress to university, competing with higher schools and other professional schools to attract quality applicants from among the middle school graduates.

Examinations in the Professional Schools

In order to understand the actual use and function of examinations in the professional schools, let us begin with the government schools. Two representative government professional schools were the Tokyo Higher School for Commerce (the present Hitotsubashi University) and the Tokyo Technical Higher School (the present Tokyo Institute of Technology). The predecessor of the Tokyo Higher School for Commerce was founded as a private school by Mori Arinori in 1875. After many ups and downs, this school became the Tokyo Commerce School (Tokyo Shōgyō Gakkō) under the jurisdiction of the Ministry of Education in 1886, and in 1887 it was renamed the Higher School for Commerce (Kōtō Shōgyō Gakkō). As its name indicates, it had a standard equal to a higher middle school, and in 1891 it had a three-year main course to which graduates of a higher middle school were admitted without examination, while graduates of the ordinary middle schools were given preliminary admission to a two-year preparatory course.

The school catalogue of 1895 indicates four bases for admission to the preparatory course (which had been shortened by then to one year): (1) admission without examination for a limited number of students who had graduated from the public and private middle schools approved by the school and who were recommended by their principals; (2) admission by examination in four subjects including English for graduates of middle schools whose academic ability did not qualify them for the first type of admission; (3) admission by examination for students who were recommended by the public and private commercial schools approved by the school; and (4) admission of those whose average score was no less than sixty-five in an examination that measured the academic ability expected of a graduate of a middle school. This admission system did not change throughout the early years of the 1900s.

It is apparent that the Tokyo Higher School for Commerce had a good reputation from its early days, and it was considered one of the most desirable schools. According to Sakai Toshihiko, who entered the First Higher Middle School in 1887: "Facing each other on the opposite sides of the First Bridge (Hitotsubashi), the First Higher Middle School and the Tokyo Higher School for Commerce were the two most popular gateways to success for boys of that era" (Sakai 1978). The ratio of those taking the entrance examination to vacancies was already 3.2 in 1898 and became progressively higher, rising to 3.8 in 1899 and 4.8 in 1900. The Tokyo Higher School for Commerce was one of the most difficult schools to enter for the graduates of a middle school.

The Tokyo Technical Higher School started as a government technical school in 1881. This middle-level school gradually improved itself and in 1890 changed its name to the Tokyo Engineering School (Tokyo Kōgyō Gakkō). According to the school catalogue of 1890, the sons of technical engineers or those over seventeen years of age who had a keen desire to become engineers could be admitted by an examination equivalent to the middle-school-level examination. In addition, those graduates from public middle schools with the governor's certificate showing that they had achieved over two-thirds of the full score on science and mathematics-related subjects in the graduation examination could be admitted without an examination. This school relied on prefectural governments for recruiting and conducting the examination. The school catalogue of 1895 shows that about the same number of entrants were chosen by each method.

Until the late 1880s, Tokyo Engineering School was not a popular school for middle school graduates, and this may have been one reason it turned to the prefectural government for help in admissions. However, after the Sino-Japanese War (1894-95), as the nation's industrialization speeded up and the job market for technical graduates improved, the number of applicants steadily increased. The competition ratio, for instance, rose to 3.8 in 1898, 2.8 in 1899, and 3.4 in 1900, which was nearly as high as the rate at the Tokyo Higher Commercial School. By 1900, in principle all the students were middle school graduates who passed an academic entrance examination; only in the unlikely event that the number of applicants did not exceed the number of places would other applicants be selected by examinations from among applicants who had not completed middle school. In 1901 the school changed its name to the Technical Higher School (Kōtō Kōgyō Gakkō).

Private Professional Schools

While the government professional schools around the turn of the century had introduced the principle of examination-based admissions for middle school graduates, many of the private professional schools still did not rely on examinations. As we have seen, the origins of the private professional schools varied. Some schools such as Meiji, Hōsei, and Chūō started as preparatory schools for the national licensing examination for the legal profesions and the civil service, while others like Keiō Gijuku, Waseda, and Dōshisha were founded to prepare young people for new middle-class occupations by providing Western-style liberal education. There were also schools founded by Buddhist, Shinto, and Christian religious groups. With the development of middle-level education for young women, women's professional schools for languages and liberal arts and teacher education also began to be established.

At least until the 1880s these private schools had much more liberal examination policies than the government schools. For example, the 1883 school rules of Meiji Law School (now Meiji University) stated that all (males) over sixteen should be admitted. No examination for either admission or graduation was stipulated; the rule simply stated that two major examinations, for which the passing score was six out of ten points, were conducted each year.

At Keiō Gijiku in 1888, the school's centenary history says, students decided to boycott classes when a procedure for a passing and failing system based on scores on examinations was announced, for until then "the teachers customarily decided the qualifications and promotion of each student based on their judgment and discussion with other teachers." The students objected that "such a scoring system is for those schools that train government officials, and it would be like pouring ice on hot charcoal and contrary to the philosophy of Mita Juku [Keiō], where freedom and independence are highly valued." This shows a basic difference in the approach to the examinations of the government and private schools of that era.

When an examination is used not only for evaluating ability but also as a selection measure, it acquires important meaning in the process of entrance, promotion to higher grades, and graduation. In the schools for training government officers, which were founded for the clear purpose of educating able people to become the driving force in Japan's modernization, the students underwent relentless evaluation and selection from entrance to graduation. The prestigious position and status promised to them after completion were sufficient reward for the effort and stress caused by this competition.

But this was not the case with the private schools, where the focus was on the national licensing examinations. Private school students were more concerned with external examinations conducted by the state, and thus the schools themselves did not need to evaluate and rank students internally. Since tuition fees were the schools' sole source of income, all applicants were admitted and there was no need for a selection process. The one important function of examinations at private schools was, therefore, as training to strengthen the students' ability in taking the state examinations.

In other schools, examinations were not necessary as measures for social selection, though they were useful to measure the effect of the school's education. Usually there was neither a limit on the number admitted nor an excess of applicants over the number that could be accommodated. In contrast to the government schools, the diplomas of these private schools did not promise a prestigious job or status in the future. In fact, few of the students at these schools studied very hard to obtain their diplomas. They studied merely to acquire sufficient ability to pass a national license examination, or to acquaint themselves with the modern culture of the West. The diploma was not the prime objective.

Private Schools and the Civil Service Examinations

As we have seen, it was a series of government policies from 1886 to 1888 that brought about a dramatic change in the orientation of private schools to examinations. These initiatives tended to incorporate private law schools as part of the training system for civil servants. In order to provide their graduates the same privileges as government schools—access to the civil service examinations and employment without an examination—these private schools had to introduce academic examinations to ensure control over the quality of their admissions, promotion, and graduation decisions. Once the government approved this policy, all the major private law schools started to adopt selection by examination.

According to the regulations of the Meiji Law School, which became one of the "specially authorized schools" in 1888, (1) admission was limited to ordinary middle school graduates or those who passed an entrance examination of a level equal to the standard of an ordinary middle school; (2) promotion to higher grades was not approved without passing the regular examination; (3) a graduation thesis was required, and in addition the students were required to achieve an average of sixty points in all the subjects they studied in the oral examination; finally, (4) upon passing the graduation examination, a diploma would be awarded in accordance with the Ministry of Education Order. As a result, only those private school students who were selected by an examination and succeeded in obtaining the diploma enjoyed the privilege of employment in the civil service. Thus, from the late 1880s the diploma awarded by private schools also became socially useful as part of an academic career.

Only a limited number of schools were granted the privilege of having their students take the national examinations, and until the early years of the 1900s only a fraction of the students in these schools were awarded the privilege. At the private law schools, one of the few cases where the privilege had been granted, applicants could be admitted to one of two courses: a "regular" course, for normal middle school graduates or those who could demonstrate equivalent academic performance in an examination; or a "separate" course, for applicants, regardless of qualifications, who could pass a simple admission test. In 1888, for example, eighty-five percent of the students of the Tokyo Law School (the present Chūō University) were enrolled in the separate course. During the period from 1888 to 1892, only 24% of the law department graduates of the six authorized schools were from the regular course.

Private law schools represented the highest quality in the private sector, yet until the late 1890s, admission of a mix of middle school graduates and elementary school graduates continued. Their ambiguous relation to middle-level education was clarified by the Professional School Law of 1903, for after that only those schools with a regular course for middle school graduates or those who succeeded in an equivalence examination could be called professional schools. Also, the ratio between regular and separate-course students improved. These developments, however, did not necessarily mean that examinations for selection to private professional schools became as difficult as those for government schools. The separate course without special qualifications persisted, and only a few schools could attract a sufficient number of applicants for the regular course to justify strict selection.

For the young people who sought higher education, a distinctive ranking of desirability emerged among the various institutions of higher education, and the ranking reflected the rigor of the entrance examination of each school. As this pyramid with the First Higher School at the summit and the private professional schools at the base was being established, Japan's examination hell also began to heat up.

Chapter Nine

The World of Examinations Before and After 1900

School Guides and Examinations

Tokyo Yūgaku Annai

In 1890, *Tokyo Yūgaku Annai* (Guide to Schools in Tokyo), edited by a company called Shōnen'en (A Boy's Garden), was first published. This book can be considered the ancestor of the contemporary guides to college and university entrance examinations. After the first release it was revised annually and became a bible for young people who dreamed of studying in Tokyo.

Before the Second World War, and particularly during the Meiji period, Japan's schools and students were highly concentrated in Tokyo—a trend that can still be observed today. In 1902 sixty-three percent of all the students who studied at higher educational institutions and eighty percent of all the students who studied at private schools were in Tokyo (Fujiwara 1982). Moreover, though a firm statistic is not available, most of the preparatory schools for entering these higher educational institutions and for succeeding in the various occupational licensing examinations were also there. Tokyo was the mecca for ambitious young people who wished to pursue a modern occupation and achieve higher social status through education.

For example, a report from the Matsue Middle School during the late 1880s notes that it had become quite fashionable for ambitious young people to quit the local school in order to study in Tokyo, since leisurely study at a rural school was thought to be shameful. A common ploy of young people was to run away from home and, after a trip of one or two days, to send a telegram to their parents asking for money, since it was difficult to get permission in advance from parents to go to Tokyo to study

(Sakurai 1942). *Tokyo Yūgaku Annai* was published in response to this craze for going to the big city to study.

Yūgaku Annai consisted of three parts: (1) notes on going to Tokyo and living there, (2) the regulations of each school, and (3) the examination questions for the leading schools. Reflecting what was clearly thought to offer the most certain route to success, the third part included questions only from government schools. The first part became more detailed with each successive edition. For instance, the seventeenth issue, published in 1902, covers such items as preparation for going to Tokyo, rules for taking an examination, approximate tuition, how many years one should stay in each school, precautions on arriving in Tokyo, selection of accommodations, and sanitary precautions. From this advice we can gain a good picture of how students were living.

Most revealing for understanding the lively world of examinations during the Meiji period, however, are the names of the schools and the rules covered in the guidebook. *Tokyo Yūgaku Annai* of 1892 begins with information on fifteen government schools ranging from the Imperial University to the Higher Teachers' Training School (Kōto Shihan Gakkō) and the Higher Commercial School (Kōto Shōgyō Gakkō). Most are schools under the jurisdiction of the Ministry of Education, but others include the Military Academy and the Tokyo Posts and Telecommunications School under the jurisdiction of the Ministry of Posts and Telecommunications. Following the government schools is a section for specially authorized schools, which covers the seven private law schools that enjoyed the privilege of having their graduates take the civil service examination. The contemporary names of these schools are Meiji, Senshū, Chūō, Nihon, Hōsei, Waseda, and Dokkyō universities.

Next the middle schools preparing students for entrance examinations are covered. Of the twelve mentioned, only three are official middle schools; the rest are preparatory schools for examinations. In the paragraph on Tokyo English School, a typical example, the guidebook states that "this school is well known for its superior facilities and careful teaching" and that this is "the best school to train a student to succeed in the entrance examinations for the higher middle schools, the Higher Commercial School, and the various professional schools including the Naval

Academy." Among the preparatory schools were a number which prepared students for the examinations of specific schools. Seijō Gakkō provided a "preparatory course for gaining admittance to the military academies," and Shōgyō Soshū Gakkō prepared students "for entering the Higher Commercial School and the Accounting School attached to it." But as we reported in the previous chapter, by this time the government higher educational institutions were largely admitting the graduates of middle schools, so the leading preparatory schools were already beginning to transform themselves into official middle schools.

Finally the names of twenty-one private professional schools outside the "specially authorized schools" group are listed. Keiō Gijuku is at the top of this list, and included in it are schools which were later classified by the Professional School Law of 1903 as professional schools. Many of the schools in this last group only provided preparation for the licensing examinations to become middle school teachers, medical doctors, and pharmacists. Leading examples are Kokugakuin (the present Kokugakuin University), Tokyo Butsuri Gakkō (the present Science University of Tokyo), and Yakugakkō (the present Tokyo College of Pharmacy). There were also language schools for English, German, French, and Russian, and schools for training professionals in engineering, agriculture, fishery, and business. These professional and preparatory schools, which all appeared after the Meiji Restoration, also provided young people intending to study in Tokyo with a way to move up the social ladder.

The Examination World of 1902

The edition of *Tokyo Yūgaku Annai* published in 1902 is a much bulkier volume, up from the two hundred pages of the 1892 edition to nearly three hundred fifty pages. This is mainly because the number of schools had increased dramatically over the ten-year period.

First, the number of government schools increased to thirty-two, due to the increase in the number of military-related schools. There were ten new army and four navy schools, reflecting the increasing importance of a military career for ambitious young people.

Twenty-six schools were listed as government and private middle schools and others equivalent to them, of which twenty-two were private schools. Several of these had once been exclusively preparatory schools. However, reflecting the continuing demand for examination preparation, a number of these official middle schools retained a special preparatory course along with the regular course.

At that time in Tokyo there were only four public middle schools, which was, needless to say, inadequate to serve even the resident population. Thus many private schools were created to respond to the shortage, and the *Annai* indicates that these private middle schools also functioned as preparatory schools.

In fact, the *Annai* offers the following advice: "Allow your child to study in Tokyo after he has finished at the local middle school. Although local middle schools generally have better facilities than the private schools in Tokyo, when it comes to certain fields, such as the teaching of foreign languages, they cannot compare to the schools in the capital." With the strong emphasis on proficiency in foreign languages in entrance examinations, "for those coming to Tokyo from the country, it would be most useful to enroll in a private middle school to undertake further study in English or German."

Not a few of the students from the local public middle schools had come to Tokyo after completing three or four years' study to transfer to these private middle schools so they could prepare for the government schools, and especially the highly regarded First Higher School located in Tokyo. This tendency can be illustrated by looking at the enrollments by grade level in the middle schools.

As shown in the previous chapter, the middle school dropout rate during this period was extraordinarily high. In 1902 at public middle schools, for example, for every one hundred students in the first grade, there were eighty-three in the second, sixty-five in the third, forty-seven in the fourth, and thirty-four in the fifth. In fact, the fifth grade had only slightly more than one third the number of students in the first grade. But at the private schools the picture was different. Starting with one hundred students in the first grade, there were ninety-nine in the second, one hundred one in the third, ninety-six in the fourth, and one hundred four in the fifth grade. The ratios are almost constant, and actually the fifth grade had even more students than the first grade. In fact, "private schools during this period customarily accepted students for each grade at any time in the school year until they reached their capacity, even though formal admission took place at the beginning of each school year."

The largest group of schools described in the guidebook are the forty-seven public and private professional schools and miscellaneous schools which now included the former "specially authorized schools." During the early 1900s, a clear distinction began to emerge between the schools which restricted their goals as preparatory schools for national license examination or as training schools for practical occupations, and those schools striving to develop into full-scale higher educational institutions.

The Professional School Law of 1903 formalized the distinction between the professional schools and the miscellaneous schools, and set standards for their classification in which yet another examination, the schools' own entrance examinations, had an influence. In addition to Keiō and Waseda, which from their early years had set their sights on becoming universities, several of the private law schools that had started as preparatory schools for the bar and civil service examinations began quickly shifting their educational objectives to training businessmen and providing a liberal education. One reason was that the national licensing examination for attorneys and government officials was becoming more difficult. Also, several of the preparatory schools for such professions as middle school teacher, doctor, and pharmacist began to broaden their curricula, patterning themselves after government schools, as they became dissatisfied with a narrow focus on preparatory education for the professional examinations. And the Christian and Buddhist schools, which from the beginning had not been concerned with the national examinations, also began trying to improve their reputations as higher educational institutions.

Privileges Associated with Examinations
In approving private higher educational institutions, what the Ministry of Education emphasized most was the academic abilities or qualifications of the schools' entering students. Only the schools which admitted middle school graduates or students of equivalent ability were granted the status and related benefits of government schools.

Apart from the privilege of taking professional license examinations, perhaps the most significant benefit was exemption from the draft system: only those students with a middle school diploma or who succeeded in an examination that required equivalent academic ability enjoyed the privilege of temporary exemption from conscription.

The description of the Meiji Law School in *Tokyo Yūgaku Annai* of 1902 noted that those who wanted to study at this school must be males over seventeen who had passed either of the following categories of examinations: (1) Japanese language, Chinese writing, and mathematics; or (2) ethics, mathematics, Japanese language, Chinese writing, history, geography, calligraphy, natural history, physics, chemistry, art, gymnastics, and foreign language. In addition, by the special provisions of Articles 13 and 23 of the Conscription Order, enrolled students who were middle school graduates and those who had passed the second category of examination were entitled to the privilege of temporary exemption from conscription.

Young people are almost always reluctant to join the armed forces. In this period, the Sino-Japanese and the Russo-Japanese Wars occurred in rapid succession. Admission to a regular course of a higher educational institution was one of the most legitimate and effective ways to escape the military draft.

The majority of private schools could not have survived if they had not been able to offer exemption from conscription, for they depended solely on student fees for their income. During this period most of the still small number of middle school graduates went on to various government and public schools, so most of those who came to the private professional schools were either higher elementary school graduates or middle school dropouts. It was for these applicants that the first category of examination was created. As the summary of the content of the examination suggests, it was little more than a test of basic reading and writing, and, in fact, was so easy that nearly anyone could pass.

The way a private school could develop from a professional school into a university was to decrease the number of admissions based on this first category of examination and to increase admissions based on either the second category or the possession of a middle school diploma. Conversely, from the young person's point of view, it was important to enter the regular course of the private schools by either obtaining a middle school diploma or succeeding in the entrance qualification exam in order to enjoy the privilege of draft exemption.

In authorizing schools and students, the rigorous position the Ministry of Education took is clearly portrayed in the Rules on Authorizing Public and Private Schools issued in 1899. According to these rules, the Ministry of Education had the authority to send a responsible official to witness the entrance examinations of the authorized school and to inspect the examination questions and answers. Furthermore, if there was a violation or unsatisfactory performance, the Ministry could deprive the school of this privilege. Schools were not allowed to give an entrance examination of their own design without the authorization of the Ministry.

Academic Credentials and the Occupational Qualification Examination

Entering the regular course affected privileges not only during school days but also after graduation, for only those with a regular course diploma were entitled to take national licensing examinations for the various professions.

The subtitle "Guide to Success in Life" of the seven-hundred-page *Risshin Kaitei Genkō Shiken Kisoku Taizen* (Complete Book of Contemporary Examination Rules) accurately describes the social importance of examinations during the late 1890s. It is amusing to look at the kinds of examinations included in the book, but what we must consider here is the relation between these occupational licensing exams and the various school diplomas.

As we have seen already, the diploma of the Imperial University, particularly its Faculty of Law, had extremely high value in the civil service examination. Though this diploma did not lead to specific benefits in the case of the foreign service examination, an Imperial University Law Faculty graduate was exempted from the preliminary examination for becoming an administrative official and could become a judicial officer without any examination at all. The diploma was also an unconditional passport to most other government positions, for which no examination was required.

The holder of a diploma from a public middle school was also exempted from the qualification examination for middle-level government offices. The holder of a diploma from a private school, however, could not enjoy this privilege once the "specially authorized school" system was abolished, in 1893. The only benefit available to the private schools was the Minister of Justice's extension of the qualification to take the examination for the judicial service to the graduates of the regular course of the law departments of approved schools.

According to the Attorney Law which was issued in 1893 to replace the previous Attorney Rules, only the graduates of the Law Faculty of the Imperial University were granted the privilege of practicing without an examination. All other applicants for a license to practice had to take the examination. However, since there were no specified academic qualifications for eligibility for the examination, the passage to the profession of attorney was, exceptionally, open to all private school students, even those who had not graduated from a regular law course.

The Licensing Regulations for Teaching at an Ordinary Teachers' Training School, an Ordinary Middle School and a Women's High School were first issued in 1886 and periodically revised thereafter. In these regulations, graduates from higher schools for teaching were given a license without an official certification examination. Graduates from various government schools, including the Imperial University and the higher schools, were also given official certification without examination, but a certification examination was required for everyone else. Here again, the privilege was awarded only to the graduates of government schools.

In 1899, the Ministry of Education changed its policy on teacher certification, awarding the privilege of certification without a licensing examination to the graduates of both public and private schools which met certain conditions. Still, only those who graduated from middle schools and professional schools authorized by the Ministry of Education could enjoy the privilege. In addition, the Ministry insisted not only on controlling the admissions requirements of the authorized schools but also on exercising strict supervision over their graduation exams by sending observers and reserving the authority to request changes in the examining method.

As of 1902, only six private schools were authorized for "certification without examination": the Literature Department of the

Tokyo Professional School (Tokyo Senmon Gakkō), Kokuga-kuin, Aoyama Gakuin, the Normal School of Nihon Hōritsu Gakkō (the present Nihon University), the Literature Department of Keiō Gijuku, and Tetsugakukan (the present Tōyō University). The small number indicates how difficult it was to become an authorized school. The Tokyo School of Physics (Tokyo Butsuri Gakkō, presently Tokyo University of Science) is a good example of a school that played an important role as a training institution for teachers but could not meet the conditions for authorization. The *Yūgaku Annai* of 1902 lists many schools of this kind, which continued to serve as preparatory schools for licensing examinations.

For medical occupations such as doctor, dentist, and pharmacist, only the graduates of public schools including the Imperial Universities received the privilege of a license without an examination. However, ironically, there was no public institution for dental education. And in the case of medical doctors and pharmacists, the social demand far exceeded the number of graduates of the public schools, and thus the system of licensing by examination became an important way of meeting the shortage. Saiseigakusha, the Tokyo Jikeikai Medical School (today's Tokyo Jikeikai Medical University), Tokyo Pharmaceutical School (today's Tokyo Pharmaceutical University) and the Tokyo Dental School (today's Tokyo Dental University) are several of the schools mentioned in the 1902 *Yūgaku Annai* as preparatory schools for the licensing examination.

However, there was already a tendency to extend the scope of "licensing without examination" through controlling and upgrading the quality of private schools while also eliminating the opportunity to obtain licenses for practitioners who lacked formal education. The revised Regulations on Medical Licenses of 1905 stated that the graduates of "private medical professional schools which are authorized by the Minister of Education" would be entitled to a license without an examination. Jikeikai Medical School received the first authorization that same year. A similar measure was adopted for dental schools in 1906 and for pharmaceutical schools in 1910.

The differentiation of professional schools and miscellaneous schools was sharpened by these developments. Saiseigakusha, the best preparatory school for medicine of that time, refused to comply with the conditions for authorization and was forced to close in 1903.

From Academic Ability to Academic Credentialism

This was the world of examination that opened to the young people of the 1890s and 1900s. It was obviously different from the previous period. The change could be summarized as a shift from the age of "academic ability" to "academic credentialism."

During the period when the school system was in chaos, pure ability made a difference. No matter where an individual studied, he had the opportunity for further studies and could obtain professional qualifications if he was able to succeed in the relevant examinations. However, once the school system was set in order and the various academic tracks established, the situation changed. "Ability" came to be tested and evaluated every day by the school system, and the result summed up in certificates. Further academic opportunity and access to professional qualifications came to depend on the correct "academic credential" rather than on an examination that directly measured ability. This was the change that evolved from the late 1890s to the beginning of the new century.

An article in the 1902 *Tokyo Yūgaku Annai* describes the change: "When you open your local newspaper and read a grand invitation to register at such and such a private school in Tokyo, you naturally feel like you want to get there as soon as possible and are already wondering how fast you can complete the course and how quickly you will achieve success, as if a lark had fallen ready-roasted into your mouth. But, readers, please realize that knowledge cannot be absorbed in our poor human brains as quickly as is claimed in the advertisements. How is it possible that one can achieve the same result in a private school from studying a foreign language, or any subject, for two or three months, or at the longest for a year, when a student at a government school studies the same subject for three to five years, step by step, in the proper order? If that were possible, who would bother to take the long journey through a public school where he has to work so hard?"

At the beginning of the Meiji period, when the age of examinations started, there were two ways to succeed in life. One was academic credentialism and the other academic ability. Which should be the main road? The government's answer was academic credentialism. But the work of building this "main road" did not proceed smoothly. There was a long period when, at each level of the system, the schools had to reevaluate the academic ability of the applicants for admission because they could not trust the diplomas of the lower levels. But that period of uncertainty was coming to an end. The age when one could take the regular course in order to move up socially, to advance step by step along the main road, had arrived.

The Examination Experience

Taking an Examination

Until now our discussion of the age of examinations has mainly focused on the system. The main objective has been to clarify the impact of this systematization of exams on the state, the society, and the schools. However, it is obvious that the rise of examinations also affected the everyday lives of the individuals who took them.

Autobiographies and biographies are a rich source of information through which we can understand the human impact of examinations in Japanese society of the Meiji era.

Hasegawa Nyozekan was an eminent journalist who was born in downtown Tokyo in 1875 and who had an active public life well into the mid-twentieth century. His *Aru Kokoro no Jiden* (Autobiography from the Heart) paints a vivid picture of the world of examinations around 1890. Hasegawa began his elementary education at the age of seven in 1881 and finished when he was twelve. Next he studied at Dōjinsha, a private school of the English language run by Nakamura Masanao. While at Dōjinsha, he did not have a clear personal goal for the future, and he did not study very hard. After failing in Dōjinsha's promotion exam, he moved to Kyōritsu Gakkō, another well-known private preparatory school. At this school students could skipped one grade if they performed well in the final examination, and, responding to the challenge, Hasegawa studied seriously and skipped a year. He only stayed at Kyōritsu for two years, however, and then he decided to follow his father's recommendation and become a lawyer.

It seems that his father, like most Edo merchants, did not like the clique from Satsuma and Chōshū that was running the country, and also despised the government's schools. So he enrolled his son, who was now an excellent student, in the preparatory course of the Meiji Law School rather than in the main stream which led from the First Higher School to the Imperial University. Hasegawa described his experience at the school as follows: "I was struck by the fact that all the students were grownups. If the age difference was not so great I would not have been so surprised, for I knew that the ages of students at many middle schools varied so widely that some of them looked like they were suitable for elementary school while others looked like today's university students. But at this preparatory course at Meiji the age gap between myself at fifteen and the oldest student was like that between a father and his son. And no wonder. Most of the students had long ago finished their early years of education and engaged in some kind of job before deciding to review law in preparation for the entrance examination."

Again, after staying less than one year, Hasegawa moved to the preparatory course of the Tokyo Hōgakuin (the present Chūō University). In the fall of 1889 he was transferred to the Tokyo English School, where he probably remained until 1893. While there, he also studied at Kokumin Eigokai (the National Society of English) and at Kokugo Denshūjo (Japanese Language Learning Center), two single-subject cram schools mentioned in *Tokyo Yūgaku Annai* as helpful in preparing for the licensing exam for middle school teachers.

After trying a variety of middle-level schools, Hasegawa finally passed the entrance examination and entered Tokyo Hōgakuin in July 1893. While he passed the second category examination, indicating his preparation was equivalent to that of a middle school graduate, once admitted, he found that the students who passed the examinations for the first and second categories attended the same classes. He had this to say about his fellow students: "I admired their efforts. Maybe because it was a private school, there was absolutely nobody I met who intended to discard his law training once he graduated and was there simply to pick up a diploma for his vita. Everyone seemed determined to utilize law as the foundation for his future." He presents a vivid picture of the purposefulness of the private law school in preparing ambitious youth for the national licensing examinaion. Hasegawa finally finished this school in 1898, taking five years because of a temporary absence due to illness. After all of that effort, however, he did not bother to take the bar exam for attorneys and moved instead into the world of journalism.

Next let us look at Yamazaki Kesaya, a well-known socialist lawyer, as an example of a private student who actually took the bar exam and became a practicing attorney (Morinaga 1972). Yamazaki was born in Nagano Prefecture in 1877 and completed his higher elementary schooling in 1892. Until 1899 he worked at his former school as a substitute teacher while also helping on the family farm and working at a silk mill run by his brother. Then in 1899 he went to Tokyo and passed the entrance examination of Meiji Law School (possibly after studying at a preparatory school for six months or so). Passing the examination was equivalent to completing the regular course of the middle school. Once admitted to Meiji, he completed the curriculum in two and a half years and graduated in July 1901. In November of the same year he also passed the examination to become a judge and prosecutor, and in December he passed the bar examination. Compared to Hasegawa, who after completing the elementary-level school wandered from one middle-level school to another and who took five years to complete the program of a law school, Yamazaki's navigation through the examination system was surprisingly efficient. If Yamazaki had remained a prosecutor, instead of choosing to practice as a lawyer after just three months in the position, his case would have been considered an ideal success story.

Effort in the Face of Difficulties

The individual most representative of the age of examinations is Noguchi Hideyo, whom I have already mentioned. Noguchi was born in Fukushima Prefecture in 1876 into an extremely poor farm family. Entering school in 1883, he completed his higher elementary schooling in 1893.

Nakayama Shigeru, the author of a biography of Noguchi, writes: "He rose to the fore from dire poverty by making maximum use of the examination system" (Nakayama 1978). While in elementary school, he was consistently outstanding in the examinations, which were still very competitive, and this enabled him to gain backing and support from his local community to help him move up. For example, though Noguchi was the son of a poor farmer, he was invited to study at the higher elementary school because a teacher who happened to be at the final examination for the lower elementary school was favorably impressed by his excellent performance.

Since Noguchi did not have sufficient means to support his dream of becoming a medical doctor, after completing the higher elementary school, he decided to study on his own for the medical examination while serving a medical practitioner as a *shosei*, or live-in working student. After three years of independent study, he went to Tokyo in 1896 to take the examination, and he scored very well in the first examination, which covered physics, chemistry, physiology, and anatomy. That was in October.

The examination for the second part, including a clinical demonstration as well as various professional subjects, was to be held in October of the following year. Noguchi recognized that independent study would not be enough to pass the second exam, so with financial support from a backer he studied at Saiseigakusha for half a year. Though only one out of twenty passed the second part of the examination, Noguchi managed to pass on his first try and to obtain the license for practicing medicine at the age of twenty. As it was usually considered necessary to spend at least three years preparing for the first examination and seven years for the latter, Noguchi obviously had an exceptional talent for taking examinations.

Nakajima Tokuzō was another student who did well on the examinations. At the height of his career Nakajima became the President of Tōyō University, but he is perhaps best known for his involvement in the so-called Tetsugakukan Incident, which took place in 1902. Tetsugakukan, the predecessor of today's Tōyō University, was one of the schools whose graduates were authorized to receive a middle school teacher's license without the licensing examination. In 1902 the Ministry of Education deprived Tetusgakukan of this privilege because the ministry officer who had been sent to observe the graduation exam found some of the questions Nakajima asked in his ethics examination to be based on "a subversive theory that is not acceptable to the national polity."

Nakajima was born in 1864, four years before the Meiji Restoration, into a farming family of Gunma Prefecture. At the age of ten he entered a newly established elementary school and was educated there until he was fifteen. Upon completion of the fourth grade of the higher elementary course and because of his excellent performance, he was hired as a substitute teacher for the school. While working as a substitute teacher, he also received one month of training at a teaching school and passed the examination for a license to teach in the regular course of the elementary schools.

Despite the poor circumstances of his family, in 1881, when he was eighteen, he was able to enter the prefectural middle school at Maebashi thanks to the recommendation and support of those who were impressed by his intelligence. There, with hard work, he completed the entire course in four years and graduated in February of 1885. His outstanding ability is well illustrated by the fact that during his first year he was able to advance from the eighth grade to the fifth; also, over the course of his studies he managed to obtain a license for teaching the middle grades.

Upon graduation from the middle school, he went to Tokyo with the promise of a four-year tuition grant from a wealthy patron, and there he brilliantly succeeded in his first attempt at the entrance examination for the preparatory course of Tokyo University. (Only seven out of eighty-eight who sat for the exam passed.) But soon thereafter his benefactor withdrew the offer of support, and Nakajima had to leave school again to become an elementary school teacher. Though by 1889 he had become a principal, he still could not suppress his passion for study. In the fall of the following year he took and passed the examination for the "nonregular course" (*senka*) in philosophy at the Imperial University's Faculty of Letters, and four years later he graduated from that institution.

The Nonregular Course of the Imperial University

The nonregular course, *senka*, was an important option for bright students like Nakajima who could not take the main road from the middle school to the higher school. Nishida Kitarō, a philosopher, was another who studied in this nonregular course (Takeuchi 1970). Born in 1870 into a landlord family of Ishikawa Prefecture, he entered elementary school at the age of five and graduated when he was twelve. After studying English and mathematics at a private school for one year, he succeeded in the entrance examination for the prefectural teaching school in the spring of 1883, soon after he had turned thirteen. He stayed at this school for slightly more than a year, eventually leaving due to poor health. Once he had recovered, he renewed his studies at a private preparatory school in the area, and was admitted in 1886 to an advanced grade of the Professional School of Ishikawa Prefecture. He became dissatisfied with the new atmosphere, however, when in the following year this school was reorganized as the central government's Fourth Higher Middle School. He left the school without completing the curriculum, and one year later entered the nonregular course of the Imperial University's Faculty of Letters. From this course, one could move to the regular course by passing all the subjects of the higher school graduation examination. Takane Yoshito, who became a law professor at the Imperial University of Kyoto, for example, entered the nonregular course in 1889 after graduating from Tokyo Professional School (the present Waseda University), and in 1891 he was admitted to the regular course by passing these examinations. Nishida, however, decided to complete the nonregular course.

Ogura Kinnosuke, a mathematician, was also one of those who was admitted to the nonregular course—though a bit later than Nishida. Born in Yamagata Prefecture in 1885, he entered his prefectural Shōnai Middle School in 1898. His family, which ran a shipping company, was relatively wealthy. Since he was not satisfied with his middle school education, he entered Tokyo Butsuri Gakkō in 1902 when he was a fourth grader. He found it difficult to study for extended periods of time in a conventional school, as he had to devote most of his time to the family business.

Tokyo Butsuri Gakkō, a well-known training school for middle school teachers, was easy to enter because it only required entrants to be over fourteen years of age with a practical understanding of arithmetic and a basic writing ability. In addition, almost all the classes took place in the evening. However, the school's promotion and graduation exams were said to be very difficult. According to Ogura, out of the two hundred eighteen students admitted in 1902 only twenty-four—eleven percent—graduated three years later (Ogura 1982). Ogura was among the small number who managed to do so. During this period Ogura also attended the private Taisei Middle School so he could obtain a middle school diploma. According to Ogura, "the fifth graders of middle schools in Tokyo then, especially at the private schools, only had their hearts set on passing the examinations." Despite playing hooky as often as possible, except for the physical education class where absence was strictly prohibited, Ogura managed to pass the middle school examination and pick up his second diploma.

After graduating from Tokyo Butsuri Gakkō, Ogura decided to try to get into the nonregular course in chemistry of the Faculty of Science of the Imperial University. Since the entrance examination included English along with chemistry and physics, he enrolled in a cram school for English. Six months later, he passed the examination, for which six had sat and only two passed. Ogura had to give up school after half a year, however, because of family circumstances.

Admission to the nonregular course was approved only when the number of students admitted to the regular course was less than the number of vacancies. While the classes were identical, the nonregular students obviously faced some discrimination. Nishida, for example, who attended the Faculty of Letters, writes in his memoirs that the nonregular course students, unlike the regular course students, had to read at desks in the corridor of the library since they were allowed neither to enter the stacks nor to read in the reading room.

The Road to Tokyo University

Thus far we have taken a look at several people who were able to move up by using the examination system, but now let us turn to those who took the main road from the higher school to the Imperial University.

Our first example is Nagaoka Hantarō, a physicist who was born to a samurai family from Nagasaki Prefecture in 1685, three years before the Meiji Restoration (Fujioka 1973). Nagaoka received his first lessons in Chinese classics at a fief school which he entered at the age of six. He entered an elementary school in 1874 in Tokyo, where his family had moved, but he failed in the promotion examination of this school. After studying English for a half year at the Kyōritsu Gakkō, he entered the government's Tokyo English Language School, a predecessor of the preparatory course for the Imperial University, when he was twelve. Nagaoka had an outstanding record in the monthly examinations there: it is said that he received the honor of moving up a grade at each examination. He was also raised in a favorable environment for study, since his father, a former samurai of the Ōmura clan, had been overseas with his lord prior to the Restoration and now was a high-ranking government official.

Due to his father's transfer, Nagaoka transferred to the government's Osaka English School, which later became the Osaka Middle School. In 1881 he passed the entrance exam and entered the first grade of the preparatory school of Tokyo University. As only nineteen of fifty-one students were able to complete the course after one year's study, Nagaoka undoubtedly was a bright student.

Upon graduating he enrolled in the Science Faculty of Tokyo University, from which he graduated in 1887. Despite a one-year absence, Nagaoka completed the course by the age of twenty-two. While at the university, he was also selected, in 1886, as "an excellent student to receive special treatment in the coming school year." The award consisted of tuition exemption plus an annual scholarship of from 48 to 72 yen, which was a substantial amount at that time. This "selection was by the faculty on the basis of his performance in the final examination."

Kishi Seiichi was born to a Matsue samurai family in 1867, two years later than Nagaoka. He entered a newly established elementary school in 1873, and graduated six years later, at the age of thirteen. He was always a top student and, according to his autobiography, on several occasions "received an honor or a book or stationery as a prize for his performance in the interschool competitive examinations that were held in the presence of a high government official" (Kishi 1939, 37).

In the same year that he graduated from elementary school, he passed the entrance exam for Matsue Middle School. This school at that time had a three-year course in Japanese and a four-year course in English. Kishi entered the English course, while also studying Chinese classics at a private school. He graduated in 1883 at the top of his class.

In the summer of that year, with aid from the prefectural government and following the advice of his father and brother, Kishi went to Tokyo to enroll at a preparatory school, Seiritsu

Gakusha. He also took private lessons in mathematics. In January of the following year, when he was seventeen, Kishi took the entrance examination for the Preparatory School of Tokyo University, and he was the only student out of 122 applicants to succeed. He was admitted to the second trimester of the second year of the three-year course. As he writes in his autobiography, "I took the exam for the second grade intending to save one year's tuition since I did not have much money."

Graduating in 1885, he moved to the Law Faculty of the Imperial University, from which he graduated four years later in 1889 with the second-best performance out of twenty-four. Immediately he started working as a licensed attorney; he was the eighth attorney in the country to have a B.A. in law. Later Kishi became a well-known non-governmental jurist.

The Road to the Imperial Universities

Onozuka Kiheiji, a scholar of political science who eventually became the president of Tokyo Imperial University, was born in 1870 to a wealthy family of Niigata Prefecture. It is said that he studied at a private school before he entered the local elementary school in 1877. He apparently received a special education, as he was considered a brilliant child. Finishing the eight-year curriculum in six years, he entered the private Nagaoka Middle School. In 1886, he enrolled at the Kyōritsu Gakkō in Tokyo to prepare for his entrance examination while also studying English at a private school. In 1887 he entered the Preparatory Course of the First Higher Middle School, and after completing both this and the Regular Course in the prescribed five years, he moved to the Law Faculty of the Imperial University in 1892. At the Law Faculty. Onozuka continuously competed for the top score with Hamaguchi Osachi, who later became prime minister. "This competition was called the battle between the First and Third Higher Schools as Onozuka was a graduate of the First Higher School while Hamaguchi was from the Third Higher School" (Nambara et al. 1963). Both were scholarship students.

The final example is Nagayo Matao, a medical scholar who later became another president of the Imperial University of Tokyo. He was born in Tokyo in 1878 into an elite family, as the third son of Nagayo Sensai, who was the Director of the Public Health Bureau of the Ministry of the Interior. Entering elementary school in 1885, he completed the ordinary elementary course in four years and transferred to Gakushūin. However, he stayed there less than a year before transferring to the Keiō Gijuku Yochisa (Keiō Gijuku's higher-school level preparatory course), from which he graduated in 1893 at the age of 16. Although graduates of the course usually entered the Keiō Gijuku regular courses, Nagayo chose a different route and enrolled himself in the third grade of a private institution. The school he chose was Seisoku Gakkō, which, after being founded in 1889 as a preparatory school, had become a middle school in 1892 and had a strong reputation for preparing students for entrance examinations.

After graduating from this school in March 1896, Nagayo took the entrance examination for the First Higher School. His biography describes the process in detail. The practice at the time, as Nagayo relates it, was for the higher schools to announce a list of the subjects, to be tested one week before the entrance examination. Nagayo had been concentrating his efforts mostly on subjects such as "chemistry, and the history of China and other countries," but "the six subjects listed on the noticeboard were English, Chinese classics, mathematics, Japanese history, the Japanese language, and physics." His preparation having been completely off course, he had to "study these subjects at the eleventh hour." Out of fourteen applicants from the Seisoku Gakkō, five including Nagayo were admitted.

Unfortunately, after he entered, he found that he was in the wrong course for preparing to become a medical doctor. So once again he left school, this time with the goal of learning German so he could enter the higher school appropriate for prospective medical doctors. The school gave him a note saying he could be readmitted if he succeeded in the German language exam. After he studied German with great intensity for two months at a private school, he succeeded in the exam. Three years later he entered the Medical Faculty, from which he graduated in 1904 at the age of twenty-six.

In his autobiography, he notes, concerning the examination at the Medical Faculty: "At the University then, unlike the contemporary University where students are simply required to pass a series of courses in order to graduate, there was a promotion examination for each grade, similar to those of the middle and higher schools. Additionally, during the last semester, there was a graduation examination on all the subjects studied during these four years." Though the diploma automatically entitled graduates to practice medicine without a licensing examination, the school nevertheless had the students take the medical examination before they graduated.

Chapter Ten

Examinations as a Way to Climb the Social Ladder

From the Samurai Class to the Commoners

The Desire to Move Up the Social Ladder

Michael Young, in *The Rise of Meritocracy*, states that merit can be expressed as IQ plus effort (Young 1958). Each person has his own intellectual capacity at birth, and this is measured and expressed as IQ. Merit, however, is determined not only by IQ but also by the amount of effort a person exerts. A meritocratic society, according to Young, is one in which an individual is evaluated in terms of his innate intelligence and the merit he has acquired through elements of effort.

The effort on which Young places importance is not only the exertions made by an individual, but also those of his parents and family (including their heritage). How much one develops his inborn intellectual ability and how widely he is able to utilize it largely depends on birth and upbringng, in respect of financial resources and social and cultural background. Not all families are alike: some are wealthy and place a high value on education, others do not; some poorer families also value education highly, while others do not. How much effort individuals with the same natural intellectual ability need to devote to intellectual competition differs according to their family circumstances. The examples we have considered in previous chapters of people who rose to high social positions through success in the examination system well illustrate the importance of this.

In the Meiji era, when a much smaller proportion of young people than today advanced beyond basic education and aspired to an occupation requiring success in the examinations, individual effort undoubtedly had a much more important impact than did family support. What motivated individuals to devote extraordinary effort to pass the examinations was their strong desire to move up in a society that admired success. We should not overlook the fact, however, that the desire for success comes not only from the individual but also from his social background (Takeuchi 1978; Kinmonth 1981). In other words, the class or social group of the individual has a powerful influence on the quality of his or her participation in the competition.

Which class or social group made the best use of the examination system? Various materials show that the former samurai class — that is, the former ruling class — was the first to take advantage of this system. The Japanese population structure in the early Meiji era consisted of six percent samurai, eighty percent peasants, and the remainder from the commercial, industrial, and artisan classes. But the majority of those studying at the various schools were from the samurai class. This is best illustrated by looking at the government schools, where strict admission procedures were observed (see Table 2).

For example, eighty-four percent of those admitted to the Law School of the Ministry of Justice in 1880 were from the former samurai class, while only sixteen percent were commoners. Similarly seventy-two percent of the students of the Engineering College in 1885 were from the samurai class, and of the seventy who graduated from the Sapporo College of Agriculture between 1880 and 1885, fifty-three (seventy-six percent) were from the samurai class. The pattern was the same at Tokyo University: in 1882 seventy-one percent of those studying at the preparatory course of the university were from the samurai class, and seventy-four percent of all the students in the Faculties of Law, Science, and Letters were also from the samurai class. In the Faculty of Medicine, however, from the early days commoners made up a large proportion of the students, and already by 1882 the share of the samurai class had decreased to forty-six percent, less than half.

Even in 1900, approximately thirty years after the Meiji Restoration and a quarter century since the new school system had been implemented with the proclamation of the *Gakusei*, the number of students from the samurai class was still remarkably high. It is doubtful that this was because the children of the former samurai class were blessed with an exceptionally high

Table 2. Social Class of Graduates of Higher Educational Institutions

	1890		1895		1900	
	Samurai	Com-moners	Samurai	Com-moners	Samurai	Com-moners
Imperial universities	63.3	36.7	59.0	41.0	˙ 50.8	49.0
Higher schools	61.6	38.4	59.3	40.7	47.7	42.3
National government professional schools						
Medicine	35.0	65.0	35.2	64.8	27.3	72.7
Commerce	49.1	50.9	48.0	52.0	43.0	57.0
Engineering	71.4	28.6	54.2	45.8	55.9	44.1
Agriculture	48.1	51.0	39.5	60.5	28.6	71.4
Local government professional schools						
Medicine	27.6	72.4	13.6	86.4	24.0	76.0
Private professional schools						
Medicine	26.6	73.4	24.0	76.0	25.1	74.0
Law	27.7	72.3	32.9	67.1	34.1	65.9
Liberal Arts & Sciences	59.8	40.2	44.1	55.9	35.3	64.7

Notes:
1. Based on the government's Official Gazette.
2. Figures for national government professional schools are based on the number of graduates for the year.
3. Figures for local government professional schools are based on the number of registrations for medical practice for the year.
4. Figures for private professional schools are derived as follows: for medicine, the number of candidates who passed, in addition to the qualifying examination for medical practice, the accreditation examination for opening a private clinic; for law, the number of successful candidates in the Higher Civil Servants, Judicial Officers and Attorneys national examinations; for liberal arts and sciences, the number of successful candidates in the Middle School Teachers Certification Examination.
Source: Amano, 1989.

intellectual capacity. While it is known that a high proportion of intelligence is inherited, for centuries individuals had entered the samurai class by birth and not because of their high intelligence. In the early Meiji era, the former samurai had the advantage of a better educational background, albeit in traditional studies. But thirty years after the restoration, the effect of that advantage should have been lost. What remained was the strength of their desire to rise socially: the drive to succeed in life enabled the children of the former samurai class to make the necessary effort (Kinmonth 1981).

The Children of the Former Samurai Class

It was undoubtedly the samurai class whose social status was most significantly affected by the Meiji Restoration. They lost their hereditary claim to work and to stipends, becoming in effect unemployed. Some of them tried to find their way in agriculture, commerce, or craft industries. Instead of these traditional occupations, however, many in the samurai class aspired to take up the new occupations which emerged as full-scale modernization unfolded and new systems were created. A critical feature of these new occupations was that most required the qualifications that come from school education.

The modernization of underdeveloped countries like Meiji Japan is usually carried out by creating small islands of modernity—government offices, industrial enterprises, schools, and the like—in the midst of the large ocean of traditional society, and then gradually enlarging these islands. If we can borrow an image Ronald Dore uses in *The Diploma Disease*, admission to these islands required a "passport" in the form of academic credentials (Dore 1976, 8). In order to obtain this passport, a strict screening for qualifications is imposed, and an examination system is often relied on for this screening. The sons of the former samurai class were attracted to this examination system because of its promise of the diplomas which would be their passports to jobs in the modern sector. The various government schools, with Tokyo University at the top, played the role of passport agencies for these ambitious young people of the former samurai class who had scholastic ability but no economic power.

In the government schools modeled after France's *grandes écoles*, such as the Engineering College and the Law School of the Ministry of Justice, the students were, as a rule, subsidized by the government and were guaranteed high-ranking posts upon graduation. While no post was promised students of Tokyo University, nearly sixty percent of its graduates in the three faculties of law, science, and letters received support from the government. Admission based on examinations was rigorous, but once students were admitted, both their student livelihood and their future upon graduating were virtually guaranteed.

Another noteworthy feature of the youth from the samurai class was that they clearly considered a career in public organizations as their first choice. They preferred the University to professional schools, government schools to private schools, and courses of study which led to bureaucratic careers over those leading to an independent profession such as medical doctor. In other words, they preferred the schools and faculties which promised the greatest privileges both while at school and after graduating. These preferences played an important role in creating a ranking among schools and departments, thereby intensifying the competition in examinations and crystallizing the academic credential system.

The Children of Commoners
As the mid-1880s approached, the government began to modify its policy of choosing ambitious youth with high intellectual ability and providing them with financial support for their studies. One after another, government schools started to decrease the number of scholarship students; some schools abolished scholarships altogether. In 1885, sixty-five percent of the students of Tokyo University in the departments of law, science, engineering, and letters were sponsored by the government, but the next year this system was discontinued. Simultaneously, tuition was suddenly raised two hundred fifty percent (from 1 yen to 2.5 yen).

Why was there such a policy change? While one of the reasons was surely the financial difficulties being experienced by the government, a more important reason is reflected in remarks made by Hamao Arata, a high-ranking officer of the Ministry of Education, which appeared in the July 5, 1885, issue of the magazine *Kyōiku Jiron* (Current Views on Education).

What would be necessary from that time on, said Hamao, was "to accept for university training only those who have at least a middle school education and sufficient economic resources, while it is unnecessary to strain ourselves to give the poor the opportunity for education, for they obviously cannot achieve a truly professional approach as their minds always tend to focus on their monthly salary, which is their only means to maintain their livelihood." Fukuzawa Yukichi of Keiō Gijuku expressed a similar opinion.

According to Fukuzawa, schools should be divided into two kinds based on the wealth and ability of the students. Those who wished to advance to the higher schools should be the sons of wealthy and upright families such as rich merchants and land-lords or former high-ranking samurai. Fukuzawa believed it was quite natural for economic power to determine who should re-ceive educational opportunities—for a family with wealth and educational zeal to buy its sons superior education while a family with less wealth had access to education at a middle level (Yasu-kawa 1970, 264-65).

Yet during the Edo period, when the samurai class enjoyed the position of ruling class and practically monopolized the opportu-nities for higher education, there were not a few farmers, mer-chants, and craftsmen who sought education, both to improve their livelihood and to raise their level of learning. Many com-moners learned the "three R's" and even went on to study the Chinese classics or Japanese classical literature at the temple schools and private academies. And once modernization started, the commoners' desire for education obviously grew stronger. New knowledge and skills became necessary in order to take advantage of the new products and systems which were intro-duced in quick succession. It was only a matter of time before the commoners began to challenge the dominance of the former samurai in the modern school system where the new knowledge and skills were systematically taught. Actually, from the begin-ning, more than half of the students at the medical departments of the public and government schools were the sons of common-ers. Even before the Restoration, medicine had been the most important intellectual occupation open to commoners, and now with modernization an entirely new body of knowledge and skills was expected of medical doctors.

With freedom of occupational choice now assured, there was a steady increase in the number of applicants from the common-ers' class to high-level institutions in every field, not just medi-cine. However, the educational desires of the commoners were not as closely connected to the desire for a diploma as were those of the samurai. The occupations in the modern sector of govern-ment offices, schools, and the professions required a diploma as an indication of occupational qualification, and this gave the rigorous examinations their meaning. The sons of the former samurai class, now "unemployed," dedicated themselves totally to passing these examinations so they could enter one of these new occupations. However, the commoners, especially the more affluent such as the wealthy farmers and merchants who already possessed a family business and hereditary wealth, had less need to struggle for a diploma or an occupational qualification, although education was needed for their children.

This can be seen in the types of schools and departments to which they sent their offspring. The commoners' sons preferred private schools to government schools, liberal arts education to professional education, and an easy course to a regular course.

As Fukuzawa said, those with wealth could buy their children superior education. (Table 3 lists the costs of schooling at several Tokyo institutions.) But superior education was not necessarily equated with specialized education leading to a diploma and an occupational certificate. At the government schools such as the Imperial University, students received superior professional education leading to a diploma, and this diploma became their passport to modern jobs. But the passport was absolutely useless for succeeding in a family business. On the contrary, the children who obtained such a passport might never return to their family business. In fact a comparison of the native place and residence of the graduates from higher educational institutions during this time shows that very few with such diplomas returned to their home towns (Amano 1965).

From the Periphery to Tokyo
During this period most of the modern-sector organizations, including government offices, private enterprises, and advanced educational institutions, were concentrated in Tokyo. In other words, Tokyo was a microcosm of modern society floating in the midst of the large ocean of traditional society. The young people who wanted to experience "modern times" directly and who wanted to acquire new knowledge and skills swarmed to this center from all over the country. At the end of 1888 there were more than ninety private schools of some note and thirty thousand students in Tokyo, most of whom were from other parts of the country. For example, at Keiō Gijuku, which was relatively popular with the Tokyo elite, only nineteen percent of the students were Tokyo-born; this compares with eleven percent at Saiseigakusha, ten percent at the Tokyo Professional School, and only six percent at the Meiji Law School.

Many of these students from other parts of Japan studied very

Table 3.   Monthly Educational Expenses (1898)

Institution	No. of years required for graduation	Monthly tuition/ fees (yen)	Personal expenses/ allowance		Accommodation	Total	Books
Imperial University	3	2.50	High	6.00	9.00	17.50	1.00
			Middle	5.00	8.00	15.50	1.00
			Low	4.00	7.00	13.50	1.00
First Higher Middle School	3	2.00	High	5.60	9.00	16.60	1.00
			Middle	4.10	8.00	14.10	1.00
			Low	3.60	7.00	12.60	1.00
Commercial High School	3	20.00 (annual lump sum)	High	5.60	9.00	16.26	1.00
			Middle	4.10	8.00	13.76	1.00
			Low	3.60	7.00	12.26	1.00
Tokyo Engineering School	3	15.00 (lump sum paid twice)	High	5.60	9.00	17.10	1.00
			Middle	4.10	8.00	14.60	1.00
			Low	3.60	7.00	13.10	1.00
Keiō Gijuku	5	10.00 (paid three times p.a.)	High	5.60	9.00	17.10	1.00
			Middle	4.10	8.00	14.60	1.00
			Low	3.60	7.00	13.10	1.00
Tokyo Professional School	3	1.80+0.6	High	5.60	9.00	17.00	1.00
			Middle	4.10	8.00	14.50	1.00
			Low	3.60	7.00	13.00	1.00
Meiji Law School	3	1.3	High	5.60	9.00	15.90	1.00
			Middle	4.10	8.00	13.40	1.00
			Low	3.60	7.00	11.90	1.00
Tokyo Metropolitan Middle School	5	1.5	High	5.60	9.00	16.10	1.00
			Middle	4.10	8.00	13.60	1.00
			Low	3.60	7.00	12.10	1.00
Tokyo Metropolitan Women's High School	4	1.0	High	5.60	9.00	15.60	
			Middle	4.10	8.00	13.10	
			Low	3.60	7.00	11.90	
Atomi Women's School	4	3.75	High	5.60	9.00	18.35	
			Middle	4.10	8.00	15.85	
			Low	3.60	7.00	14.35	

Extracted from *Kyōiku Jiron* (Current Education Report), September 15, 1898. The preamble to the table states that it is provided to give a general idea of costs for tuition and personal and other expenses, since some students "...indulge in drinking, some frequent the licensed quarters, and lead a dissolute life not appropriate to students.... Such students are talented in making excuses, and with the false explanation that they are required to buy more books" they manage to get their parents to "quite unknowingly support them in lavishing money on drinking."

hard under adverse conditions to obtain a passport out of the traditional society and into the modern sector. However, the majority were young people whose wealthy parents wished to buy them superior education. These affluent youths tended to choose private law schools as a source of modern education, but they had little interest in the examination for becoming a government or judicial officer.

For example, the positive reception given to the Rules for Special Students which were issued by Meiji Law School in 1888 is a good indication of the numbers of young people of this kind who were pursuing their studies in Tokyo. According to the fifty-year history of the school, upon payment of two hundred yen as three years' tuition, the school would "take responsibility in supervising and taking care of the students so that they can complete their study and go home with honors." The school was concerned that "not a few students from other parts of the country wander around Tokyo enjoying themselves, drinking and wenching while arguing about the state of the world, and end up failing to complete their studies." The plan evidently appealed to a number of parents: thanks to its wide subscription the school's management became stable. It was hard on the students, however: the school managed their money, giving each only the "necessary amount" each month; and the dean of students stayed in a room near the dormitories in order to keep an eye on them.

The July 5, 1897, issue of *Kyōiku Jiron* describes an independent company created for the same purpose. The advertisement for this non-profit company, Tokyo Gakushi Hoken Kaisha (Tokyo School-Expense Trust Company), declared: "For your son's successful study in Tokyo, we will manage the money you send and pay tuition so that you can keep your son from addiction to dissipation and from excessive freedom. Without any commission, we will introduce your son to a good school and will become your son's guarantor. We will also assume responsibility for informing you about your son's conduct and academic progress."

The Stabilization of the Examination System

The "new" middle class in any country shows the strongest desire for higher education and is especially oriented to the competitive schools that open the doors to the professional occupations and the higher civil service (Amano 1982). Though the "old" middle class of affluent merchants and farmers with their family businesses and private wealth recognized that the intelligence and status associated with education enhanced an individual's social desirability, education was not usually necessary for maintaining or improving their social status. This was not true, however, for the new middle class, whose members worked in various types of organizations and whose occupational qualifications were obtained through national licensing examinations. The members of the new middle class had neither a family business nor private wealth to pass on to their children. Their social status could only be maintained by educating their children to pass the examinations for obtaining a superior academic credential (a diploma) and the appropriate occupational certification. And conversely, the personnel for the new middle class of civil servants, the staffs for public and private enterprises, and the professional groups, including teachers—especially in Japan, where modernization started late—could only be produced through the school and examination systems.

The various government schools have functioned mainly as organizations to produce this new middle class. These schools carried out the education of staff for modern organizations and professions, mainly by attracting the sons of the former samurai class, who lacked a family fortune or business. In contrast, many of the old middle class used private schools to acquire culture, studying law, political science, or economics rather than professional subjects, and after completing their studies most went back to their home towns to inherit their family business or launch a new venture.

When looked at in terms of the examination system, the early 1900s can be said to have been a time of great transition in the relationships between examinations and the school system and various social groups and classes. Not only did the school and examination system become firmly rooted and the number of people receiving a school education rapidly increase, but Japan's modern sector embarked on its industrial revolution at this time, and the number of new middle-class jobs in that sector rapidly expanded. Of greatest significance was the increase in private enterprises and hence the increase in the number of white-collar workers that were required. A mere increase in the number of public sector and professional jobs would have led to but modest expansion in the scale of the modern sector and the new middle class. Due to industrialization and the demand for this new class of office workers, both the modern sector and the new middle class began to experience sustained growth.

This change also had a great impact on the school and the examination system, for Japanese schools, and particularly the universities and professional schools, were the chief suppliers of the rapidly expanding office-worker class (Amano 1982, ch. 9). Unlike government organizations, private enterprises often do not demand a diploma or occupational license when selecting staff for employment. In Japan, however, private enterprises adopted the policy of employing individuals based on school careers; more precisely, Japanese businesses sought recruits with specific diplomas. Moreover, they based salaries and promotions on each employee's academic history and diploma. The diplomas which were given the most value and preference were those awarded by the schools that were hardest to enter and graduate from—in other words, those whose entrance examinations were the most difficult.

Already by the early 1900s the second and even the third generations of the new middle class, who were largely from the former samurai class, were ready to enter school. In addition, an increasing number of the old middle class started to utilize the schools and the examination system in pursuit of new occupations and higher social status. Just around the corner was the period when the craze for advanced education, especially at schools with prestigious diplomas, would become attractive to a widening social stratum, leading to an overheating of the examination competition.

Two Roads to the Examinations

The Main Road

So far we have focused on who participated in the newly created school and examination system. But how many could leap the hurdle of the examinations and win the race in the age of examinations?

There were two distinct roads through the examination system. One was to build an impressive academic career by passing the series of examinations that were part of the school system. The second was to bypass the school system and aim directly at the qualification examinations. Because of strong criticism, in the late 1890s examinations were eliminated as the basis for promotion and graduation in the elementary schools, and admission by examination was postponed until young people entered a middle school. From then until a student completed the Imperial

University, a series of examinations continued to determine entrance, promotion, and graduation. Let us first look at the admission by examination process for the middle school.

At the middle school level, sixty to seventy percent of applicants were admitted to some school through entrance examinations, with a competition ratio of approximately 1.7. The actual number admitted was about seven thousand in 1893 and slightly over thirty thousand in 1902, which is less than one-third of the number admitted to today's national universities. During this period, those admitted to the middle schools were already a carefully selected group. Furthermore, an 1898 Ministry of Education survey shows that only fourteen percent of those admitted had only the minimum required six years of elementary education; nearly half had eight or more years.

What awaited those who were admitted was an even harder process of selection. For example, from a starting middle school class of one hundred in 1900, only fifty had advanced to the fifth grade four years later in 1904. This means that half either failed or dropped out. Undoubtedly, the examinations were not the only reason for these losses, but it certainly was one of the most important factors.

An evaluation method based on absolute scores was used at the middle school during this period. One could neither advance to a higher grade nor graduate unless his average score was no less than 60 and the number of failing subjects was less than a prescribed number. Moreover, if the same grade had to be repeated more than once, the student was expelled. Finally in 1902 the number of graduates of the middle schools came to slightly exceed ten thousand.

The competitive entrance examination for higher schools was even harder. The admission rate up to 1899 was about fifty percent, including various affiliated courses such as the departments of medicine. After 1900, when the higher schools began to focus only on the university preparatory course, the admission ratio dropped below forty percent. According to a survey of 1903, of those admitted only sixty-three percent of those who passed the entrance examination had come directly from a middle school (see Table 4). The remainder had had to spend a year or more studying before they passed; ten percent spent two or more years. Students in isolated parts of the country found it essential to abandon their local schools and move to Tokyo to study at a private middle school or a private preparatory school in order to acquire sufficient ability to pass the entrance examinations.

Table 4.   Admission Rates to Major Schools (%)

	Middle[1] schools	High[2] schools	Medical schools	Commercial high schools	Engineering high schools
1893	70.8				
1894	72.5				
1895	66.3	66.4			
1896	71.3	56.4		38.5	31.8
1897	69.4	45.8		35.4	30.7
1898	63.4	48.7		33.9	26.6
1899	61.5	49.3		26.6	35.4
1900	60.0	37.2	61.6	22.7	29.1
1901	58.6	32.9	48.2	23.2	28.1
1902	59.6	35.7	46.6	23.2	25.2

Source: Ministry of Education Yearbooks.
Notes:
1.   Figures for the years 1893 and 1894 are for public schools only.
1985 figures include public and private schools.
2.   Figures for the years 1895-99 include medical, law, and engineering departments, in addition to university preliminary course admissions.

In 1902 there were about sixteen hundred students who were successful in moving to one of the national higher schools. Once admitted, the journey through the higher schools was not as perilous as that through the middle schools. Still, thirty to forty percent either failed or dropped out. The total graduating in 1902 was about nine hundred. Advancement and graduation were all determined by examinations.

In principle, advancement from a higher school to the Imperial University did not require an entrance examination. But this principle could not always be observed. The higher school had three divisions: the first division prepared students in law and letters, the second prepared them for engineering, science, agriculture, and pharmacy, and the third focused exclusively on medicine. Since the number admitted to each division was determined in relation to the capacity of the Imperial University, repeated examinations to select students for the universities were unnecessary. When too many applicants from the first or second division focused on a particular university course, however, selection became necessary. To accommodate such a development, in 1896 a regulation was issued stating: "When the number of applicants surpasses the number expected by a faculty of the university based on its capacity, admission should be determined based a competitive examination covering the subjects taught in the university preparatory course." In 1904 at the Engineering Faculty of Tokyo Imperial University, the number of applicants was fifty over the limit. The time when yet another entrance examination would be necessary between the higher schools and the university was just around the corner.

The examination system in the universities was also quite demanding. As in the higher schools, advancement and graduation were based on the results of examinations which attempted to evaluate mastery relative to some absolute criterion. Unless the average score of semester and final examinations was at least 60, unconditional advancement and graduation were not approved. If a student failed he had to retake all the subjects. Two continuous years of failure resulted in expulsion.

In courses such as law, engineering, medicine, and veterinary medicine, where the diploma also served as a license for professional practice, the respective faculties had their own examination rules. For example, at the Medical Faculty the graduation examination extended over half a year from September to March and covered three major subject areas—anatomy and physiology, surgery and ophthalmology, and internal medicine and obstetrics. The graduation examination of the law school, which included an oral examination, was also very difficult. A special examination committee was selected at a faculty meeting, and at least two members of the committee had to be present for each oral examination.

Since the list of graduates was ranked in order of performance on this graduation examination, the annual catalogue of the Imperial University clearly revealed who did best. The top graduate was also awarded a silver watch by the Emperor.

Various Bypasses

What we have just looked at was the so-called main road for social mobility through passing the examinations of the school system. Even in the early 1900s, fewer than one thousand were able to reach the end of this road and become alumni of the Imperial University.

It took seventeen or eighteen years to graduate from a university, counting from the time a youth began elementary school, if there were no interruptions. Even among the students of the Imperial University, where only the brightest students were accepted, there were students who had repeatedly failed and retaken the examinations before passing and gaining entry (*rōnin*) and repeaters, so the average age of freshmen was twenty-two to twenty-three, and the average graduate was twenty-six to twenty-seven. Counting from the time of entering elementary school, many young people spent some twenty years in the school system. A student needed economic support, intellectual ability, physical strength, and above all extraordinary ambition and perseverance to reach the vaunted goal.

With the development of the school system, however, various bypasses emerged alongside the main road leading from middle school to higher school to the Imperial University. And these bypasses provided opportunities to those who did not have sufficient time, money, ability, or ambition to walk the main road.

One bypass led through a government professional school in commerce, engineering, or medicine. By 1902 there were about twenty of these schools, and they admitted approximately two thousand students—more than the number admitted to the higher schools. As in the case of the higher schools, entry to these schools required a proof of graduation from a middle school, though graduation from a vocational school was also acceptable. In general, the entrance examinations were not as difficult as those for the higher schools; however, the competition for admission to the Tokyo Commercial Higher School (Tokyo Kōto Shōgyō Gakkō) and the Tokyo Engineering Higher School (Tokyo Kōto Kōgyō Gakkō) became as stiff as that for admission to the academic higher schools as the status of these schools improved and the number of applicants increased.

Though it was a bypass, this route swung progressively closer to the main road as the graduates of these government and public schools received the privilege of exemption from the license examination for medical doctors and middle school teachers, on a par with the graduates of the Imperial University. By 1902, the number of graduates of these schools was approximately one thousand, or slightly above the total for the Imperial universities.

Another bypass was the private school. According to the statistics compiled for 1904, thirty-six of these schools met the standards outlined in the Professional Schools Law, and they admitted sixty-five hundred students to their regular courses with an overall competition rate of 1.2. Approximately seventy percent of the regular-course students had completed middle school education, and the rest passed an equivalency examination. In the same year, these schools graduated about fifteen hundred students from their regular course, and the graduates were entitled to the various privileges accorded the graduates of government and public schools.

According to these statistics, the number admitted only to the regular courses of the private professional schools exceeded the number admitted to all of the government and public schools, and the number of graduates was about the same. Over thirty percent of those admitted to the private schools had completed only the higher elementary school, but through independent study had acquired ability equivalent to a middle school graduate. In addition to the regular courses there were other private schools and courses with no requirements whatsoever. Until the mid-1890s, these open schools had been the mainstream of the private sector, and even as late as 1902 many schools retained that system. From the beginning these schools and courses had been established as preparatory schools for national licensing examinations, so they did not have their own entrance or graduation examinations. While the scale of operation of these schools is not clear, it is apparent that from the mid-1890s they rapidly declined relative to the "regular" courses.

We have, then, a rough indication of the number of people who successfully managed to travel the road of examinations within the school system. Let us now look at the situation of the occupational licensing examinations.

The Civil Service and the Legal Profession
First let us look at the national examinations for the civil service profession, which was considered to be the best path for getting ahead during this period. Table 5 shows the numbers of those who succeeded in the various national licensing examinations. We have already studied the origin of these examinations. The examination for attorneys was revised in 1893, and in 1894 the

examination for administrative officials was also revised, while in the same year the examination for foreign service officers was instituted.

Table 5. Education of Those Who Passed the Examinations for Official Positions

	Administrative Officers		Foreign Service Officers		Judicial officers		Attorneys	
	Imperial Univ.	Other	Imperial Univ.	Other	Imperial Univ.	Other	Imperial Univ.	Other
1888	11	0			37	9	*	41
1889	15	4			13	13	*	50
1890	44	5			24	42	*	132
1891	18	-			18	20	*	201
1892	*	-			-	-	*	108
1893	*	-			-	67	*	59
1894	0	6	3	1	79	44	0	28
1895	25	12	4	1	49	22	2	29
1896	41	9	5	1	66	33	1	15
1897	25	29	3	4	45	42	1	29
1898	23	18	3	5	31	81	4	88
1899	22	9	2	6	56	51	5	39
1900	40	18			18	77	1	47
1901	18	24	1	4	25	81	5	63
1902	28	13	2	4	31	138	2	91

*Not known.
Sources: Spaulding 1967, Okudaira 1913, Hata 1981, and Ministry of Education annual statistics.

Until 1893 the numbers in the columns for judicial officers, attorneys, and administrative officers from the Imperial University indicate the graduates who were employed or who obtained their licenses without taking these examinations. The graduates of the Imperial universities, despite being exempt from the examinations, showed relatively little interest in becoming attorneys and also gradually began to sidestep the examination for the foreign service. With few exceptions, their eyes were focused on the civil service. They were so determined to become higher civil servants that, if they once failed the exam, they would repeat it rather than become judicial officers, which would have been possible even without taking an examination.

In 1900, for example, of the hundred twenty-nine graduates from the Law Faculty, twenty-three became administrative civil servants, eighteen became judicial officers, eleven went to private enterprises, and the majority—fifty-eight—had been graduate students, so they could repeat the civil service examination the following years. Actually, one-third of the Imperial University graduates who succeeded in the exam to become civil servants between 1900 and 1902 had spent at least a year preparing to retake the exam (Hata 1981).

The gateway to the higher civil service, the pinnacle of success, was not automatically open even to the graduates of the Imperial universities. The rate of passing the examination for employment of Imperial University graduates between 1894 and 1901 was forty-seven percent, or only one out of two. For other applicants, the gate was much narrower. At the preliminary examination two-thirds were dropped, and finally only six percent of the applicants passed the main examination (Spaulding 1967, 131). Three hundred sixty found employment in the executive civil service between 1894 and 1902, for a yearly average of forty. Among these, sixty-two percent were graduates of Imperial universities, thirty-four percent were from private law schools, and only four percent came from other backgrounds. Half this four percent were graduates of government institutions of higher education such as the commercial and normal schools, and the remaining half were those who succeeded with no more formal education than middle school. The graduates of private law schools, the second most successful category, found it almost impossible to pass directly upon graduation, and most spent a number of years preparing for the examinations.

Graduates of private law schools found the gateway to becoming judicial officers and attorneys much wider. From 1894 to 1902, for example, while the average annual number of those other than Imperial University graduates who succeeded in the civil service examination was about fifteen, sixty-three passed the judicial officer examination and an average of forty-eight passed the examination for attorneys.

Nevertheless it was not easy to pass these examinations. Seventy-four percent of the judges and prosecutors who began working between 1891 and 1895 passed an interlude of two years or more between graduation and employment; similarly, sixty-one percent of those employed between 1896 and 1900 spent at least a two-year interlude. Generally the applicants spent this interlude preparing for the exams.

In the 1894 examination for attorneys, twenty-eight of eight hundred ninety-five applicants, or only three percent, passed (Okudaira 1971, 816). In 1897, when the names of the schools of successful applicants were made available, it became evident that nine of the forty-two candidates who passed the examination for judges and prosecutors had been enrolled at two or more schools; four of the twenty-eight who passed the examination for attorney had attended two or more schools. Obviously, many of those who sought to pass these examinations enrolled in more than one private law school in order to prepare.

To conclude this discussion of the national licensing examinations, let us consider the careers of the 5,651 graduates of the seven private law schools from the time of their founding until 1897. Only 990 (17.5 percent) engaged in occupations for which a license examination was required, of which 139 were higher civil service officers (2.5 percent), 387 were judges and prosecutors (6.8 percent), and 464 were lawyers (8.2 percent). In comparison, of the 1,368 graduates of the law faculties of the Imperial universities, 375 were higher civil service officers (27.4 percent) and 300 became judges and prosecutors (21.9 percent). The sharp contrast between the main road and the bypass is apparent.

Medical Doctors and Middle School Teachers
From the early years, the government sponsored public training organizations to prepare medical doctors and allowed the graduates of these organizations to practice medicine without taking a licensing examination. The graduates from the Medical Faculty of the Imperial University and the eight other public and government institutions were insufficient to meet the demand, however, and even at the turn of the century many doctors received their training at private schools and had their qualifications validated by the licensing examination. Table 6 shows the figures for those who obtained their medical license on the basis of their educational backgrounds or by passing the qualifying examination. The figures show that there were consistently more who qualified by examination: sixty-five percent in 1890, and ten years later, in 1990, still sixty-three percent.

Looking at the average annual number of newly licensed medical doctors during the ten years between 1891 and 1900, we find that fifteen were university graduates, three hundred were graduates of government medical training institutions, and as many as four hundred seventy obtained their licenses through the qualifying examination.

Thus the licensing exam accredited about five hundred doctors annually, far more than those graduated from medical institutions. These doctors naturally received some kind of education before taking the licensing examination. As we have already seen, most of them obtained their medical education at private medical schools; to be more precise, they studied at private preparatory schools for the licensing examination. These schools, unlike the private law schools, were not full-scale institutions for higher education where systematic professional education was provided.

Table 6.   Qualification Routes for Medical Practitioners and Pharmacists

| | Medical Practitioners | | | Pharmacists | | |
Year	Universities	Private Medical Schools	Licensing Examination	Universities	Private Medical Schools	Licensing Examination
1886	865	476	3,745			
1887	1,041	753	4,072			
1888	1,155	1,134	4,680			
1889	1,287	1,310	5,215			
1890	1,340	1,621	5,595	142	-	2,547
1891	1,367	1,928	6,046	150	-	2,542
1892	1,422	2,307	6,373	152	14	2,550
1893	1,428	2,504	6,621	154	16	2,575
1894	1,433	2,800	7,065	158	48	2,619
1895	1,437	3,068	7,478	162	81	2,696
1896	1,462	3,343	7,874	165	100	2,754
1897	1,470	3,666	8,467	165	124	2,797
1898	1,482	4,082	9,232	165	142	2,851
1899	1,503	4,525	9,884	166	161	2,940
1900	1,514	4,929	10,779	165	197	3,000

Source: Ministry of Health and Welfare, *Eighty-Year History of the Medical System*, 1955.

It was only after the enactment of the Law on Medical Doctors of 1906 that a systematic four-year medical education at a formal medical school conforming to the guidelines of the Professional School Law was recommended for those seeking to become medical doctors. At the same time, the graduates of private medical schools that could meet acceptable standards were given the privilege of a license without an examination. Finally, in

1916 the licensing exam for medical doctors was completely abolished.

Essentially the same pattern can be observed in the case of dentists and pharmacists. The pharmaceutical course of the Imperial universities and the government schools for medicine trained only a small number of pharmacists, so in 1890 ninety-five percent of those who obtained a license did so by passing the examination, and even in 1900 the proportion was virtually unchanged (eighty-nine percent). The number who succeeded in the examination was also low, averaging forty-six a year between 1890 and 1900. Most were from private pharmacy schools designed specifically for the licensing examination, and in 1910 their graduates were given the privilege of practicing without taking the licensing examination so long as the schools conformed with the Professional School Law. For the profession of dentistry, there was neither a formal public institution for professional education nor a private preparatory school for the examination. Even the licensing examination system was not established until 1906. To become a dentist, the aspirant usually underwent a lengthy apprenticeship or took a short, simple course (Ministry of Health and Welfare, 1955, 153).

Until the early 1900s, the gateway to becoming a middle school teacher was wide open to those who took the examination based on ability. The government recognized several formal training organizations for middle school teachers, including the government higher schools for teaching and the various other government institutions for higher education, including even the Imperial universities. One of the principal early functions of the Tokyo Commercial Higher School and the Tokyo Engineering Higher School was to train teachers for the vocational middle schools. Almost all of these government schools were authorized to give their graduates the privilege of becoming middle school teachers without taking the licensing examination.

These government schools could not provide enough teachers, however, so the government attempted to fill the shortage by establishing temporary teacher training courses. Even this measure was not enough, and a considerable proportion of the teachers had to be recruited from those who passed the licensing examination.

According to a survey in 1904, thirty-nine percent of the middle school teachers were still unlicensed, and of the 1,882 licensed teachers, exactly half had been licensed through the examination.

Until 1898, there was not much difference between the numbers licensed by the examination and without the examination; from 1899, however, those licensed without the examination began to dominate. This is because from 1899 on the Ministry of Education extended to private professional schools the privilege of licensing without an examination (see Table 7). Up to that time, most of the teachers licensed by the examination had studied at private professional schools and miscellaneous schools.

Table 7.   Licensing of Middle School Teachers

Year	Private professional school graduation (exempt from examination)	Licensing examination	Success rate in licensing examination (%)
1893	157	156	21.2
1894	174	148	21.2
1895	172	165	20.3
1896	230	163	17.5
1897	264	207	19.1
1898	248	289	19.9
1899	418	359	17.1
1900	505	375	12.8

Source: Sakurai 1942, 288, 374-5.

We have already seen that there were many preparatory schools for training teachers at that time in Tokyo. A report on middle school teachers in Tokyo of this period lists a surprising variety of schools that appeared on the vitae of those who obtained teaching licenses, including Kokumin Eigakkai (National English Society), Seisoku Eigo Gakkō (Seisoku English School) and Eastlake English Conversation School; Kokugo Denshujo (Japanese Language Teaching Center), Nishō Gakusha, and Kokugakuin for studying Japanese language; the Tokyo Butsuri Gakkō (Tokyo Physics School) and Junten Kyugōsha for studying mathematics. In the late 1890s, as many as three hundred each year who did not even have a diploma from a middle school but had acquired ability at these preparatory schools succeeded in the licensing examination; however, four out of five who took the examination failed.

Towards the Institution of Entrance Examinations

The Death of Murray

David Murray, who in his commencement speech at Tokyo University in 1877 had emphasized the importance of examinations as a step to measure progress in education and society, returned to the United States in 1879. Many years later, in 1905, he died at the age of seventy-five, without revisiting Japan. This was precisely the time when the Japanese school system was consolidating Murray's proposal and beginning to move into a new phase in the institutionalization of examination.

As we have seen so far, a variety of examination systems entered Japan, which had no history or tradition in these matters, and took root in an extremely short time, becoming an indispensable institution for both school and society. Murray, who continued to be interested in Japan, must have died with a sense of great satisfaction that his ideal had been realized.

Of course, the examination system was not without its problems or critics. By the mid-1880s, as we have seen, criticism arose concerning the elementary school examinations, and in the 1890s the Ministry of Education began making efforts to improve them. Though not as strong, similar criticism was heard concerning the middle school system. And with respect to the Imperial universities, a book titled *Tōzai Ryōkyō no Daigaku* (The Universities in Two Major Cities, Tokyo and Kyoto) made quite a stir. This book focused on the examination system as one of the major differences between the two Imperial universities, and went so far as to say: "What kills a person in Tokyo Imperial University is its examination system. The examination system there is more harmful to the students than opium is to the human body" (Zanba 1903). There were also calls at this time for reforming the examination system for employing government officers and the licensing examinations for the medical and legal professions.

These criticisms, however, were insignificant compared to the fatal flaw in the examination system that was to reveal itself at the end of the 1890s. The excesses of the elementary school examination system had been substantially alleviated by then. While there was still a tough selection process for admission by examination at the advanced levels of the education system, this problem only affected a handful who aspired to join the elite and it was considered a matter of course that they should endure this hardship, since they would enjoy great privilege later. Even though unqualified optimism for examinations had disappeared, very few doubted that they were an indispensable means for the progress of education and society.

The Graduation Examination and the Entrance Examination

The fatal flaw mentioned above is the emerging need to introduce entrance examinations. A situation emerged in Japan that had not been faced in the West.

Competitive entrance examinations were not unknown in the West. The intensity of France's *grandes écoles* examination, for one, was well known. But in no country except Japan did entrance examinations to higher education institutions play such a critical role in a student's future, after he had completed an accredited course of advanced secondary education. In the West, a certificate showing success in the middle-school graduation examination was required to advance to the universities. If the West could be described as the home of graduation examinations, Japan gave birth to entrance examinations. Japan, which had imported its examination system from the West, naturally was familiar with graduation examinations. We have already observed that the *Gakusei* regulations included several rules on graduation examinations. But special graduation examinations did not take firm root in Japan, though in principle a diploma from an elementary or a middle school was meant to guarantee admission to a middle or higher school without examination. Why then didn't this guiding principle, which had been clearly defined in the regulations of each school, hold fast? Several reasons can be suggested.

First, schools of all levels were established simultaneously in Japan, so the schools at the higher levels could not count on standardized quality of students from lower-level schools. They had to establish their own entrance standards based on the educational programs they sought to carry out. It was to ensure the admission of appropriately trained students that the entrance examination started. In this sense, the entrance examination could be regarded as a transitional strategy for selecting students in the early stages of establishing the system. But it was not abolished even after elementary and secondary education became well organized and the standard of academic ability of the students at these levels became generally high. Careful examination of the situation reveals that the root of the problem lies in the very structure of the country's education system.

Izawa Shūji, a prominent advocate for the reform of the educational system during this period, employed a helpful metaphor: The school system of Japan was formed from two streams. "The head" was the university while the "tail" was the elementary schools, and various problems resulted from the imperfect connection between these two parts (Izawa 1958, 49-50).

The university started as a training institution for the elite, who were the support and driving force for modernization. At the university, the learning of the West was taught directly in Western languages. This university, for the sake of Japan's national pride, could not be academically inferior to the universities of the West, which is why the standard of academic ability required of the students was set so high. Regardless of the level of education in the schools below the university, this standard had to be upheld in order to equal the West. The difficult entrance examinations of the middle and higher schools were indispensable as a means of bridging the wide gap between the high standard required by "the head" and the variable standards of "the tail." And while the entrance examination system provided a link between these two parts, it had to be fortified by lengthy preparatory education including the preparatory schools and the extra years of study after graduation before attempting the examination.

A second factor seems to have emerged from the chain of events following from the early policy of limiting admission to the middle and higher schools. At the early stages in the founding of the school system, those who sought education at the elementary schools, to say nothing of the middle schools and universities, were mainly the sons of the samurai class. But as soon as the general public came to realize that schools were the most important route to success in life, the number seeking higher education began to increase rapidly, with wealthy commoners in the lead. Especially in the late 1890s and early 1900s, the number of youths seeking higher education but unable to enter higher schools began to increase. The Proposition Regarding the Establishment of Higher Schools and Imperial Universities, which was introduced to the House of Peers in January 1899, for example, presents a harsh criticism of this situation, observing: "With the recent progress in education, increasingly large numbers try to enter the higher schools and then the universities after completing middle school, but not infrequently the aspirations of these youths are betrayed because of the limited capacity of the higher schools" (Abe 1932, 86). But the government, facing a financial pinch, could not easily support major increases in the capacities of the upper level schools, particularly the higher schools and the universities. Proposals to expand the government's higher educational institutions were repeatedly submitted to the Imperial Diet. The five original higher schools were only increased to seven by the mid-1990s, and there were only two Imperial universities, one in Tokyo and another in Kyoto. An entrance examination became indispensable to respond to the surging wave of students preparing themselves for higher education.

Change in the Entrance Examination

These are some of the reasons the entrance examination, which originally had been thought of as a transitional measure, became so deeply rooted in the Japanese school system. This did not occur without public criticism of the increasingly severe competition to pass the examinations. The following comments are from the Diet Record for February 1902: "By the time they finish elementary school and try to enter middle school, they usually spend an extra year or two preparing for the competitive examination, and prior to entering the higher school from middle school, they usually spend one or two extra years. . . . Only a small number graduate from universities at the age of twenty-four or twenty-five while many graduate at twenty-seven or twenty-eight. Some even graduate when they are over thirty." In the discussions of the Lower House of March 1907 there was more sharp criticism of the situation: "After finishing the middle school graduation examination, the very next day they have to begin to prepare for the competitive entrance examination with their exhausted and battered brains. It is no wonder that only one out of ten of those young people pass. Even among those living in the Tokyo metropolitan area are many unfortunate students who have been taking the entrance examination for a higher school each year for five to seven years."

Despite such criticisms, most concerned observers did not think the problem lay with the entrance examination itself. Indeed, the criticism of the entrance examination presented to the Imperial Diet was part of a larger argument for the reform of the school system and the expansion of educational opportunities. The shortage of capacity was thought to be the major problem, not the entrance examination itself. At the time, both the nature and the degree of severity of the problem of entrance examinations were quite different from the situation that the nation would experience later on. It was not until the end of the decade that the situation with regard to entrance examinations began to change.

What brought this change? The most important factor was the full-scale institutionalization of academic credentialism. As we have already seen, the regulations relating to the employment of civil servants were the first instance of stressing particular academic careers. Similar privileges were extended to those studying at government schools who wanted to become medical doctors and teachers, and the education system itself gradually placed more and more stress on educational background in assessing qualifications for admission to courses and eligibility for examinations. In other words, while ability to pass examinations was initially all that was required to seek various occupational and educational opportunities, as the school system developed, the individual's academic career became more important than any specific test of ability. The granting of the privilege of exemption from various licensing examinations to the better private schools furthered the reliance on academic credentials.

The decision by Japanese enterprises to stress the importance of the applicant's diploma when considering him for employment, however, played the most critical role in the institutionalization of academic credentialism. Since professional education is one of the main objectives of higher education in modern societies, it is quite natural that educational background should be linked with the qualifying standards for professional occupations and for the employment of government officials. Indeed, it is desirable from the standpoint of social justice that some objective process such as academic achievement become a condition for qualification. Credentialism, in this sense, was first established in Western countries, and Japan only transplanted the foreign practice to its soil. But the reliance on academic credentials for recruitment to the business world is different. In the European countries of the late nineteenth century, it was unusual for university graduates to be employed as business staff members. The graduates of higher educational institutions usually became professionals or government officials and almost never entered business.

Academic Careers and the Age of Entrance Examinations

Japan was different. Japanese businesses from the very beginning of the modern period aggressively recruited so-called *gakkōde* (graduates of higher educational institutions), and these graduates did not resist becoming white-collar workers. An important reason for this must be the special character of Japanese modernization. In contrast to the European countries, modernization started late in Japan, and there were no places except the schools to train the populace in the necessary knowledge and skills for operating such modern organizations as factories and offices; the graduates of higher schools from the beginning looked to the business world as an acceptable goal for their ambitions. In fact, quite a few of the graduates of the Imperial universities, to say nothing of the graduates of such professional schools as Keiō Gijuku, Tokyo Commercial Higher School, and Tokyo Engineering Higher School found employment in private businesses, especially those belonging to the *zaibatsu* groups. Thus from an early stage, the school an individual attended came to be regarded as a job qualification not only for government and professional jobs but also for the world of business.

Indeed, it might be said that Japanese businesses placed even greater reliance on an applicant's academic career than did the public sector. While the academic career was important in the case of government offices, employment examinations were also usually relied on. Unless candidates passed the examination, regardless of whether they held a diploma from an Imperial University or not, they could not join the civil service; conversely, if an individual succeeded in the examination, even if his academic credentials were weak he could obtain a government position. However, in business applicants usually did not have to face the hurdle of an employment examination. It was only during the 1920s that enterprises began to make use of employment examinations in hiring workers, but these examinations stressed a variety of skills along with academic ability. And the possession of an appropriate diploma was a precondition for being eligible for these examinations. Furthermore, in the eyes of a particular enterprise, diplomas were not all accorded the same value. Each enterprise made its own decisions about the preferred academic careers of its employees, and these decisions shaped a host of decisions from recruitment to promotions and salaries.

It was some time after the early 1900s, when significant numbers of graduates of high-level educational institutions chose to become white-collar workers in business rather than enter the bureaucracy or the professions, that people came to hold some general concept of the ranking of different educational backgrounds. The yardstick for this ranking was the severity of the selection process at each stage along the path from entrance to graduation from a school. In a country where a system of qualifying graduation examinations never took root, it was reasonable that the toughness of an institution's entrance examination was taken as the most concrete indication of its quality and the basis for selection of employees.

If companies use an individual's educational background, including consideration of the ranking of the institution which issued his graduation certificate, as the basis for selection of employees and determination of their starting salaries, then people seeking a career in business will naturally compete to enter a school recognized as the most advantageous gateway to his chosen field. The race for a better career intensifies as a society becomes more industrialized, as growing numbers of applicants seek to enter companies requiring more highly developed skills. In Japan it was in the first decade of the 1900s that the school entrance examination clearly began to function as the starting gate in the race for a higher-level career. It became evident that the practice had become deeply rooted in the nation's basic social structure, and that measures such as reform of the educational system or increasing the number of student places could not cope with the problem.

In 1905, the same year that Murray died in his American homeland, Japan was entering a new phase in the Age of Examinations. Over the years the leaders of Japan had actively adopted and implemented the examination system as a means to promote the advancement of education and society, in the very manner that Murray had stressed in his address at Tokyo University. They had been sucessful—perhaps too successful—in institutionalizing examinations. As Japan moved into the second decade of the twentieth century, the first signs of its peculiar "examination hell" were appearing. It may be that Murray, had he lived long enough to hear of the problems caused by the promotion of examinations for Japanese education, would not have been altogether pleased with his handiwork.

Bibliography

Abe Isō (ed.). *Teikoku Gikai Kyōiku Giji Sōran* (Record of Educational Debates in the Imperial Diet), Vol. 2. Tokyo: Kōseikaku Shoten, 1932, pp. 86-87.

Abe Shigetaka. *Kyōiku Kaikakuron* (The Reformation of Education), 1937; reprint edition, Tokyo: Meiji Tosho, 1971.

Akagi Akio. *Rangaku no Jidai* (The Period of Dutch Studies). Tokyo: Chūō Kōron Sha, 1980, pp. 32-33.

Amano Ikuo. *Kindai Nihon Kōtō Kyōiku Kenkyū* (Higher Education in Modern Japan). Tokyo: Tamagawa University Press, 1989.

Amano Ikuo. "Kindai Nihon ni okeru Gaikokuhō no Juyō to Hōgaku Kyōiku no Seiritsu" (The Acceptance of Foreign Law in Modern Japan and the Establishment of Legal Education), *Nagoya Daigaku Kyōiku Gakubu Kiyō* (Journal of the Faculty of Education, Nagoya University), Vol. 18, 1971.

Amano Ikuo. "Kindai Nihon ni okeru Kōtō Kyōiku to Shakai Idō" (Social Mobility and Higher Education in Modern Japan), *Kyōiku Shakaigaku Kenkyū* (Journal of Educational Sociology), No. 24, 1965.

Amano Ikuo. *Kōtō Kyōiku no Nihonteki Kōzō* (The Structure of Japanese Higher Education). Tokyo: Tamagawa University Press, 1986.

Amano Ikuo. *Kyōiku Kaikaku o Kangaeru.* (On Educational Reform). Tokyo: University of Tokyo Press, 1985.

Amano Ikuo. *Kyōiku to Senbatsu* (Education and Selection). Tokyo: Dai-ichi Hōki Shuppan, 1982.

Amano Ikuo. *Kyūsei Senmon Gakkō* (Professional Colleges in the Prewar Educational System). Tokyo: Nihon Keizai Shinbunsha, 1978, pp. 57-63.

Amano Ikuo. "Nihon ni okeru Kyōiku Kakushin no Keifu to Kanōsei" (The Heritage and Future of Educational Reform in

Japan). In Kōno Shigeo and Shinbori Michiya (eds.), *Kyōiku Kakushin no Sekaiteki Dōko* (International Trends in Educational Reform). Tokyo: Gakken, 1979.

Amano Ikuo. "Tokyo Daigaku no Meiji Jūnen" (Tokyo University in 1877). UP, December 1977.

Aries, Philippe. *L'enfant et la vie familiale sous l'ancien régime* (The Culture of Childhood). Paris: Editions du Seuil, 1960.

Asō Makoto. *Daigaku to Jinzai Yōsei* Universities and Skill Development). Tokyo: Chūō Kōronsha, 1970.

Asō Makoto. *Erīto Keisei to Kyōiku* (Education and the Making of Elites). Tokyo: Fukumura Shuppan, 1978.

Asō Makoto and Amano Ikuo. *Education and Japan's Modernization*. Tokyo: Japan Times Co., 1983.

Asō Makoto and Ushiogi Morikazu (eds.). *Gakureki Kōyōron* (The Utility of Educational Credentials). Tokyo: Yūhikaku, 1977.

Azumi Koya. *Higher Education and Business Recruitment in Japan*. New York: Columbia University Teachers College Press, 1970.

Bledstein, Burton. *The Culture of Professionalism*. New York: W. W. Norton, 1976, p. 271.

Bowman, Mary Jean. *Educational Choice and Labor Markets in Japan*. Chicago: University of Chicago Press, 1981.

Cummings, William K. *Education and Equality in Japan*. Princeton: Princeton University Press, 1980.

Cummings, William K., Amano Ikuo, and Kitamura Kazuyuki (eds.). *Changes in the Japanese University*. New York: Praeger, 1979.

Curtius, Ernst Robert. *Die französische Kultur* (French Culture). Stuttgart/Berlin: Deutsche Verlags-Anstalt, 1930.

Dore, Ronald P. *The Diploma Disease: Education, Qualification and Development*. London: Allen & Unwin, 1976.

Dore, Ronald P. *Education in Tokugawa Japan*. Berkeley: University of California Press, 1965.

Durkheim, Émile. *L'evolution pédagogique en France*. Paris: Presses Universitaires de France, 1938. Quotations from the translation by Peter Collins: *The Evolution of Educational Thought*. London: Routledge & Kegan Paul, 1979.

Ebina Kenzō. *Sapporo Nōgakkō* (Sapporo Agricultural College). Tokyo: Tosho Shuppan, 1980, p. 125.

Etō Jun. *Sōseki to Sono Jidai* (Sōseki and His Era), Part 1. Tokyo:

Shinchōsha, 1970, p. 56.

Fujioka Yoshio (ed.). *Nagaoka Hantarō Den* (Biography of Nagaoka Hantarō). Tokyo: Asahi Shinbunsha, 1973.

Fujiwara Yoshiki. *Kindai Nihon Kōtō Kyōiku Kikan Chiiki Haichiseisakushi Kenkyū* (Regional History of Japanese High School Education in the Modern Period). Tokyo: Meiji Tosho, 1982, p. 167.

Fukaya Masashi. *Gakurekishugi no Keifu* (The Lineage of Credentialism). Tokyo: Reimei Shobō, 1969, p. 182.

Fukuzawa Yukichi. *Fukuō Jiden* (The Autobiography of Fukuzawa Yukichi). Quotations from the English translation by Kiyooka Eiichi. Tokyo: Hokuseidō, 1960, pp. 80-81. Fuse Shōichi. *Ishi no Rekishi* (A History of Medical Practitioners). Tokyo: Chuokoronsha, 1979.

Fuse Shoichi. *Ishi no Rekishi* (The History of Physicians). Tokyo: Chūō Kōronsha, 1979.

Gaxotte, Pierre. *Histoire des Francqis* (History of the French People). Paris: Flammarion, 1958.

Hata Ikuhiko. *Senzenki Nihon Kanryōsei no Seido, Soshiki, Jinji* (Japan's Prewar Bureaucratic System: Organization and Personnel). Tokyo: University of Tokyo Press, 1981.

Hirakawa Sukehiro. *Mateo Ritchi Den* (Biography of Matteo Ricci). Vol. 1. Tokyo: Heibonsha, 1969, pp. 100-122.

Hirakawa Sukehiro. *Seiyō no Shōgeki to Nihon* (The Western Shock and Japan). Tokyo: Kōdansha, 1974, pp. 46-53.

Horimatsu Buichi. "Meiji Zenki ni okeru Shōgakkō Shikenhō no Jittai" (The Reality of Elementary School Examination Procedures in the Early Meiji Period). *Kyōikugaku Kenkyū*, Vol. 38 No. 2, 1971.

Inoue Yoshimi. *Nihon Kyōikushisō Shi no Kenkyū* (Studies in the History of Japanese Educational Thought). Tokyo: Keisō Shobō, 1978.

Ishida Takeshi. *Nihon no Seiji Bunka* (Japan's Political Culture). Tokyo: University of Tokyo Press, 1970, pp. 104-107.

Ishidoya Tetsuo. *Nihon Kyōinshi Kenkyū* (A History of Japanese Teachers). Tokyo: Kōdansha, 1967, p. 223.

Ishikawa Matsutarō. *Hankō to Terakoya* (Fief and Temple Schools). Tokyo: Kyōikusha, 1978.

Itō Hitoshi. *Nihon Bundan Shi* (Japan's Literary Circles: A History), Vol. 1. Tokyo: Shinchōsha, 1952.

Iwata Ryūshi. *Gakurekishugi no Hatten Kōzo* (The Structure and Development of Academic Credentialism). Tokyo: Nihon Hyōronsha, 1981.

Izawa Shūji. "Kokka Kyōiku no Keitai" (The Form of National Education). In *Izawa Shūji Zenshū* (The Complete Works of Izawa Shūji), 1958, pp. 49-50.

Kaigo Tokiomi. *Inoue Kowashi no Kyōiku Seisaku* (The Educational Policies of Inoue Kowashi). Tokyo: University of Tokyo Press, 1968, p. 226.

Karasawa Tomitarō. *Kōshinsei* (Recommended Students). Tokyo: Gyōsei, 1974.

Kawakami Takeshi. *Gendai Nihon Iryōshi* (A History of Medical Care in Modern Japan). Tokyo: Keisō Shobō, 1965.

Kinmonth, E. H. *The Self-made Man in Meiji Japanese Thought.* Berkeley: University of California Press, 1981. Kishi Seiichi. *Kishi Seiichi Den.* Tokyo, 1939.

Kobayashi Tetsuya. *Society, Schools, and Progress in Japan.* London: Pergamon Press, 1978.

Koike Kazuo and Watanabe Yukirō. *Gakureki Shakai no Kōzō* (Credentialism and Society). Tokyo: Tōyō Keizai Shinpō-sha, 1979.

Kokuritsu Kyōiku Kenkyūjo (ed.). *Nihon Kindai Kyōiku Hyakunenshi* (One Hundred Years of Modern Education in Japan), Vol. 3: *Gakkō Kyōiku 1* (School Education 1), 1974.

Kokuritsu Kyōiku Kenkyūjo (ed.). *Nihon Kindai Kyōiku Hyakunenshi*(One Hundred Years of Modern Education in Japan), Vol. 4: *Gakkō Kyōiku 2* (School Education 2), 1974.

Koma Toshirō. "Tekijuku — Ogata Kōan." In Naramoto, *Nihon no Shijuku.*

Kurasawa Takashi. *Gakusei no Kenkyū* (The Educational Ordinance). Tokyo: Kōdansha, 1973.

Kurasawa Takashi. *Kyōikurei no Kenkyū* (A Study of Education Law). Tokyo: Kōdansha, 1975, pp. 219-222.

Kurihara Shin'ichi. *Fenollosa to Meiji Bunka* (Fenollosa and Meiji Culture). Tokyo: Rokugei Shobō, 1968, pp. 118-119.

Kuroha Ryōichi. *Rinkyōshin: Dōnaru Kyōiku Kaikaku* (The Ad Hoc Council on Education: Prospects for Educational Reform). Tokyo: Nihon Keizai Shimbunsha, 1985.

Kyōiku Zasshi. Number 82, 1878, Appendix, pp. 1-63.

Kyōikushi Hensankai (Editorial Committee for Educational

History) (ed.). *Meiji Ikō Kyōiku Seido Hattatsushi* (History of the Development of Japanese Education System Since the Meiji Restoration), Vol. 1, 1938, p. 118.

Maki Masami. *Nihon Kyōin Shikaku Seidoshi Kenkyū* (The Development of the System for Certifying Teachers). Tokyo: Kazama Shobō, 1971, Chs. 1 and 2.

Masumi Junnosuke. *Nihon Seitōshi Ron* (The History of Japanese Political Parties), Vol. 2. Tokyo: University of Tokyo Press, 1966, pp. 26-27.

Matsukuma Toshiko. *Nitobe Inazō*. Tokyo: Misuzu Shobō, 1969, p. 57.

Matsuura Juntarō. "Meiji Shonen no Shotō Kyōiku" (Education at the Beginning of the Meiji Period). In *Kyōiku Gojūnenshi* (Fifty-Year History of Education), Kokumin Kyōiku Shōreikai, 1922.

Meiji Bunka Zenshū (The Complete Collection of Meiji Culture). Tokyo, 1950.

Ministry of Health and Welfare. *Ishi Hachijūnenshi* (Eighty Years of Professional Medicine). 1955.

Mitamura Taisuke. *Naitō Konan*. Tokyo: Chūō Kōronsha, 1972.

Montgomery, R. J. *Examinations*. London: Longman, 1965.

Mori Ōgai. *Nihon Iryōron* (On Japanese Medicine). Reprinted in Vol. 27 of *Ōgai Zenshū* (Complete Works of Mori Ōgai). Tokyo: Iwanami Shoten, 1957.

Morinaga Eizaburō. *Yamazaki Kesaya*. Tokyo: Kinokuniya Shoten, 1972.

Morokuzu Nobuzumi. *Shōgakkō Kyōshi Hikkei* (The Indispensable Book for Primary School Teachers), 1873.

Murakami Tetsumi. *Kagaku no Hanashi* (About Science). Tokyo: Kōdansha, 1980.

Nagai Michio. *Higher Education in Japan: Its Take-Off and Crash*. Tokyo: University of Tokyo Press, 1971.

Nagao Tomiji. "Puroisen Ōkoku ni okeru Han-kakumeiteki Chūtō Kyōiku Seisaku" (Anti-Revolutionary Secondary Education Policy in the Prussian Empire). In *Sekai Kyōikushi Taikei* (World Educational History), Vol. 24: *Chūtō Kyōikushi 1* (Secondary Education 1). Tokyo: Kōdansha, 1975.

Nagayo Sensai. *Shōkō Shishi* (A Private History), 1904.

Nakayama Shigeru. *Noguchi Hideyo*. Tokyo: Asahi Shinbunsha, 1978.

Nakayama Shigeru. *Rekishi to shite no Gakumon* (History as a Science). Tokyo: Chūō Kōronsha, 1974.

Nakayama Shigeru. *Teikoku Daigaku no Tanjō* (The Birth of the Imperial University). Tokyo: Chūō Kōronsha, 1978.

Nanbara Shigeru et al. (eds.). *Onozuka Kiheiji: Hito to Gyōseki* (Onozuka Kiheiji: The Man and His Career). Tokyo: Iwanami Shoten, 1963.

Naramoto Tatsuya (ed.) *Nihon no Shijuku* (Private Schools in the Tokugawa Period). Kyoto: Tankōsha, 1969.

Narita Katsuya. *Igirisu Kyōiku Seisakushi Kenkyū* (The History of British Educational Policy). Tokyo: Ochanomizu Shobō, 1966.

Nihon Bengoshi Rengōkai (ed.). *Nihon Bengoshi Henkakushi* (The Transformation of the Legal Profession), 1959.

Nihon Iji Shinpōsha (ed.). "Hasegawa Shin Sensei" (Professor Shin Hasegawa). In *Kindai Mei-i Hitoyo-banashi* (Accounts of Famous Modern Physicians), 1937.

Noda Yoshio. *Meiji Kyōikushi* (A History of Education in the Meiji Period). Tokyo: Ikueikai, 1907, p. 247.

Ogura Kinnosuke. *Sūgakusha no Kaisō* (The Making of a Mathematician). No. 14 of *Nihonjin no Jiden* (Autobiographies of Japanese). Tokyo: Heibonsha, 1982.

Ōkubo Toshikane. *Nihon no Daigaku* (The Japanese University). Tokyo: Sōgensha, 1943, p. 104.

Okudaira Masahiro. *Nihon Bengoshishi* (A History of the Japanese Legal Profession), 1913; reprint edition, Tokyo: Gennandō Shoten, 1971.

Organization for Economic Cooperation and Development. *Reviews of National Policies for Education: Japan.* 1977.

Ōsawa Kenji. "Tōei Chūgo" (A Speech by Lawplight). In *Nihon Kagaku Gijutsushi Taikei* (Comprehensive History of Japanese Science and Technology), Vol. 8: *Kyōiku 1* (Education 1). Tokyo: Dai-ichi Hōki Shuppan, 1964.

Ōta Yūzō. *Eigo to Nihonjin* (English and the Japanese). Tokyo: TBS Britannica, 1981, p. 82.

Passin, Herbert. *Society and Education in Japan.* New York: Columbia University Teachers College Press, 1965.

Piobetta, J.-B. *Les institutions universitaires en France* (French Universities). Paris: Presses Universitaires de France, 1961.

Ringer, Fritz K. "Cultural Transmission in German Education

in the 19th Century." In Karabel and Halsay (eds.), *Power and Ideology in Education*. Oxford: Oxford University Press, 1977, p. 540.

Ringer, Fritz K. *The Decline of the German Mandarins*. Cambridge: Harvard University Press, 1974.

Ringer, Fritz K. *Education and Society in Modern Europe*. Bloomington: Indiana University Press, 1979.

Rohlen, Thomas P. *Japan's High Schools*. Berkeley: University of California Press, 1983.

Sakai Toshihiko. *Sakai Toshihiko Den* (Autobiography). Tokyo: Chukō Bunko, 1978.

Sakurai Mamoru. *Chūgakkō Kyōikushi Kō* (History of Middle School Education). 1943, p. 140.

Sakurai Mamoru. *Chūtō Kyōikushi Kō* (History of Secondary Education). 1942; reprint edition, Tokyo: Rinsen Shoten, 1975.

Shimizu Yoshihiro. *Shiken* (Tests). Tokyo: Iwanami Shoten, 1957.

Shimura Kyōichirō. "Furansu Chūtō Kyōiku no Anshan Rejīmu" (The Ancien Régime and France's Secondry Education). In *Sekai Kyōikushi Taikei* (World Educational History), Vol. 24: *Chūtō kyōiku shi 1 (Secondary Education 1)*. Tokyo: Kōdansha, 1975.

Shinbori Michiya. *Gakureki* (Educational Credentials). Tokyo: Daiamondsha, 1966.

Sonoda Hidehiro. "Gakurekishugi no Rekishiteki Kigen" (Historical Review of Academic Credentialism). In *Gakureki Kōyōron* (Essays on Credentialism). Tokyo: Yūhikaku, 1976.

Spaulding, Robert M., Jr. *Imperial Japan's Higher Civil Service Examinations*. Princeton: Princeton University Press, 1967.

Takahashi Korekiyo. *Takahashi Korekiyo Jiden* (Autobiography). Tokyo: Chūō Bunko, 1975 (reprint), pp. 172-73.

Takahashi Toshinori. *Nihon Kyōiku Bunkashi* (A Cultural History of Japanese Education), Vol. 1. Tokyo: Kōdansha Gakujutsu Bunko, 1978.

Takano Kiyoshi. "Kangien — Hirose Tansō." In Naramoto, *Nihon no Shijuku*.

Takenaka Teruo. "Kokka Shiken Seido to Teidai Hōka Tokken-"(The National Examination System and the Imperial University Law Faculty), in Motoyama Yukihiko (ed.), *Teikoku*

Gikai to Kyōiku Seisaku (The Imperial Diet and Education Policy). Tokyo: Shibunkaku Shuppan, 1981, pp. 393-394.

Takeuchi Hiroshi. *Kyōsō no Shakaigaku: Gakureki to Shōshin* (The Sociology of Competition: Educational Credentials and Career Success). Kyoto: Sekai Shisōsha, 1981.

Takeuchi Hiroshi. *Nihonjin no Shussekan* (The Japanese Idea of Success). Tokyo: Gakubunsha, 1978.

Takeuchi Yoshitomo. *Nishida Kitarō.* Tokyo: University of Tokyo Press, 1970.

Têng Ssu-Yü. "Chinese Influences on the Western Examination System." *Harvard Journal of Asiatic Studies,* Vol. 7, 1943.

Terasaki Masao and Sakai Yutaka. "Tokyo Daigaku Shozō Shiritsu Hōritsu Gakkō Tokubetsu Kantoku Kankei Shiryō" (Materials on the Special Administration of Private Law Schools at Tokyo University). *In Tokyo Daigakushi Kiyō* (Journal of the History of the University of Tokyo), No. 3, 1980.

Tezuka Yutaka. "Shihōshō Hōgakkō Shōshi 1 –3" (History of the Law School of the Ministry of Justice 1, 2, 3), *Hōgaku Kenkyū,* Vol. 40, Nos. 6–7, 1967.

Toita Tomoyoshi. *Kyūsei Kōtōgakkō Kyōiku no Seiritsu* (The Establishment of the Prewar High Schools). Tokyo: Minerva Shobō, 1975, pp. 112, 115.

Tsunogae Hiroshi. "Igirisu no Sangyō Kakumei to Chūtō Kyōiku Kaikaku" (England's Industrial Revolution and the Reform of Secondary Education). In *Sekai Kyōikushi Taikei* (World Educational History), Vol. 24: *Chūtō Kyōikushi 1* (Secondary Education 1). Tokyo: Kōdansha, 1975.

Uchida Tadasu. *Meiji-ki Gakusei Kaikaku no Kenkyū* (The Reform of the Meiji Education Ordinance), 1968, p. 235 (privately published).

Ueyama Yasutoshi. *Doitsu Kanryōsei Seiritsu Ron* (The Establishment of the German Bureaucracy). Tokyo: Yūhikaku, 1964.

Uno Toshikazu. "Itō Hirobumi." In Tōyama Shigeki (ed.), *Kindai Nihon no Seijika* (Political Leaders of Modern Japan). Tokyo: Kōdansha, 1964, pp. 121-123.

Ushiogi Morikazu. *Gakureki Shakai no Tenkan* (Educational Credentials: Society at a Turning Point). Tokyo: University of Tokyo Press, 1978.

Vogel, Ezra. *Japan As Number One.* Cambridge: Harvard University Press, 1977.

Wada Yoshikazu. "Bunkan Senkō Seido no Hensen 3" (Evolution of the System for the selection of Civil Servants), *Shiken Kenkyū*, No. 13, July 1955, p. 56.

Watsuji Tetsurō. *Jijoden no Kokoromi* (An Attempt at Autobiography). Tokyo: Iwanami Shoten, 1961.

Yasuhara Yoshihito. *Oxford Daigaku ni okeru Yūtō Gakui Seido no Seiritsu* (The Establishment of Oxford University's Honor System), *Daigakushi Kenkyū*, Tokyo: 1981.

Yasukawa Hisanosuke. *Nihon Kindai Kyōiku no Shisō Kōzō* (The Structure of Modern Japanese Educational Thought). Tokyo: Shin Hyōronsha, 1970, pp. 264-265.

Yokoo Takahide. "Gakui Seido no Kigen" (The Origin of the Degree System), *Daigaku Ronshū*, Vol. 5. Hiroshima Daigaku Daigaku Kyōiku Kenkyū Center, 1977.

Yoshimura Tadashi. *Gendai Seiji ni okeru Kanryō no Chii* (The Position of Civil Servants in Modern Politics). Tokyo: Maeno Shoten, 1950, p. 128.

Young, Michael. *The Rise of Meritocracy*. London, 1958.

Zanba Kenzen. *Tōzai Ryōkyō no Daigaku* (The Universities in Tokyo and Kyoto). Tokyo: Yomiuri Shinbunsha, 1903, p. 14.

Index